"Thought-provoking, well researched and well written, the book presents information rather than strongly arguing for a point of view. In doing so, Holst builds a persuasive case. He has collected a great deal of information from numerous sources and provides a fine overview of events which forever changed the world."

-- Scottish Rite Journal

"*Sworn in Secret* is a work of outstanding clarity, analytical style, and superb good sense."

-- Eduardo Estrada, PM

"The author takes you on a fascinating journey through time and place, drawing on his amazing knowledge and research of Freemasonry and the Knights Templar. He explores the impact Freemasons have had on world science, philosophy, art and history. Painstakingly researched, this book offers impressive details on a multitude of topics including Solomon's Temple, Rosslyn Chapel, the St. Clairs of Scotland, and even the roots of the masonry trade, all in an entertaining writing style. He gives life to heroic characters whose principles of brotherly love, morality, loyalty and charity have left a permanent imprint on modern day Freemasonry."

-- Gudrun Stutz

"Fascinating. I really enjoyed how ancient history is interwoven with Freemasonry and modern society. This book really filled in some gaps I had about Freemasons, and provided me with a greater understanding of the life and times of biblical people."

John Whiteknight

PHOENICIAN SECRETS
Exploring the Ancient Mediterranean

Sworn in Secret

Freemasonry and the Knights Templar

Sanford Holst

SANTORINI
BOOKS

Santorini Publishing
14622 Ventura Boulevard, #800
Los Angeles, California 91403

First Edition
1st Printing: April 2012
2nd Printing: July 2014

On the cover "The Admission of a Novice
to the Vows of the Order of the Temple" by
C. G. Addison, *The Knights Templars*, 1852.

Publisher's Cataloging-In-Publication Data

Holst, Sanford.
    Sworn in secret : Freemasonry and the Knights Templar /
Sanford Holst. — 1st ed.

    p. : ill. ; cm.
    Includes bibliographical references and index.
    ISBN: 978-0-9833279-3-6

    1. Freemasonry—History. 2. Freemasons—History.
3. Templars—History. I. Title.

HS403 .H65 2012
366/.1   2012932203

Acknowledgments

This book is dedicated to

Allen Price 33° (1929-2010) friend and mentor, who introduced me to the ways and secrets of Freemasonry.

And special thanks are given to

Eduardo Estrada for his valued guidance. Helene Price—Allen's wife and partner—as well as Fred Price—his older and, I'm told, wiser brother. Good friend Norm Leeper whose many years of experience helped to leaven some of my exuberance and keep things on an even keel.

In the Grand Lodges of England, Scotland and Ireland appreciation is due to Nigel Brown, David Begg, Barry Lyons, Robert L.D. Cooper and Martin Cherry. And at York, to the keeper of history David Hughes.

Thanks also to Howard "Bud" Ramsey Jr, Richard Cooper, Carlos Gonzalez, Paul McElwain, Robert Akin, Nick Khatch, Gudrun Stutz, Torien Blackwolf, Brett Fisher, Harvey Lyman, John Whiteknight, Dr. Douglas Roberts, Dr. Victor Helo, David Rush, Robert Borden, Steven Eberhardt, Gary Leavitt, Michael David, Scott Weber, Edwin Balao, Rick Baca, Simon McIlroy, Jim Hoerricks, Antony Kubichan, Daniel Hood, David Williams, Lyle Sorensen, Danny Witherspoon, Brett Fisher, John L. Cooper III and Russ Charvonia.

For Mediterranean and Lebanese insights I thank Judge James Kaddo, Amira Matar, Joumana Medlej, Antonia Kanaan, Dr. Antoine Khoury Harb, Salim Khalaf, Dr. Christos Doumas, Reuben Grima, Dr. Patricia Bikai and Dr. Felipe Fernandez-Armesto.

Living history was shown to me by Rev. Robin Griffith-Jones who is the current Master of the Temple at Temple Church in London, and by Geoff Pavitt at Gresham College. I also must acknowledge Dr. Malcolm Barber, John Robinson, Charles Addison and Dr. Albert Mackey, whose works were invaluable in this exploration down ancient corridors.

And of course I acknowledge the Great Architect of the universe, who is the actual Author of all these things.

Contents

Appendix

We have now reached the most interesting portion of the history of Freemasonry. We are getting away from the regions of legend and tradition, and are passing into the realm of authentic records. [1]

Albert G. Mackey

Fig. 1 George Washington attired as Master

To Aid a Distressed Brother

One of the most often-repeated promises made in Masonic lodge rooms is that each brother will come to the aid of a distressed Master Mason. This is reinforced by the ritual that raises a brother to the degree of Master Mason. In that ceremony he is taught how to give the Grand Hailing Sign of distress. This Hailing Sign can be shown in a public place and is immediately recognized by other Master Masons, who are then obliged to provide whatever relief they can.

That obligation echoes the practice of the Knights Templar concerning their brothers. No knight of that Order could leave a brother in distress on the field of battle. While any remained, all had to remain. Only when all the knights were brought to the Templars' Beauceant banner could they then leave, all the brothers together. Similarities between Freemasons and Templars seem to be part of the reason why questions of a connection between these two secretive orders keep being raised.

Among Freemasons, that strong commitment to brothers found expression not only in the lodge room but also on the battlefield, as George Washington amply demonstrated. He became a Mason at the young age of twenty, long before distinguishing himself on fields of war and in the seat of government. He was even said to have shown favoritism by choosing fellow travelers as his officers during the American Revolutionary War. Washington unabashedly displayed his attachment to the rules of this invisible brotherhood on more than one public occasion, including the aftermath of a battle.

> In the 46th regiment of the British army there was a traveling Lodge, holding its Warrant of Constitution under the jurisdiction of the Grand Lodge of Ireland. After an engagement between the American and British forces, in which the latter were defeated, the private chest of the Lodge, containing its jewels, furniture and implements, fell into the hands of the Americans. The captors reported the circumstances to General Washington, who at once ordered the chest to be returned to the Lodge and the regiment, under a guard of honor. "The surprise," says the historian of the event, himself an Englishman and a Mason, "the feeling of both officers and men may be imagined, when they perceived the flag of truce that announced this elegant compliment from their noble opponent, but still more noble brother. The guard of honor, with their music playing a sacred march [carried] the chest containing the Constitution and implements of the Craft borne aloft, like another ark of the covenant, equally by Englishmen and Americans, who lately engaged in the strife of war."[2]
>
> Albert G. Mackey

To aid the enemy in time of war is commonly regarded as treason. This is a simple rule understood in every nation on Earth. But Freemasonry seems to have always marched to the beat of a different drummer and lived by a different set of rules.

George Washington did not appear to concern himself that some might question his loyalty because of this action after battle. His commitment to help brothers in distress overcame other considerations. Since he was later elected President of the United

States, the people of his day apparently accepted these actions and his deep involvement in the practices of Masonry.

How did these practices begin? What driving force behind Freemasonry caused it to survive for so many centuries, first in secret and then partially revealed as it is today? And what was contained in the other obligations its members swore in secret to always conceal and never reveal? In truth, much of the mystery-shrouded activities of Freemasonry's early years were so tightly bound and so little shared that they eventually fell from view. That simple reality is commemorated in Masonic ritual today by the lament that the original Master Mason's secrets have been lost, and only a substitute for them remains. The inciting things responsible for creating and propelling this clandestine society to great heights of membership and influence are now no longer consciously known by Freemasons. Yet traces of them remain in the curious words, symbols, and pieces of ritual that are still used and practiced despite having little or no known meaning today.

When asked, most people inside and outside of Freemasonry readily admit they do not know much about the early days of Masonry prior to 1717. Outside of Masonry, people tend to fill this gap by embracing a broad spectrum of assumptions that are influenced by everything from anti-Masonic tirades to novels that show Masons protecting the bloodline of Jesus Christ. The people and actions responsible for Freemasonry's rise to a position of considerable influence have to compete with all those things. Fortunately, the reality is sometimes even more intriguing than many of those other stories, as you will soon see.

Freemasons have made up for the lack of records about their society's early days by launching a veritable cottage industry of creative story-making. In these accounts Freemasonry has been traced back to almost every famous man in history—even to Adam in the Garden of Eden. Masons usually call these stories "traditions" rather than history, as a nod to their questionable nature. Even so, a surprising number of Masons treat many parts of them as being factual.

The actual history of Freemasonry is strange enough already. This widespread organization for many years quietly exerted a

strong influence on society, magnified by the fact that it was, and
still is, the largest fraternal society in the world. And with this
came controversy. Accusations against Freemasons included
charges of treason. Were those condemnations true or false?
George Washington was not the only one affected by this. No
doubt the king of England felt justified in viewing all perpetrators
of the American Revolution as being guilty of treason. Whether
individuals agreed or not depended on which side of the battle
lines they stood.

Freemasons were also accused of heresy. Clearly the popes in
Rome viewed Protestants as being guilty of heresy. And Freemasonry included Protestants as well as Catholics and members of
other religious groups. Again, those charges were valid or not
depending on which side of these lines you stood.

For better or worse, the many conflicts and confrontations that
occurred over the years steadily shaped Freemasonry, and helped
shape the society in which we live.

In early Freemasonry the obligations of secrecy were so well followed that it really was a secret society, as many have noted.

> Prior to the year 1717 the Masonic order was a true
> secret society; not just an organization with secret
> signs and secret handgrips, but a widespread society
> whose very *existence* was a secret.[3]
>
> John J. Robinson

When Freemasonry came out into the open in that year and
shed some surface layers of secrecy, it entered a new manner of
existence. It became what has aptly been called a society with secrets. Yet its remaining layers of secrecy still ran deep. While more
of these have been revealed over the years, it turns out that the
most fascinating secrets still remain. They go beyond the rituals
and observances of the lodge to encompass all the unspoken acts
and practices of the secret society whose heritage is continued in
Masonry today.

The legacy of Freemasonry included the deeds of remarkable people who shaped and guided this society. To experience the emergence of Freemasonry into public view, we follow one of the men instrumental in causing that to happen. Striding into the Apple-Tree Tavern to negotiate this major step that occurred in 1717, he probably had a more far-reaching involvement with the about-to-be-created Grand Lodge than any of the others. His name was John Desaguliers, one of the early Grand Masters.

A graduate of the University of Oxford in 1709, he moved to London and became an assistant to Sir Isaac Newton. The venerable Sir Isaac took John under his wing and sponsored him for membership in the prestigious Royal Society, then introduced him to many members of London's higher social circles.

Around this time Desaguliers became active as a Freemason in the lodge that met at the Rummer and Grapes Tavern in Channel Row, Westminster.[4] When four of the old lodges held a preliminary meeting to discuss forming a Grand Lodge, the Rummer and Grapes was one of them. The other instigators were from the lodge that met at the Goose and Gridiron Ale-house in St. Paul's Churchyard, the lodge at the Crown Ale-house near Drury Lane, and the one at the Apple-Tree Tavern in Covent Garden.[5] James Anderson described the events of those times in his *New Book of Constitutions* produced in 1738.[6]

> They and some old Brothers met at the said *Apple-Tree*, and having put into the Chair the *oldest Master* Mason (now the *Master* of a *Lodge*) they constituted themselves a GRAND LODGE pro Tempore in *Due Form*, and forthwith revived the Quarterly *Communication* of the *Officers* of Lodges (call'd the Grand Lodge) resolv'd to hold the *Annual* ASSEMBLY *and Feast*, and then to chuse a GRAND MASTER from among themselves, till they should have the Honour of a *Noble Brother* at their Head.

Accordingly

On St. *John Baptist's* Day, in the 3d Year of King George I. *A.D.* 1717. the ASSEMBLY and *Feast* of the *Free and accepted Masons* was held at the foresaid *Goose and Gridiron* Ale-house.

Before Dinner, the *oldest Master* Mason (now the *Master of a Lodge*) in the Chair, proposed a list of proper Candidates; and the Brethren by a Majority of Hands elected

Mr. ANTONY SAYER Gentleman, Grand Master of Masons, who being forthwith invested $\left\{ \begin{array}{l} \text{Capt. } \textit{Joseph Elliot.} \\ \text{Mr. } \textit{Jacob Lamball,} \\ \textit{Carpenter} \end{array} \right\}$ $\begin{array}{l} \textit{Grand} \\ \textit{Wardens.} \end{array}$

with the Badges of Office and Power by the said *oldest Master*, and install'd, was duly congratulated by the Assembly who pay'd him the *Homage*.

With that grand event, Freemasonry emerged from secrecy and became a visible member of society. Two years later John Desaguliers was chosen by his peers to serve as Grand Master. With his acceptance of this position, the Grand Lodge seemed to take a significant leap forward. Aristocratic members of the London community showed more interest and began to join, elevating the public perception of Masonry. He also served as Master of various Occasional Lodges[7] where members of nobility were made Freemasons.

> Desaguliers was considered, from his position in Freemasonry, as the most fitting person to confer the Degrees on the Prince of Wales, who was accordingly entered, pass and raised in an Occasional Lodge, held on two occasions at Kew, over which Dr. Desaguliers presided as Master.[8]

In addition to exchanging gloves with nobility, John also had a strong commitment to his family. He married Joanna Pudsey and she gave him seven children. Unfortunately the happiness she brought him was tempered by the tragic loss of many of their children. Only two of them survived infancy and lived to adulthood. When John's own time came on the 29th of February in 1744, the Royal Society noted with proper respect that he was buried at the Savoy Chapel on the Strand, Westminster.

These newly-emergent Freemasons drew many of their symbols from the working craft of stonemasons, and used stories based on stoneworking as allegories for how to live a good life. In more recent years Freemasons have come to distinguish themselves from working stonemasons by referring to the latter as "operative masons." They then refer to themselves as "speculative masons." Since people less familiar with Freemasonry seem to have difficulty working with those expressions, the original terms are used here. The men who worked with stone are referred to as "stonemasons" or "masons." Members of the secretive society are referred to as "Freemasons" or "Masons."

We know there was some relationship between Freemasons and stonemasons. But new evidence suggests this early connection was quite different than what we had imagined. The generally-held assumption has been that this relationship began in Medieval times. Yet there is unexplained evidence that seems to go back to ancient times as well.

Some of these recurring issues from antiquity surround the building of Solomon's Temple and the Great Pyramid, which are often associated with Freemasonry. How did they come to be connected in this manner? And did some esoteric practices come into Masonry by this route and affect the Christian heritage usually associated with it? This includes practices such as Kabbalah, from which we get the word cabal, for secret plotters.

One way or another, something happened that caused a deep respect for stonemasons to develop among gentlemen who had never shaped a squared stone with their own hands.

Like many others who became Master Masons, I hoped all the secrets and history of Freemasonry would become clear on the day I was raised to the Third Degree. However it did not turn out that way. Working through the Scottish Rite and becoming a 32°

Mason helped, then entering the York Rite and receiving the degree of Knight Templar was eye-opening. Yet the more I learned, the more it revealed things we did not know, and that bothered me.

This happened once before, when I was studying the mysterious Phoenicians of the ancient Mediterranean. Most of their history was unknown and was widely accepted as having been lost.[9] It took thirty years of work, but I finally produced a book showing their full, rich heritage.[10] For this I was elected a member of the Royal Historical Society, a greatly appreciated honor.

That work described two men from the Phoenician city of Tyre named King Hiram and Hiram Abiff, who helped raise Solomon's Temple. They also figured prominently in the lore of Freemasonry. Seeing this, I was struck by the many similarities between Phoenicians, Freemasons, and the Knights Templar. All three were connected to Solomon's Temple. All were accused of terrible atrocities and perverted beliefs. All of them were praised for great accomplishments and remarkable contributions to society. All became known as mysterious and having closely-held secrets.

A major breakthrough came in 2008 when I was in London presenting an academic paper at Queen Mary College and stayed on to add a month of exploration in the land where Freemasonry emerged in the early 1700s. This intensive expedition took me to Masonic lodges, libraries, and historic sites all across England, Scotland and Ireland.

Grand Secretary Nigel Brown at the United Grand Lodge of England considerately put his resources at my disposal, and librarian Martin Cherry brought out original parchment manuscripts from the 1600s for examination. In ancient York, former lodge Secretary David Hughes revealed materials preserved from their brief reign as a Grand Lodge. In Edinburgh, Scottish Grand Secretary David Begg encouraged my research into new areas, asking only that the results be presented fairly, while librarian Robert L. D. Cooper added information on Rosslyn Chapel. In Dublin, Irish Grand Secretary Barry Lyons produced helpful records and sent me onward to Clontarf Castle, the Knights Templar preceptory just outside the city.

*Fig. 2   Old Charges manuscripts from the archives
of the United Grand Lodge of England*

Answers began to coalesce as more pieces fell into place. They involved the officers of the craft lodge, the words they spoke in ritual, and the ornamentation they wore, which began to take on new significance and meaning. They also began to give shape to the driving forces at play in Masonry's early rise.

Included in that early heritage was the recurring question of whether a relationship existed between Freemasonry and the Knights Templar. Several possible connections were suggested over the years, but each was later disproved or found to have little supporting evidence. As a result, many people have concluded no such relationship existed. Yet there are several other possible connections between the two that now seem to have elements of support, making them worthy of a deeper look. The serious charges and controversies that surrounded the last years of the Knights Templar may also have colored perceptions of Freemasonry, whether rightfully or wrongfully.

One thing that is already emerging is the realization that such a relationship would have been with the Templars *after* arrest warrants were issued for them on 13 October 1307, when they became fugitives. This is significant because the Templars at their peak were devout Roman Catholics and would reasonably have conveyed that same world-view to Freemasonry if such a connection existed at that time. That clearly did not happen. However the *fugitive* Templars had seen their brothers arrested, brutally tortured by the pope's inquisitors, and burned alive at the stake. The ones who avoided capture faced those same arrest warrants. It would have been understandable if refugee Templars became devoutly anti-Catholic. No doubt some did and some did not. To remain brothers, they needed to accept the fact that some brothers' views differed from their own, and yet still find a way to be brothers. It would be to those fugitive brothers that traces of connection would have existed.

Among the similarities between Freemasons and the Templars was their treatment by the pope in Rome. For centuries the Vatican and members of the public seem to have literally feared Freemasonry and the "dark secrets" believed to be in its possession.

Pope Clement XII put his fear of Masonry's secrecy into words in 1738 when he condemned the society in his pontifical letter *In eminenti.*

> [Freemasons have] a strict and unbreakable bond which obliges them, both by an oath upon the Holy Bible and by a host of grievous punishment, **to an inviolable silence about all that they do in secret together....** [They] have caused in the minds of the faithful the greatest suspicion, and all prudent and upright men have passed the same judgment on them as being depraved and perverted.[11]

This attack on Freemasonry echoed similar Vatican attacks on the Knights Templar in the 1300s. In those earlier years the power of the pope was vastly stronger, and its full force was felt in the extreme actions taken against the Templars. Many of their number were subjected to trials that lasted for years, accompanied by unbearable tortures, death in flames at the stake, or a slower death in dark dungeons. If all that misery had any small benefit for society, it was that these trials lifted a corner of the impenetrable secrecy that surrounded the internal practices of the Knights Templar. One such trial was that of Walter de Clifton.

Sir Walter was led through the streets of Edinburgh and into Holyrood Abbey for trial on the 17th of November in 1309, with only his white mantle and its blood-red cross for protection. Jacques de Molay, his Grand Master, was weighed down by chains in the confinement of a French prison and could give him no assistance. The pope whom they both served had yielded to the machinations of the king of France and sanctioned their imprisonment, along with that of their companions.

If there was fault for Walter being in jeopardy, it did not rest with the sovereign of Scotland. Robert the Bruce was preoccupied with defending his throne when a papal order for arrest of the Knights Templar was placed in his hand. Reluctantly, he allowed a porous net to be cast that caught only two Templars in all of Scotland.[12] Since the charges of heresy leveled against Walter de Clifton and William de Middleton could incur the penalty of death by immolation, scrupulous records of their trial were kept by church scribes.

Walter's testimony during these proceedings proved to be particularly revealing of the Templar initiation ritual, oaths made in secret, and other events of those days. His obligations and vows within the brotherhood normally would have prevented him from answering at all, but the pope's office was higher than that of the Templar Grand Master, and the pope had ordered the Templars to respond to the charges against them. Under duress, de Clifton described his initiation into the Order.

> He states that they then led him to the chamber of the Master, where they held their chapter [meeting], and that there, on his bended knees, and with his hands clasped, he again prayed for the habit and the fellowship of the Temple; that the Master and the brethren then required him to answer questions to the following effect: Whether he had a dispute with any man, or owed any debts? Whether he was betrothed to any woman? And whether he had any secret infirmity of body? Or knew of anything to prevent him from remaining within the bosom of the fraternity? And having answered all those questions satisfactorily, the Master then asked of the surrounding brethren, "Do ye give your consent to the reception of brother Walter?" who unanimously answered that they did; and the Master and the brethren then standing up, received him the said Walter in this manner. On his bended knees, and with his hands joined, he solemnly promised that he would be the perpetual servant of the Master, and of the order, and of the brethren, for the purpose of defending the Holy Land. Having done this, the Master took out of the hands of a brother chaplain of the order the book of the holy gospels, upon which was depicted a cross, and laying his hands upon the book and upon the cross, he swore to God....
>
> Being asked where he had passed his time since his reception, he replied that he had dwelt three years at

the preceptory of Blancradok [Balantrodoch] in Scotland; three years at Temple Newsom in England; one year at the Temple at London, and three years at Aslakeby. Being asked concerning the other brothers in Scotland, he stated that John de Hueflete was Preceptor of Blancradok, the chief house of the order in that country, and that he and the other brethren, having heard of the arrest of the Templars, threw off their habits and fled, and that he had not since heard aught concerning them.[13]

Walter's imprisoned Templar brethren—who suffered their own trials in England, France and other countries—provided many more details of the initiations and events that took place within their Order. Thus it seems clear that he did not reveal all he knew about these clandestine proceedings, nor where the Templars went as they departed the preceptory for the last time and went underground. As far as their neighbors and the local officials knew, the Templars simply disappeared behind a cloak of remarkably tight secrecy.

During the course of this journey into the early days of Freemasonry and the Knights Templar, a number of surprising discoveries come to light. Some of them became critical moments in the lives of these societies.

For example in the Holy Land the Knights Templar were driven into the arms of Lebanese Christians, where they found much-needed mutual support. These Lebanese people were descended from the Phoenicians who helped build Solomon's Temple. Their society continued to be as secretive and tightly-knit as it had been during those earlier centuries. In time, the Templars became known for having those same characteristics.

When the Templars were attacked in the 1300s, only a few hundred of them were arrested, out of the several thousand people in their Order. The rest disappeared behind a veil of complete privacy, becoming fugitives from powerful leaders of church and state.

Surprisingly enough, it is seen that Freemasonry also began in the 1300s, as shown by documents that are still in existence. These include the Regius and Cooke manuscripts. This was a secretive and tightly-knit brotherhood whose members depended on each other for their survival. They included members of nobility as well as educated clerics and workingmen. And it gradually became evident that they lived parallel to, but apart from, the stonemasons. Only when stonemason lodges were dying in the 1600s did gentlemen become members in significant numbers and take over lodges rather than let them disappear.

We come to see the work of Freemasons from the 1300s onward as related to the protection of fugitives from powerful leaders of church and state. For their efforts they became accused of heresy and treason. When at labor in these works, they were not builders of stone walls but builders of free men. We experience all these things in vivid detail drawn from actual documents and historical sources—often told in the words of people who were there.

One thing is already certain, and it is that the combination of practices which constituted Freemasonry often put it at odds with heads of nations and heads of religions. Much like the black and white squares on the floor of a Masonic lodge room, Masonry has had a long and checkered career of being caught in the middle of conflicts and confrontations.

We now go back to experience those major conflicts and events that shaped Freemasonry, even to the days of antiquity leading up to the building of Solomon's Temple.

Ancient Temple,
Great Pyramid

$\mathcal{T}$he symbols of Freemasonry reflect much of its heritage, and reach back far into antiquity. Solomon's Temple was well represented among these symbols, as was the Great Pyramid with its all-seeing eye, along with the simple tools of stonemasons that have existed since time immemorial. How did these symbols and heritage come to Freemasonry, and what might they reveal to us about how Freemasonry came into existence? It turns out that the people who held those tools and helped to build Solomon's Temple—the Phoenicians from the city of Tyre—may be able to shed some light on these things. Among them were King Hiram, Hiram Abiff, and other masons from that city who shared a legacy they brought to their work. This heritage included a small yet magnificent temple at Tyre that long preceded the one they helped build for Solomon.

Herodotus, the ancient Greek historian, was one of those who described this earlier temple.

> In the wish to get the best information that I could on these matters, I made a voyage to Tyre in Phoenicia, hearing there was a temple of Hercules at that place,

very highly venerated. I visited the temple, and found
it richly adorned with a number of offerings, among
which were two pillars, one of pure gold, the other of
emerald, shining with great brilliancy at night.

Herodotus 2:44

The two pillars standing in front of this temple would later be
echoed in two towering pillars that received the names *Jachin* and
Boaz and came to be the most visible symbols of Solomon's Temple.

In addition, this smaller temple opened the way for us to see
back into the earliest days of the city of Tyre and the secretive society that it harbored. Curious about the age of this beautiful Tyrian temple, Herodotus asked its priests when this edifice had been
built. They replied that it had been raised in the same year Tyre
was founded, which they said was 2300 years earlier. Naturally
that seemed to leap into the realm of mythology, especially since
Herodotus visited Tyre around 450 BC, which would have put the
founding of the city at the year 2750 BC.

Seeking something more substantial, I looked through the archaeological explorations performed at Tyre—in what is today the
southern part of Lebanon—and discovered Patricia Bikai had
done a detailed excavation in 1974 that went all the way down to
bedrock. By examining the pottery found at each level unearthed,
she was able to reliably date the building of the city to the first
part of the third millennium BC. In other words, she showed the
city was founded around 2750 BC. Incredibly enough, the archaeological evidence verified the date given to us by Herodotus. This
has now become the commonly accepted date for the origin of
Tyre, a city that would come to have an impact felt all across the
Mediterranean.

Yet our search for the roots of Solomon's Temple and the
Phoenician masons who worked on it was not yet over, for the
society that created Tyre had come from a city sixty-nine miles to
the north known as Byblos.[14] It was there that the mysterious society we know as the Phoenicians first took shape, fueled by the
building of yet another ancient temple.

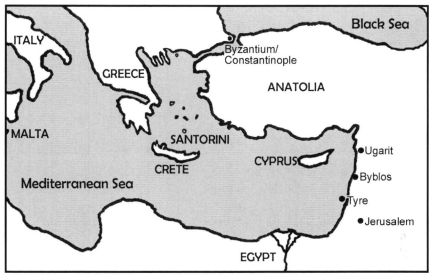

Fig. 3 Eastern Mediterranean region

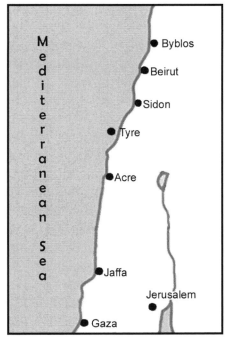

Fig. 4 East coast of the Mediterranean Sea

Byblos rested on a high point of land where the Lebanon Mountains came down to the Mediterranean shore. Blessed with a vast supply of tall, sturdy cedar trees, the wandering Canaanites who settled there formed those giant tree trunks into fishing boats and became fishermen upon the sea. To augment their income, they began to carry some goods on board their rustic craft and traded these items for luxury goods up and down the coast. Their ventures farther from home eventually brought them south to Egypt where a remarkable event took place.

Egypt was a land virtually without useful wood. The soft and pulpy palm trees were useless for construction, and the small acacia trees could produce boards only three feet long.[15] Into this land in 3200 BC were rowed wooden ships from Byblos built of strong cedar planks and carrying stores of heavy cedar beams they were willing to trade. The demand for their wares was immediate, and word of these sea traders with their remarkable cedar wood traveled far up the Nile River to the city of Hierakonpolis.[16] It was the capital of Upper Egypt—as that half of the country was known—and had the wealth to engage in a large and daring project that could produce immense benefit in terms of civic pride.

So they contracted with the traders from Byblos to bring four huge cedar logs measuring roughly forty feet (twelve meters) in length and three feet in diameter to create a magnificent addition to their temple. We know this ambitious project was actually built in Hierakonpolis because its remains were discovered there in 1985 by archaeologist Michael Hoffman. Yet—as with so many temples built in antiquity—this brought with it another mystery. Given the small size of boats and the limited ability of pack animals in those days, how could pillars as massive as these have been brought almost 400 miles across the sea and another 400 miles into the interior of Egypt? It was a staggering problem for the ship captain from Byblos who received the offer. But the rewards accompanying it were great, and his small town on the coast of Lebanon rallied to the challenge.

The shipping problem was soon solved by arranging to drag each massive pillar behind a boat, a method that became part of their folklore and tradition. It was even used many years later by King Hiram of Tyre, who said to Solomon:

I will do all thy desire concerning timber of cedar, and concerning timber of fir. My servants shall bring them down from Lebanon unto the sea; and I will convey them by sea in floats unto the place that thou shalt appoint me, and will cause them to be discharged there....

1 Kings 5:9

The major difficulty was that this solution required four boats, whose rowers would need to be replaced from time to time as they struggled with the prevailing sea current that would be trying to push the floating pillars to shore, pulling the rear of the boats with them. Then each night the tow-boats and supporting craft would need to put in to shore for food and rest before beginning again the next day. Several weeks would have been required to accomplish this mission. Somehow the whole town managed to pool its manpower and resources to accomplish this daunting task. The huge pillars were delivered to the mouth of the Nile then towed hundreds of miles upriver by the Egyptians. There they were placed in the post holes that arrayed them in front of the temple. Looming several stories high, they served a role much like cathedral towers would serve many centuries later, being visible for miles around and instilling a sense of awe. In a world without wood, the temple with these four massive cedar pillars would have been a marvel in its day.

The impact on the people of Byblos was no less profound. Instead of being fishermen who performed some trades on the side, the riches of this Egyptian expedition and the years of trade that followed it quickly transformed the sleepy town into a major city. A thick wall was built around the young city to protect its new wealth, civic buildings were endowed, and the rush was on to build more cedar boats to meet the demand for trade from all those cities along the Nile.[17]

With this transformation into the life of sea traders, the society we know as the Phoenicians officially began. Many of the characteristics formed in these people during those early days would remain active throughout their society's long existence. The interdependence they learned in those early times became stronger as the years went by. Sea trading was a risky business. If one ship sailed over the horizon filled with valuable goods and never came back, its owner and relatives could be completely wiped out. By sharing the risks and the rewards, the close brotherhood among them became so strong that by the time of Alexander the Great this bond among Phoenicians was unshakable.

Being ruled by cooperative commerce rather than force, they chose their own leaders, and tended to move the leadership role among the leading families rather than submit to a hereditary monarch. Even when they decided to imitate their neighbors and call their leader a king, his major actions were still subject to approval by the town council. He served more as a Managing Director or CEO with a board of directors, rather than as an absolute king.

There was another characteristic of these early Phoenician people that found expression in King Hiram and Hiram Abiff many years later. And it would also find its way into Freemasonry. This was the practice of religious tolerance. It was a most unusual characteristic at that time, and would continue to be so for much of the long and ragged history of civilization.

We see this in the temple built to the goddess of the city, who was known as Baalat Gebal, which meant Our Lady of Byblos. The small house and enclosed yard they had set aside for her when they were fishermen became a grand temple of rough-hewn stone now that they had their trading wealth to support it. But beyond the beauty of the edifice was also its use. The Phoenicians allowed any visitor to call this feminine deity by whatever name they were comfortable. Egyptian visitors were allowed, and even encouraged, to call her Hathor, the goddess most similar to Baalat Gebal in the Egyptian pantheon. Canaanite visitors from other cities could, and did, call her Astarte. Greeks would later call her Aphrodite, and the Romans, Venus. All these names were acceptable to the Phoenicians without hesitation. Gifts from foreign dignitaries have been found in Byblos addressed to one or more of these names.

A lesser temple was built to male deities in Byblos, and again any male god could be worshiped there. One of the ways the Phoenicians were able to accomplish this was by having no graven image of the deity in their temples. They used a simple stone marker instead to identify this as a sacred place where prayers could be offered. This stone had a square base and tapered as it went higher, being capped with a small pyramid. They called this marker a *maṣṣebah*. The same shape was used by the Egyptians but usually on a larger scale, and it became known as an obelisk. Since the shape and appearance of the *maṣṣebah* was the same for all deities, every worshiper could pray in the temple with equal comfort.

This was not so much an altruistic or enlightened practice by the Phoenicians as it was an astute and practical one. A leading cause of war in those days—and even today—was fighting over differences in religion. The Phoenicians were a small society and in no way a military match for the nations around them. So they removed this threat to their existence by standing in prayer beside others, even if their beliefs were different. Perhaps there was something of value in this practice, because the Phoenicians survived for many centuries while those around them perished one by one.

In later years, when Solomon asked King Hiram for help in building a temple to God as worshipped by the Jewish people, there was again no hesitation. Hiram accepted the offer and sent his best mason. And as we will see, there was not only peace between them but a measure of brotherhood.

As Byblos prospered it began to establish other cities and ports to support its growing trade. Sidon was built forty-six miles to the south on the Lebanese shore, where it enjoyed good access to more forests of cedar on the Lebanon Mountains. Another twenty-three miles further south they founded Tyre on a rocky island located about a half-mile offshore. This made it well situated to service all the Phoenician ships southbound on voyages to Egypt, their major trading partner.

Yet the birth of Tyre and Sidon was only the beginning of a baby boom that put Phoenician outposts all around the Mediterranean Sea. To supply the ravenous appetite of populous Egypt for goods of all kinds, the Phoenicians sought out new sources of raw materials that could be sold to their large customer. This drove their cedar ships and enterprising crews to sail north and west in that search. That brought them to the coast of Anatolia—today called Turkey—and the islands off the coast of what would become Greece and Italy. One of these islands was Malta, just south of Sicily, which would have a particularly long and intimate relationship with the Phoenician people, and introduce them to the stonemason's craft.

In 3600 BC, for some unexplained reason, the simple farmers on Malta began to honor their ancestors in a most remarkable way. Like many other cultures, they buried their ancestors in underground caves. Then the innovation they added was to begin building above-ground "caves" where the living could go to honor these ancestors. Those stone temples above ground were quite rustic at first, being made with natural or rough-hewn stones of all sizes—some weighing up to 50 tons. These boulders were carefully and efficiently stacked one upon another, with small stones put in the crevices between them, to form remarkably stable buildings of rock. Those impressive creations towered over the green hillsides of Malta—as well as the hills of its small neighboring island of Gozo. The walls of each temple were carefully shaped to create clusters of rounded rooms, highly evocative of the caves below ground. Many of these ancient temples are still standing today, so I was able to examine them and follow the changes that happened from decade to decade after the first rustic one was built at Ggantija.

For centuries these stone temples proliferated across Malta. Then a subtle change started to occur in 3000 BC. It may or may not be a coincidence, but this was the same time the Phoenicians were expanding westward across the Mediterranean. In any event, responding to an increase in local prosperity, most reasonably from foreign trade, the people of Malta began to upgrade some of their old temples with attractive new additions. They also set out to build a number of completely new temples. Using the skills they had learned in centuries of stoneworking, the Maltese crafted these newer temples with huge stones that were ever more perfectly cut. In doing so they developed the manner of dressing stones which would become known as ashlar. These ashlar stones had perfectly flat sides, with exactly squared corners, allowing the stones to be erected into large, stable structures that required no mortar between the stones. The temple built at Tarxien, only a few miles from the city of Valletta, was an excellent example of this ashlar masonry. The Maltese people had been refining their craft of raising stone buildings for almost 1,000 years by the time this temple at Tarxien was built. This was no longer a matter of just assembling large stones. The fine art of precise masonry had been born.

The rough stonework being done by the Phoenicians in their own cities showed that they were not teachers here but were more akin to students or an appreciative audience.

At this same time, about two hundred years after the founding of Tyre, Phoenician trade with Egypt was soaring. The people of that land on the Nile had started the expensive task of building pyramids, and were about to embark on raising the Great Pyramid at Giza.

Mud from the banks of the Nile had supplied an endless stream of baked bricks that Egyptians used for their buildings since time beyond counting, and it seemed to meet all their needs. It was only in 2650 BC that they created their first significant stone structure. This was an enclosure built by King Khasekhemwy around his proposed burial site. His son Djoser carried his father's work one step further and not only built such a wall, but then had a thick layer of stone blocks placed above his underground burial chamber. He then put a smaller, second layer of blocks on the first, then added an even smaller third layer and so on. Finally he ended up with something resembling a pyramid. This is still called the Step Pyramid because of its rough design. Four pharaohs later, Snefru continued to experiment, building a step pyramid like that of Djoser, then built a second pyramid whose smooth sides were so steep the builders were forced to drastically change the angle halfway up. That resulted in what is known today as the Bent Pyramid. Still dissatisfied, Snefru had a third one built, in the shape of a true pyramid using red stones, which became known as the Red Pyramid.

After all these flawed attempts, the extremely large and perfectly proportioned Great Pyramid was built by his son Khufu.[18]

The Great Pyramid was raised only one hundred years after the first stone wall built in Egypt, and only one generation after a king fumbled repeatedly trying to do the same task. Not only was this new pyramid vast in scope—having individual stones weighing up to 80 tons—it was perfectly laid out on an east-west axis, accurately leveled, ingeniously constructed, and had perfectly indented layers even when the size of the stones changed. This incredible combination of massive size and near perfection has led many observers over the years to assume aliens or paranormal forces must have been at play in building the Great Pyramid. To a certain extent, they were raising a good point.

The development of skills such as shipbuilding, pottery-making, and masonry did not happen overnight, as history has clearly shown. In Egypt the development of riverboats proceeded from simple reed rafts, to sewn boats using small planks, then to full cedar riverboats, and took about a thousand years to accomplish this evolution. In similar manner, it took the people of Malta roughly a thousand years to develop their expertise at crafting and placing huge, perfectly-cut ashlar stones. So how did Egyptians go from building their first rustic stone wall to building the massive and precise Great Pyramid in only a hundred years? As it turns out, they did not need to seek help from space aliens. There was another, much more prosaic source closer to home.

This other source was brought to my attention by a mysterious event that occurred on the island of Malta. The Maltese people who had been building beautiful stone temples across their islands for so many generations suddenly disappeared during the twenty-sixth century BC. Investigations on Malta have found no signs of warfare, disease, economic failure or natural disaster at that time. It was as if they went down to ships one day and vanished. By extraordinary coincidence, this was the same time that work was getting under way on Khufu's Great Pyramid.

The Phoenicians were known to have been intimately involved with the Maltese. They also had been supplying cedar and other materials for the building of Egyptian temples for almost 600 years at that point. Could the Phoenicians have acted as intermediaries, bringing to Egypt masonry skills learned in Malta, while the Great Pyramid was being built? Could they have brought

Fig. 5   Cedar boat at the Great Pyramid

actual Maltese masons to Egypt, to accomplish the almost impossible feat being attempted there? Could they have brought *all* the people of Malta to Egypt to work on one of the largest structures ever attempted in antiquity? The answer to all these questions is yes, they could have. More detailed research needs to be done before it can be said that this is what actually happened. Yet it is clearly one of the most intriguing and reasonable explanations for what occurred—especially if the alternative is either the arrival of space aliens, or the possibility that hit-and-miss pyramid builders in Egypt suddenly got lucky and built an incredibly massive and nearly-perfect Great Pyramid, right after their error-prone earlier attempts. The disappearance of the Maltese stonemasons and the parallel rise of the Great Pyramid would seem to be worthy of further investigation.

Meanwhile, we do not need to guess if the Phoenicians were directly involved with the Egyptians while the Great Pyramid was being built. Remarkable physical evidence exists of their role in supplying Egypt with cedar and other materials needed for raising this majestic structure. That evidence was discovered in 1954 AD when two cedar boats were unearthed beside the Great Pyramid, where they had been buried to serve King Khufu in his afterlife. For some mysterious reason, both boats were disassembled and stored in "kit" form, with markings showing how to assemble the boats for use.[19] One of these boats was re-assembled and put on display beside the Great Pyramid. More recently, in 2008, it was announced that the other craft would also be assembled, a process which would take several years. These boats of Lebanese cedar are visible reminders of Phoenician participation in one of the greatest masonry accomplishments ever achieved, the raising of this Seventh Wonder of the Ancient World.

The all-seeing eye was known to the Egyptians as a symbol of protection. They called it the Eye of Horus, and associated it with the goddess Hathor. As we saw, they also referred to the goddess of the Phoenicians by this name. In any event, the all-seeing eye was painted on the prow of Phoenician and Egyptian boats to protect them on their journeys. The Egyptian boats primarily traveled up and down the Nile. The Phoenician ships traveled the length of the Mediterranean and out to the Atlantic coast at Morocco and Portugal. Even today, boats in the harbors of Malta and Portugal still reflect their people's long association with the Phoenicians by having all-seeing eyes painted on the prow of the boats.

The familiar Freemasonry symbol of the Great Pyramid surmounted by an all-seeing eye became an easily-recognized image of power and protection. This Masonic symbol continues to be used on American dollar bills to the present day.

As those Phoenician boats made their way around the Mediterranean after the Great Pyramid was built, the fine art of stonemasonry seemed to travel also. It soon rose to prominence as part of the miracle on Crete, and the society we know as the Minoans.

Chapter 3

Minoan Palaces and Stonemason Secrets

Many mysteries surround the rise of the spectacular Minoan society on the island of Crete, in which stonemasons appeared seemingly out of nowhere and began to build luxurious palaces. For countless years the people of this large island in the Mediterranean Sea had been shepherds and farmers. Then over a short period of time around 2000 BC they began to raise huge palaces made of perfectly-cut ashlar stones, engage in sea trade, and form vast bureaucracies to manage their business ventures. It now appears that their good fortune was strongly influenced by events transpiring in the Eastern Mediterranean.

There the Phoenician cities were enduring the opposite of prosperity. They were battered by Amorite tribes who came down from the North around 2200 BC and seized control of lands near Byblos. Not satisfied with what they already had, those Northern tribes proceeded to raid in all directions, even breaching the wall protecting Byblos to rob the city. The Phoenicians survived and repaired the damage that was done, then rebuilt their walls thicker than before. Yet the Amorites only became stronger. These restless neighbors broke through the new walls and plundered the city again. This forced the people of Byblos to realize they needed to take action of a more drastic nature. First they rebuilt the city walls yet again, higher and stronger. Then they began to look for a new place to live.

Their southern city of Tyre would have been a safe haven. It was located on an island and surrounded by a natural moat that was deep and wide. Yet the surface of the island was barely large enough to support its own population, let alone those of the other Phoenician cities. Another possibility was Cyprus. This was a spacious island barely over a hundred miles from the Lebanese coast—but unfortunately, warlike people similar to the Amorites were already there. Farther away was the Phoenician outpost on the island of Santorini in the Aegean Sea near Greece, which had to be considered. It offered more livable area than Tyre. But it had almost no sources of water, so Santorini could not support many more people than it already held. Then there was the large neighboring island of Crete.

The Phoenicians had been trading with people on Crete for many years by that time. The Cretans were relatively peaceful, and the trade with them seemed to have established reasonably good relations. While no treaties or documents have been preserved that spell out what happened next, the considerable historical and archaeological records that exist paint a fairly detailed picture of what transpired.

Around 2000 BC the people of Tyre and Sidon packed all their belongings and moved away, leaving their cities virtually abandoned. Many citizens of Byblos also joined their brethren, leaving only priests and their staffs to support the ancient temples, plus a small contingent to maintain the harbor. But where did they go?

Before the people of Crete could build their luxurious palaces they needed to create the wealth necessary to afford them. To accomplish this, the local shepherds and farmers somehow became transformed into merchants and sailors of ships, then came to dominate sea trade in the Aegean region. By remarkable coincidence—all right, maybe it was not a coincidence—those were the same skills possessed by the Phoenician sea traders who were migrating from their cities in Lebanon at this same time.

The subsequent rise in wealth led to the erection of palaces at Knossos, Phaistos, Malia and other locations. Nor were these

buildings the cobbling together of odd stones such as those shepherds and farmers had commonly used. The remains of these palaces—still visible today—show that they were built with carefully-cut ashlar stones that revealed a high skill in masonry. These
were techniques the Phoenicians had acquired from the vanished
master builders of Malta and the builders of the Great Pyramid.
These were also skills that subsequently appeared in Phoenician
buildings and harbors over the years.

The stonemasons in Minoan society were given many opportunities to hone and perfect their skills. The palaces they raised
were monumental in size—with some containing hundreds of
rooms and standing many stories high. The violent earthquakes
felt on Crete occasionally gave these masons the instructional opportunity to build the same walls again. Each new effort seemed
to improve the degree of craftsmanship in structure, solidity and
beauty. At the Knossos palace, for example, it is still possible to
see how the lowest level of stone blocks differed from the courses
of stone added later.

So did the many Phoenicians who left Tyre, Sidon and Byblos
at this time come to live among the people of Crete? A lively discussion raged around this for some time, with a number of experts
seeing an "Eastern influence" occur on Crete. Others took an "in-
digenous development" view and proposed that everything arose
exclusively from Cretan soil. As more pieces of evidence were
gathered by archaeologists and scholars, however, it became apparent that the Eastern influence was very much present. This is
reasonably ascribed to the large number of Phoenicians arriving
and taking up residence on Crete at this time. The merging of
widely-traveled Phoenicians with the rustic people of Crete gave
rise to a new society that was a blending of those two, and which
came to be known as Minoan.[20]

Minoan writings showed this process actively at work. The
heretofore illiterate people of Crete learned to read in the Phoenician fashion and began to write in a script called Linear A. The
individual words of this script have never been deciphered, but
the structure of the writing has been identified as Semitic—which
is to say, from the region in and around Lebanon.[21] In another hint
of its origin, the Minoans apparently applied this new skill not for

literature or philosophy, but for the recording of business transactions. There were many lists and quantities among the writings.

A measure of secrecy likewise became introduced into Cretan society with the appearance of the Minoans. Did the Phoenicians make this contribution? Excavations in Byblos, Tyre and other Phoenician cities have revealed their people carved virtually no monuments with laudatory commemorations of their great accomplishments. There were no busts depicting Phoenician kings or other noted leaders. No libraries presented their writings. No revelatory inscriptions on burial places noted personal or social events. The secrecy they maintained about themselves was essentially complete and impenetrable.

The Phoenicians seem to have brought this practice forward with them to their settlement on the island of Santorini. It is a virtual requirement of all secretive societies that they have initiation ceremonies in which new members take obligations to safeguard the secrets of the organization. Freemasonry does this, the Knights Templar did this, and other secretive societies have been said to do so. The Phoenicians not only performed these initiations at Santorini, but left behind images of the events surrounding these ceremonies. This outpost existed before the rise of the Minoans and retained much of its original Phoenician character,[22] yet it also thrived alongside its Minoan brethren and added luxuries at its town of Akrotiri such as the beautiful frescoes painted on the interior walls of its buildings. These vivid paintings were miraculously preserved and show us intimate moments of their social life, including the events surrounding their initiation rituals.

These are found in the temple raised for their goddess who was originally known as Our Lady of Byblos.[23] Young men are shown in various states of undress before receiving the colorful zoma kilt that went around their waist and marked them as a full member of the society. Young women went from the simple trappings of girls to the ornate skirts reserved for women. Clearly this was a pivotal moment in the life of each of these people and greatly celebrated.

The building in which these colorful frescoes were painted tells us something more about these people. The temple was built of expensive, perfectly cut ashlar stones on two sides of the structure, showing it had great status in the community. Not far away was the trading house for this town, and its importance may be deduced from the fact that it had four walls of finely-worked ashlar stone. These sea traders began this custom in Byblos, having a trading house and a temple to Our Lady in each of their cities, and keeping the two buildings separate. It further substantiates the Phoenician origin of this settlement.

This custom was modified on Crete as part of the sharing between local people and the newly-arrived Phoenicians. In Minoan society the temple and trading house were combined, and the luxurious accommodations in which they both were housed became known as palaces. At Knossos, for example, the main entrance in the north is through the trading house, after which one walks up a ramp to the open central square of the compound. The religious rooms are to the right and the king's rooms are to the left. Storage rooms for trade goods are found throughout the building, as are workrooms for the bureaucrats who maintained the business records of all the trades performed in this region. In Minoan society, much as in that of the Phoenicians, the king served as CEO of the trade business that paid for their palaces and luxurious lifestyle.

In fact among crowds of Minoan people, the close-knit Phoenicians who came to the island seemed to function like a society within the society. They managed to preserve their livelihood and most of their social practices, even while living among the much larger number of people native to the island. The trading business of the Phoenicians replaced much of the previous shepherd-farmer existence, and the Phoenician masons set to work changing the appearance of the society. Shipping became important, and the writing skills of the Phoenicians were soon widely learned. The secrecy that was part of the protection treasured and practiced by Phoenicians seemed to be honed and enhanced by this "society within a society" experience. It allowed them to control the flow of life around them without being seen to do so.

Since by definition they were not seen to be doing this, how do we know it happened? Because during the dissolution of this beautiful Minoan society we came to see its constituent parts.

Fig. 6   Young woman in Adorant fresco on Santorini

All was not paradise on the Aegean Sea, for a confrontation was slowly building. Just after Minoan society began to rise on the island of Crete, the first Greek-speaking people—known as Mycenaeans—came down from the North and arrived on the mainland. There they quickly established themselves in hilltop citadels and set about subduing the local people in the surrounding land. The Mycenaeans then mounted forays to some of the smaller islands, attacking ships for plunder along the way. The Minoans responded by holding those raiding parties at bay upon the seas, using their superior number of ships. They also prevented the raiding parties from reaching Crete. Thucydides described those events this way.

> The first person known to us by tradition as having established a navy is Minos. He made himself master of what is now called the Hellenic [Aegean] sea, and ruled over the Cyclades, into most of which he sent the first colonies, expelling the Carians and appointing his own sons governors; and thus did his best to put down piracy in those waters, a necessary step to secure the revenues for his own use.
>
> For in early times the Hellenes [Greeks] and the barbarians of the coast and islands, as communication by sea became more common, were tempted to turn pirates, under the conduct of their most powerful men; the motives being to serve their own cupidity and to support the needy. They would fall upon a town unprotected by walls, and consisting of a mere collection of villages, and would plunder it; indeed, this came to be the main source of their livelihood, no disgrace being yet attached to such an achievement, but even some glory. An illustration of this is furnished by the honour with which some of the inhabitants of the continent still regard a successful marauder, and by the question we find the old poets everywhere representing the people as asking of voyagers whether they are pirates, as if those who are asked the

question would have no idea of disclaiming the impu-
tation, or their interrogators of reproaching them for
it. The same rapine prevailed also by land.

Thucydides 1:4-5

Thus protected by its navy, the Minoans thrived. In addition to
the palace at Knossos, located at the middle of the north shore
where it faced Santorini across the sea, other regional centers
spawned their own palaces as well. Near the southern shore was
Phaistos, and on the eastern coast was the palace at Zakros. Between Zakros and Knossos on the northern shore was the palace
at Malia. But eventually, disaster struck.

Around 1628 BC[24] a series of mild earthquakes was followed by
a tremendous eruption of the volcano at Santorini. The shattering
earthquake and tidal wave that accompanied it dealt the Minoans
a mortal blow. With great difficulty they rebuilt their broken palaces, ports and roads, but the extensive damage seemed to con-
sume all their resources. When a later series of sharp earthquakes
hit, Minoan society was unable to recover in time. The Mycenaeans took advantage of this open window of opportunity. Those
mainlanders' ships and soldiers swept over the sea to Crete, taking full possession of the island around 1550 BC.

We noted earlier that the Phoenicians disappeared from Tyre,
Sidon and most of Byblos at the same time Minoan society arose
on Crete. Any doubts about their joining with the local people to
create Minoan society should have been put to rest by the Minoan
adoption of many Phoenician practices. If not, consider what happened next. As the Minoans fled before the Mycenaeans, the local
people returned to their quiet sheep-herding and farming existence, and the Phoenicians returned to their ports in Lebanon. Having maintained their customs and practices as a "society within a
society" the Phoenicians quickly restored those cities.

Archaeologists digging at Tyre and Sidon found a thick layer of
sand covered the buildings that existed at 2000 BC. Occupation of
those cities did not resume again until around 1550 BC.[25] The people of Byblos, whose city had remained small but continuously
occupied throughout the Minoan years, also welcomed returnees

home. The society re-established at Tyre and Sidon was remarkably similar to the one in which the Phoenicians had lived before.

To go one step further, the ancient legend of Europa indicated that the people of that day were fully aware of the patrimony of the Minoans. In this story the god Zeus lived on the island of Crete. One day he was said to have seen the Phoenician princess Europa walking beside the sea in Lebanon. He immediately fell in love with her and, changing himself into a white bull, approached her and knelt at her feet. Fascinated by this remarkable animal, she climbed upon his broad back. He then rushed over the sea, abducting her to Crete. Zeus then changed back into his human form, and had three children by Europa. Their eldest son became King Minos, who then ruled over Crete. Surprisingly enough, this legend popular in ancient Greece has been trying to tell us about the relationship between the Minoans and Phoenicians for about 3,500 years.

The Mycenaeans who overran Crete became a considerable power in the Aegean Sea during the years that followed. As they took over more of the sea trade, they pushed the remaining Phoenician traders far to the east. The Phoenicians' problems were compounded by the Egyptians, who had been their good trading partners for so many years. Now Egyptian armies came up from the south and declared themselves overlords of the Levant[26] and demanded tribute from the cities of Lebanon and their neighbors. Meanwhile the Hittites who ruled central Anatolia in what is today known as Turkey, came down and seized the city of Ugarit. By so doing, the Hittites placed themselves on the northern doorstep of the Phoenicians and threatened to go farther. The Egyptian king had declared his "protection" over this area, but allowed Ugarit to be taken, and seemed willing to let the Phoenicians be taken next. The Phoenicians were in danger of being destroyed before they could even consider the building of Solomon's Temple. A miracle was needed for them to survive, and fortunately one arrived in the form of the Sea Peoples. And a natural disaster.

Serious crop failures hit the Northern Mediterranean just before 1200 BC, causing famine in many areas. The Mycenaeans and Hittites were fortunate in that they could buy enough grain and

Fig. 7   Europa coming to Crete

other foods to survive. Ugarit actually flourished at this time as a pass-through port for grain from Egypt on its way to the Hittites. However the people of Western Anatolia and the Black Sea region to the north were left without food and gradually became desperate. The Phoenicians had grain from Canaan they could sell, but were shut out of the Hittite and Mycenaean markets. So it is believed that they brought grain to the beleaguered people of Western Anatolia and the Black Sea region. The Phoenicians may well have been doing this only for profit, but it seemed to gain them considerable standing among these destitute people.

A desperate attempt by a small force from Western Anatolia to establish a beachhead in grain-rich Egypt failed miserably. That event was commemorated by King Merneptah[27] as a great victory over the "Sea Peoples."

Those desperate people then staged a more successful second attack. Their ships from Western Anatolia and the Black Sea ravaged the Mycenaean seacoast in Greece, destroying many of the harbor towns. Without those harbors to bring trade and food, the Mycenaeans began to die a slow death. Their population dwindled steadily for the next one hundred years until their society finally disappeared.

These marauding Sea Peoples continued eastward from the Aegean and raided the Southern Anatolia coast held by the Hittites. Finally they reached Ugarit and Cyprus, which they sacked and thereby cut off the Hittites' food supply. Thus weakened, the Hittites were no match for the hordes of hungry people in Northern Anatolia who swept southward and destroyed the Hittite empire. Great victories had been won, but the Sea Peoples had not yet reached the lush grain fields to the south.

With victory in sight, more than a hundred thousand Sea People poured southward, with ox carts carrying their meager possessions and family members walking behind. They surged through the land now known as Syria, leaving destruction in their wake. Out of respect for whatever assistance the Phoenicians had given them, they treated the Phoenician cities like holy ground and bypassed them on that southward trek. With that sole exception, the Sea Peoples laid waste to virtually all the cities they encountered. Across the land now known as Israel their destructive path moved forward, occasionally leaving thousands of people from the caravan to settle beside the rich grain fields. Less than 200 years before the birth of King David, they marched past the city of Jerusalem which was not on their path.

At last the Sea Peoples reached Gaza and the border of Egypt. Reduced in numbers, but supported by ships able to attack the Nile Delta, they tried once more to take Egypt. In furious battles, the Egyptians under King Ramses III managed to turn back the Sea Peoples by land and sea. Yet when the fighting was done, the Egyptians were left so weak they were compelled to allow the tribes of the Sea Peoples to live in the lands they had taken. The Peleset who had settled across southern Canaan gave the name Palestine to that land. Other tribes took the middle and northern portions.

The Phoenicians were left in peace in their cities along the coast. As it turned out, all of their opponents had been defeated. The troublesome Hittites were left with only a tiny remnant by the Euphrates. The competing port of Ugarit was never rebuilt. The Mycenaeans died slowly, and in a hundred years were gone. Egypt had won the battle but lost the war—it fell into penniless obscurity for the next several centuries.

Following that major event, which changed the course of history in the Mediterranean, and before the building of Solomon's Temple, a smaller event happened in Byblos that was highly revealing. It also renewed the connection between the Phoenicians and the Great Pyramid, which had made such a deep impact on them. A man named Wenamun came from Egypt to Byblos, where he wrote a detailed account of the people he encountered in 1075 BC. Along the way he robbed some Tjekers, a Sea Peoples tribe in what is now Northern Israel. After the robbery, Wenamun fled to Byblos, intent upon completing his mission, which was to buy a ceremonial cedar boat for his Egyptian temple.

> Then he [the King of Byblos] spoke to me, saying: "On what business have you come?" I said to him: "I have come in quest of timber for the great noble [riverboat] of Amen-Re, King of Gods."

"What your father did, what the father of your father did, you too will do it." So I said to him. He said to me: "True, they did it. If you pay me for doing it, I will do it. My relations carried out this business after Pharaoh had sent six ships laden with the goods of Egypt, and they had been unloaded into their storehouses. You, what have you brought for me?"

He had the daybook of his forefathers brought and had it read before me. They found entered in his book a thousand *deben* of silver and all sorts of things....

He placed my letter in the hand of his messenger; and he loaded the keel, the prow-piece, and the stern-piece, together with four other hewn logs, seven in all, and sent them to Egypt. His messenger who had gone to Egypt returned to me in [Phoenicia] in the first month of winter, Smendes and Tentamun having sent [from Egypt]: four jars and one *kakmen*-vessel of gold; five jars of silver; ten garments of royal linen....

The prince rejoiced. He assigned three hundred men and three hundred oxen, and he set supervisors over them to have them fell the timbers. They were felled and they lay there during the winter. In the third month of summer they dragged them to the shore of the sea....

I went off to the shore of the sea, to where the logs were lying. And I saw eleven ships that had come in from the sea and belonged to the Tjeker (who were) saying: "Arrest him! Let no ship of his leave for the land of Egypt!" Then I sat down and wept....

When morning came, he [the King of Byblos] had his assembly summoned. [Note the Phoenician custom of the king consulting the town council before making important decisions.] He stood in their midst and said to the Tjeker: "What have you come for?" They said to him: "We have come after the blasted ships that you are sending to Egypt with our enemy." He said to them: "I cannot arrest the envoy of Amun in my coun-

try. Let me send him off, and you go after him to arrest him."

He had me board and sent me off from the harbor
of the sea. And the wind drove me to the land of [Cy-
prus].[28]

In this first-hand account by an Egyptian, we see an unintended testimony to the strong brand of secrecy practiced by the
Phoenicians. Wenamun said the King of Byblos took out a detailed book of Phoenician records that went far back in time. This
was but one of many observations in antiquity showing books of
Phoenician writings that have never been found. The practices
developed by the Phoenicians to cloak their affairs and conceal
their writings proved to be remarkably tight and successful.

This rare document also echoed an event that happened during
the building of the Great Pyramid some 1500 years earlier. Wenamun pointed out that the cedar boat he purchased was sent to
Egypt in pieces, to be assembled there. This mirrored the two cedar boats buried beside the Great Pyramid for Khufu's use in the
afterlife. As is well known, shipmakers normally build their vessel
to completion, then slip it into the water to sail to its new owner.
Here we saw an extremely rare occurrence: a boat was made with
cedar of Lebanon to be used for religious purposes, was cut and
shaped in pieces, then delivered in pieces to Egypt. The mystery
of why the Great Pyramid boats were stored in this strange way is
perhaps no longer such a mystery.

That the Phoenicians were able to repeat this same task 1500
years later is intriguing. Yet that seemed to be the nature of Phoenician society. Their ability to control their secrets apparently improved their ability to preserve them. The visible net result was
that the practices and fundamental principles of Phoenician society changed remarkably little over the centuries.

On the day of Wenamun's visit it had been 2100 years since
Byblos became a full-fledged city and launched the Phoenicians as
a society. Yet sea trade continued to be their main occupation.
Cedar of Lebanon was still their most coveted export. Their craft
skills, which began with precision cutting of cedar for their much-
envied boats, was continued with the precision cutting of ashlar

stones for the raising of walls and buildings. The closely guarded secrets of their early days not only continued but grew stronger and embraced more of their affairs as the years went by. Their tolerance for people of other religions—seen in their own temples—would soon become evident again as they assisted Jewish neighbors in building a great temple of their own.

And Hiram King of Tyre Sent Masons

Hiram was still young when his people in the Phoenician city of Tyre were confronted with a serious threat to their survival. King David of Israel sent troops northward to extend his authority, and they marched from victory to victory until they reached this city in what is known today as Lebanon. While the angel of death hovered over this anticipated battlefield along the Mediterranean coast, Hiram saw his father King Abibaal craft a path toward peaceful resolution of the crisis. Rich gifts were offered to the Hebrew king, and the impending devastation was avoided. Among these were the promise that Phoenician craftsmen would build a palace for David in Jerusalem.

Shortly thereafter, while Hiram was nineteen years of age, his father died and left the young man a heavy crown, along with a strong desire to do remarkable things with his life. The new ruler began by fulfilling his father's obligation.

> And Hiram king of Tyre sent messengers to David, and cedar trees, and carpenters, and masons; and they built David a house.
>
> 2 Samuel 5:11

The Tyrian king was aware that David dreamed of building a great temple to God in Jerusalem. Due to the man's tumultuous life and campaigns, however, that desire was not accomplished during David's lifetime. Instead the mission fell to his son, Solomon, who became king around 970 BC.[29] Fortunately these events were described in great detail by Hebrew scholars in the Tanakh, and later appeared in the Old Testament of the Bible.

> And Hiram king of Tyre sent his servants unto Solomon; for he had heard that they had anointed him king in the room of his father; for Hiram was ever a lover [great admirer] of David.
>
> And Solomon sent to Hiram, saying, "Thou knowest how that David my father could not build an house unto the name of the LORD his God for the wars which were about him on every side, until the LORD put them under the soles of his feet. But now the LORD my God hath given me rest on every side, so that there is neither adversary nor evil occurrent. And, behold, I purpose to build an house unto the name of the LORD my God, as the LORD spake unto David my father, saying, Thy son, whom I will set upon thy throne in thy room, he shall build an house unto my name. Now therefore command thou that they hew me cedar trees out of Lebanon; and my servants shall be with thy servants; and unto thee will I give hire for thy servants according to all that thou shalt appoint; for thou knowest that there is not among us any that can skill to hew timber like unto the Sidonians."
>
> And it came to pass, when Hiram heard the words of Solomon, that he rejoiced greatly, and said, "Blessed be the LORD this day, which hath given unto David a wise son over this great people."
>
> And Hiram sent to Solomon, saying, "I have considered the things which thou sentest to me for; and I will do all thy desire concerning timber of cedar, and concerning timber of fir. My servants shall bring them down from Lebanon unto the sea; and I will convey

them by sea in floats unto the place that thou shalt appoint me, and will cause them to be discharged there, and thou shalt receive them; and thou shalt accomplish my desire, in giving food for my household."

So Hiram gave Solomon cedar trees and fir trees according to all his desire. And Solomon gave Hiram twenty thousand measures of wheat for food to his household, and twenty measures of pure oil; thus gave Solomon to Hiram year by year. And the LORD gave Solomon wisdom, as he promised him; and there was peace between Hiram and Solomon; and they two made a league together.

1 Kings 5:1-12

This close relationship grew over the years and proved to be exceptionally beneficial for the two kings and for their people. The Phoenicians avoided a war, and instead turned their predicament into a profitable arrangement. They were able to sell large amounts of building materials to their new neighbors, who had arrived with swords at their southern border. The Hebrew tribes also benefited because they were a largely pastoral people who offered outdoor sacrifices to their God. They had never built a temple before, as illustrated by 1 Kings 3:2 "The people only sacrificed in high places, because there was no house built unto the name of the LORD, until those days [of Solomon]." So how could King Solomon hope to build the beautiful temple to God he wished to raise? He did the natural thing. He called upon his experienced Phoenician neighbors to provide a master mason and skilled artisans.

And king Solomon sent and fetched Hiram out of Tyre. He was a widow's son of the tribe of Naphtali, and his father was a man of Tyre, a worker in brass; and he was filled with wisdom, and understanding, and cunning to work all works in brass. And he came to king Solomon, and wrought all his work.

1 Kings 7:13-14

This Hiram had the same name as the king of Tyre, but there was no known family relationship between them. To distinguish between the two men, Freemasons refer to the master builder as Hiram Abiff. The above passage from the Bible told us Hiram Abiff came from the Phoenician city of Tyre. His father was from Tyre as well, so Hiram had ancestral ties in the city. His mother was descended from the tribe of Napthali, one of the twelve Hebrew tribes, so he could also have claimed Jewish heritage if he wished. Since his mother was a widow, Hiram's father must have died by the time Solomon's Temple was raised. If Hiram had wanted to immerse himself in Hebrew culture and religious practices, it would have been reasonable for him to have moved to Israel after his father's death. That he did not do so—and chose to stay in Tyre—suggested that he took over his Phoenician father's business of creating brassworks. No doubt Hiram was exceptionally well regarded as a builder and brassworker, for when the King of Israel chose to lavish huge fortunes upon the construction of a temple, and could ask the King of Tyre for anyone he wanted, Hiram was chosen.

The Phoenicians had been building temples of cut stones, beaten gold and fragrant cedar for many centuries by this time. In Tyre alone they had three temples made of masonry, with one of them being particularly striking and easily visible from the shore. This was the one that Herodotus described as having "two pillars, one of pure gold, the other of emerald, shining with great brilliancy at night."

This temple and its pair of magnificent pillars were believed to have inspired the design of Solomon's Temple. The major difference between the two was the much larger size of the temple in Jerusalem. Land was at a premium on the island of Tyre, so the footprint of its temple was necessarily small. In addition, gold, brass and cedar were much-coveted materials for building and decoration in those days, and generally were sparingly used. With that in mind, the sheer size of Solomon's Temple and its grand display of precious adornments begins to convey some of the impact which must have been felt by those fortunate enough to enter its doors.

In those days, the favored measuring unit was a "cubit," the distance from a man's elbow to the end of his extended fingers—a length of about one and a half feet, or half a meter. That reference helps us appreciate the sweeping scale of those master works, compared to the size of a person walking among them in those times.

> For he [Hiram Abiff] cast two pillars of brass, of eighteen cubits high apiece; and a line of twelve cubits did compass either of them about. And he made two chapiters [capitals] of molten brass, to set upon the tops of the pillars; the height of the one chapiter was five cubits, and the height of the other chapiter was five cubits. And nets of checker work, and wreaths of chain work, for the chapiters which were upon the top of the pillars; seven for the one chapiter, and seven for the other chapiter.
>
> And he set up the pillars in the porch of the temple; and he set up the right pillar, and called the name thereof *Jachin*; and he set up the left pillar, and called the name thereof *Boaz*. And upon the top of the pillars was lily work; so was the work of the pillars finished.
>
> And he made a molten sea [place for washing], ten cubits from the one brim to the other: it was round all about, and his height was five cubits.... It stood upon twelve oxen, three looking toward the north, and three looking toward the west, and three looking toward the south, and three looking toward the east: and the sea was set above upon them, and all their hinder parts were inward. And it was an hand breadth thick, and the brim thereof was wrought like the brim of a cup, with flowers of lilies: it contained two thousand baths.
>
> And Hiram made the lavers, and the shovels, and the basons [basins]. So Hiram made an end of doing all the work that he made king Solomon for the house of the LORD.
>
> So was ended all the work that king Solomon made for the house of the LORD. And Solomon brought in

Fig. 8   Solomon's Temple

the things which David his father had dedicated; even
the silver, and the gold, and the vessels, did he put
among the treasures of the house of the LORD.

1 Kings 7:15-17, 21-26, 40, 51

The spacious complex in which Hiram placed all these adornments was also large in scale. It consisted of a courtyard containing the great altar for sacrifices, and his "molten sea" on the backs
of twelve brass oxen as described above. At the front of the temple
itself he raised the shimmering brass pillars named *Jachin* and *Boaz*
which stood at least twenty-seven feet high. Walking past the pillars meant passing under a porch whose height was probably similar to the pillars. It was necessary to open one of the massive
doors covered with gold to gain entry into the main house of the
temple. The thirty foot width of this room was comfortable rather
than huge, yet it was also sixty feet long and soared forty-five feet
high, roughly four stories of unimpeded space lined with rich and
intricate decoration. The solid stone walls were completely covered on the inside with cedar, gold, and ornate brasswork. The
effect would likely have conjured a surpassing sense of beauty,
wealth and power.

At the far end of the room, a partition separated the Holy of
Holies from the main room. For the very few permitted to pass the
final partition and enter the inner sanctum, this holy chamber was
seen to extend thirty feet wide, thirty feet long and almost three
stories high. The ancient Ark of the Covenant rested there, protected by two angels covered in gold. These guardians stood fifteen feet high. Their wingspans were likewise fifteen feet in
length, such that together they spanned the entire width of the
room. Again, the stone walls were covered with cedar, gold and
brasswork. Additional adornment was provided by a linen veil
woven in blue, crimson and purple, with images of angels.

And the house which king Solomon built for the
LORD, the length thereof was threescore cubits,[30] and
the breadth thereof twenty cubits, and the height
thereof thirty cubits. And the porch before the temple

of the house, twenty cubits was the length thereof, according to the breadth of the house; and ten cubits was the breadth thereof before the house. And for the house he made windows of narrow lights.

And the house, when it was in building, was built of stone made ready before it was brought thither: so that there was neither hammer nor axe nor any tool of iron heard in the house, while it was in building.

The door for the middle chamber was in the right side of the house: and they went up with winding stairs into the middle chamber, and out of the middle into the third. So he built the house, and finished it; and covered the house with beams and boards of cedar. And then he built chambers against all the house, five cubits high: and they rested on the house with timber of cedar.

And the oracle [Holy of Holies] he prepared in the house within, to set there the ark of the covenant of the LORD. And the oracle in the forepart was twenty cubits in length, and twenty cubits in breadth, and twenty cubits in the height thereof: and he overlaid it with pure gold; and so covered the altar which was of cedar. So Solomon overlaid the house within with pure gold.

1 Kings 6:2-4, 7-10, 19-21

Throughout this work on the temple, which the Hebrew scribes told us took seven years to accomplish, the record-keepers followed the custom used by most of their peers—they cited the marvelous contributions of the local people, but especially of the King. This gave the impression that Solomon fastened each cedar beam into place himself. In fact, records of this nature rarely gave outsiders any credit for work on such an intensely personal part of their people's culture as Solomon's Temple proved to be. So for the Phoenician king and his mason to have been mentioned here numerous times was a strong tribute to the critical nature of their contribution. The choice of Hiram as master builder, and the importance given to him by Hebrew scholars who described those events seemed to have been a reasonable compromise between local pride and foreign credit. Among the experienced Phoenician masons needed for this work Hiram—having a Hebrew mother—was more acceptable than anyone else to give direction to the local workmen, as well as to the Phoenician workers.

Even so, might an issue have arisen among some of the workmen? The Phoenicians were well-known in antiquity for holding their secrets close to their chest and not sharing them with others. In Freemasonry, when a person becomes a Master Mason, the ritual they experience includes the reenactment of a confrontation in which local workmen demand the master builder tell his secrets.[31] He refuses to do so. Such a confrontation may have actually occurred. If it did, however, it does not seem to have had the fatal outcome for Hiram that is portrayed in the ceremony. The historical Hiram apparently lived to complete his work on the temple, as the Bible passages have told us. Even so, the atmosphere was true to life.

A wide range of secrets and things-not-to-be-seen have been attributed to Solomon's Temple by numerous sources. Over the years, these clandestine matters have been said to include the Holy Grail, the Ark of the Covenant, a record of the descendants of Jesus Christ, writings pertaining to mystical secrets, and myriad other mysterious matters. Two more were suggested by the biblical accounts cited above, so it would be appropriate to consider them now.

The first set of secrets presented were those of the Phoenician masons working on the Temple. Much like their brothers who appeared later in Europe, these masons seem to have taken steps to limit what local workmen could learn about their craft. The squaring and carving of stones for the temple apparently was done privately at a distant place, for we were told, "And the house, when it was in building, was built of stone made ready before it was brought thither: so that there was neither hammer nor axe nor any tool of iron heard in the house, while it was in building." This reflects serious amounts of extra effort being exerted to maintain secrecy around the arts being practiced by the masons.

Separate from that was the amount of care taken to keep the Holy of Holies isolated as much as possible from the outside world. This was a necessary step, since that repository had to protect the Ark of the Covenant, in which the two stone tablets of Moses were said to have been stored. These were among the most treasured Hebraic relics of antiquity. An intruder seeking to approach the Holy of Holies would have had to first cross the courtyards outside the temple, to which access was limited. Then he had to pass through the porch and down the length of the main hall, going past the temple's many priests, before coming to the only doorway that led into the sanctuary. All those things revealed a strong intent to achieve security.

Yet breach of that security could still be achieved. In fact, King Shishak of Egypt did it in 933 BC.[32] Further attacks came about 900 BC by king Asa of Judah;[33] circa 825 BC by King Jehoash of Judah;[34] circa 790 BC by King Joash of Israel;[35] circa 734 BC by King Ahaz of Judah;[36] and circa 712 BC by king Hezekiah of Judah.[37] The Temple was twice attacked and pillaged by King Nebuchadnezzar II of Babylon—once in 597 BC and again in 586 BC—after which he burned the building and carried to Babylon all the treasures that could be found.[38] Many of the Hebrew people were also seized and taken away, in what has come to be known as the Babylonian Captivity.

Since raiding the riches of a captured temple was commonly done and reasonably expected, it was natural that the builders of Solomon's Temple would have felt compelled to take additional secretive measures.

Secrecy traditionally begets concealment, and in places of worship that has often tended to be a fearful and secret place, usually a crypt. Crypts evoke places of death, ultimate isolation and the passage of eons of time.

The ancient Egyptians built secret crypts in their pyramids to conceal and protect the bodies of the pharaohs. Medieval stonemasons in Europe later built crypts under churches or temples to safeguard the remains of great leaders, or objects of value. For Solomon's Temple, the Holy of Holies was a large and visible target for any raider. The only true protection would have been a clandestine place the raider could not find.

For a large temple such as this, a modest underground crypt would have been almost invisible. If it was added when the foundation was being laid, few onlookers would have had any idea of its significance, since at that time the onlookers were unfamiliar with temple construction. Such a crypt under the Holy of Holies would only have needed to be large enough to hold the Ark of the Covenant—and possibly not even that. An enclosure of sufficient size to hold the two stone tablets would have been enough. Yet if such a crypt were being built, it would reasonably be given enough capacity to hold other valuables as well, such as scrolls containing the Mikra—the Hebrew religious writings—as well as any documents that were better kept out of public view.

The Phoenician builders were no stranger to secrecy and mysteries. Their history remained virtually unknown for many centuries, due in large part to the secrecy in which they wrapped their society. They were notorious for jealously protecting their trade sources, navigation charts, writings and other internal records. They passed these documents and pieces of information from generation to generation among themselves, but took drastic measures to prevent them from falling into the hands of others. How successful were they at doing this? Consider that they were the ones who brought the Phoenician alphabet and modern writing to lands all across the Mediterranean. Yet of all their copious records and writings, almost none have passed into the hands of others.

In terms of the physical skills of concealment, the Phoenicians had already built many crypts in their city of Byblos. Archaeologists unearthed a series of underground burial chambers in that city which were built during the ten centuries before Solomon's day. Inside one of them was the ornately-decorated sarcophagus of King Ahiram of Byblos, with its long inscription that made use of the early Phoenician alphabet. These underground chambers were situated in the religious precinct of the city, and seemed to imitate the earlier Egyptian practice. Occasional heavy stone sarcophaguses and other indicators of wealth found in the Byblos crypts suggest these vaults were for prominent members of the community and their valued relics. Clearly, then, the Phoenician builders had experience designing hidden chambers and had put this knowledge to use.

To prove that a crypt was or was not built into Solomon's Temple, it would be reasonable to simply go to that site and search for clues of such a structure. Unfortunately any manner of new excavation is extremely difficult to arrange given the current religious and political tensions that have come into play on Temple Mount. The next best source would be to determine if such underground structures had been found in any previous excavations on the Mount. In fact, numerous underground structures have been discovered there, with many subterranean rooms and passages found and explored over the years. It was even reported that the Knights Templar opened and entered some of those structures when they established their Order on the Mount. Among these underground areas that can still be seen today are the curiously named "Solomon's Stables." It should be noted that not all of these underground structures have been fully explored.

Could Hebrew priests have placed objects of value down there? Might the Knights Templar have found some of these things during their later explorations? The answer to these questions is, "Yes. They could have." But did those things actually take place? There is no agreement on that among all the divergent parties involved. However several additional clues are now bringing us much closer to answering some of those questions, and we will return to that soon.

King Hiram extended his relationship with Solomon far beyond the building of that extraordinary temple in Jerusalem. He negotiated the building of a personal palace for Solomon using fragrant cedar wood throughout. The two kings became like brothers, and that opened the way for them to undertake an ambitious trade venture. Lacking access by sea to the east, Hiram saw an opportunity in the town of Eilat at the southern tip of Israel, on the shore of the Red Sea. This sea flowed between Egypt and what is now Saudi Arabia, and then opened up to the Indian Ocean. It was an ideal route eastward. With the prospect of additional riches in front of them, Hiram and Solomon came to a mutually beneficial agreement.

The Phoenician king contributed ships, crews and his people's sea-trading expertise. Solomon's contribution was the port city of Eilat, along with some portion of the cargo to be traded, and several representatives to make sure his interests were protected. The destination of these trading ships was a mysterious land that the Phoenicians referred to as Ophir. This is usually understood to mean India, a bountiful source of gold, spices and exotic animals. The venture was launched, then it was repeated every three years. This repetition suggested both parties were happy with their share of the rich profits and readily came back for more. Even though Israel was never known to have had a great navy in antiquity, Solomon's scribes became a little carried away in drafting their account, which otherwise gave us some intriguing details on this joint venture.

> And king Solomon made a navy of ships in Eziongeber, which is beside Eloth, on the shore of the Red sea, in the land of Edom. And Hiram sent in the navy his servants, shipmen that had knowledge of the sea, with the servants of Solomon. And they came to Ophir, and fetched from thence gold, four hundred and twenty talents, and brought it to king Solomon.
>
> And the navy also of Hiram, that brought gold from Ophir, brought in from Ophir great plenty of almug trees, and precious stones. For the king had at sea a navy of Tharshish with the navy of Hiram: once in three years came the navy of Tharshish, bringing gold, and silver, ivory, and apes, and peacocks.
>
> 1 Kings 9:26-28, 1 Kings 10:11, 22

The wealth of Solomon became legendary, an outcome in which these shipments of gold would have played no small part. It is also true that the raising of Solomon's Temple had a tremendous impact on how the Hebrew people came to see themselves. It evoked a sense of pride and wonder that still lingers to some degree today. It would be reasonable to say that the Phoenicians had a noticeable effect on their southern neighbors.

During these years King Hiram was busy on a number of other projects that would impact the Hebrew people, Solomon's Temple, other secret societies, and much of the Mediterranean world. When Hiram succeeded his father as ruler of Tyre, his small realm was one of the three leading cities of the Phoenicians. The ancient port of Byblos was still active in Hiram's day, but had long since passed the baton of leadership to the younger and more energetic Sidon. This other Phoenician city, also called Saida, was to the north of Tyre and it had the advantage of being close to dense forests of cedar trees on the sides of the Lebanon Mountains. Sidon had grown up beside a natural harbor along the shore and enjoyed unlimited room to grow. Those things allowed the city to expand more quickly than Tyre, and so it had risen to the forefront of Phoenician society. But that was about to change.

Hiram's Tyre had the unique advantage of standing on an island a half-mile from the Phoenician coast. This made it well-protected from attack by land, and since Hiram's ships dominated the surrounding sea it was protected there as well. But the island was too small for all the things he hoped to accomplish. Eyeing the rocky shoal immediately to the east of his island, Hiram directed his masons to create a landfill between his island and the nearby shoal, hoping to reclaim it from the sea.[39] This marvel of engineering was accomplished in relatively short order, and Tyre rapidly expanded to cover the forty acres of land that was now available.[40] As the number of ships he put into the sea increased year by year, Tyre soon eclipsed the other Phoenician cities, and became the "first among equals" in the widespread Phoenician sea trade across the Mediterranean. No doubt the rich trade Hiram conducted with Solomon helped to finance this expansion.

Hiram filled these larger harbors with shipping and wealth by expanding the Phoenicians' few colonies overseas. Their main foreign encampment at that time was on the eastern end of the island of Cyprus, where his predecessors had planted the city of Kition.[41] This guaranteed the Phoenicians a share of the rich copper ore for which the island was famous. Copper and tin were heated together and beaten into the bronze swords and plowshares that gave the Bronze Age its name.

He greatly expanded the trade in gold, silver and other precious materials from the Phoenician outposts at Cadiz in Spain, Larache in Morocco, and Utica in North Africa.[42] Pliny, Strabo and other ancient scholars noted those trading posts were established prior to 1000 BC,[43] but the trade camps seem to have been small or seasonal at first, since archaeologists have not found substantial structures built before the tenth century BC. It was during these tentative years, when the young colonies might yet fail, that Hiram managed to send boats on risky voyages the entire length of the Mediterranean Sea, changing the temporary outposts into permanent settlements

Especially relevant to the building of Solomon's Temple was the fact that a similar building had been raised just prior to that time by the Phoenicians at Kition on Cyprus. The temple they built there was dedicated to Our Lady, and the massive stones used for her temple were cut in the Phoenician style of perfectly squared ashlar stones that fit together so precisely they required no mortar between them. Many of those great stones are still visible today, and measure about nine feet long, six feet high and six feet thick. It is striking how much the Phoenician temple at Kition resembles the description by Hebrew scribes of the great temple and other buildings raised on Mount Moriah.

> All these were of costly stones, according to the measures of hewed stones, sawed with saws, within and without, even from the foundation unto the coping, and so on the outside toward the great court. And the foundation was of costly stones, even great stones, stones of ten cubits, and stones of eight cubits.
>
> I Kings 7:9-10

Since the foundation stones of the Temple in Jerusalem were dragged away and dispersed by the Romans, they are no longer there for us to see and touch. It is possible that the great stones of Our Lady's temple in Kition—cut by Phoenician masons just before the time that Solomon's work was done—are the closest we will ever come to seeing the original walls of Solomon's Temple.

We will return soon to the Temple of Solomon, but first we must glean more from the events that shaped the Phoenician and Hebrew people after the erection of Solomon's landmark house of worship on the high hill above Jerusalem. These events, as well as the temple itself, would seriously impact the Knights Templar and Freemasons who were to follow.

Chapter 5

The People of the Temple

The secrets known by the people who built Solomon's Temple were preserved even while they passed through several of the greatest moments in Mediterranean history.

Elissa of Tyre was an unlikely person to be founder of a great city, but it is to her that Carthage owed its existence. She was only about fifteen years old when her father died. This was more than just a personal loss, for he was the King of Tyre. That meant Elissa and her eleven-year-old brother Pygmalion were among the candidates to succeed him. The late king's brother Acherbas sought to further his own ambitions by quickly marrying Elissa and rallying a portion of the city in her favor. When his efforts failed, Pygmalion received the crown. Acherbas subsequently died under mysterious circumstances. Six years after her brother' rule began, Elissa apparently slipped quietly out of Tyre with many boatloads of supporters and much of the wealth of the city. After traveling for a period of time these prospective colonists arrived at the coast of North Africa. There they began to build Carthage upon Byrsa Hill, with Elissa as their queen.

Consistent with this account of Carthage being launched by the arrival of many people and considerable wealth, the city rapidly grew to become the most dominant Phoenician colony in the Mediterranean. Yet it was far from alone. Phoenician colonies were springing up everywhere like flowers in springtime after a brisk rain.

Their older outposts at Kition on Cyprus, Utica in North Africa, Cadiz in Spain, and Larache in Morocco were joined by new colonies scattered across Sicily, Sardinia, Corsica, Malta, several Aegean islands, other parts of Spain, Morocco, Algeria and North Africa. Outside the Pillars of Hercules their explorers ventured north from Cadiz along the Atlantic coast to make settlements at Lisbon and Porto in the land that would become known as Portugal. The traders who followed them were said to have reached Brittany in France, Cornwall in England, and farther north, bringing back goods that included valuable tin for use in making bronze.

Yet among all this far-flung colonization, Carthage stood out. Located near the midpoint of the Mediterranean, halfway between Spain and Lebanon, it was embedded at the end of an arm of land that reached up from Africa toward Sicily and Italy in the middle of Europe. This placed Carthage at the crossroads of trade between East and West, as well as between North and South across the Mediterranean.

Sicily was only a short one hundred miles to the east of Carthage, with the other end of Sicily separated from Italy by a single mile of water. These were distances easily traveled. It caused classical Greece and Rome to be highly aware of Carthage when those societies emerged in the years that followed.

Thucydides, one of the leading Greek historians, told us that when the first Greek settlers arrived at Sicily around 734 BC, they found Phoenicians already settled on the island.

> There were also Phoenicians living all round Sicily, who had occupied promontories upon the sea coasts and the islets adjacent for the purpose of trading with the Sicels. But when the Hellenes [Greeks] began to arrive in considerable numbers by sea, the Phoenicians abandoned most of their stations [in Eastern Sicily], and took up their abode in [Western Sicily at] Motye,

Fig. 9 Aeneas and Elissa (Dido) at Carthage

Soloeis, and Panormus [Palermo], near the Elymi [lo-
cal people], with whom they united, confiding in their
alliance, and also because this is the nearest point for
the voyage between Carthage and Sicily.

Thucydides 6:2

Phoenician masons at all of these widespread colonies continued to build the massive and durable harbors and waterways
needed for their maritime trading operations. Carthage's extensive harbor facilities were built for commercial ships as well as for
the military vessels that protected their lifelines across the sea. On
land, many miles of defensive walls spread across Carthage's peninsula to seal off the city from the mainland. These walls were so
well built that it has been reported they were never successfully
breached. When Carthage eventually suffered misfortune, it came
through other avenues.

Meanwhile, the people of Solomon split their kingdom in two
during the reign of his son, with the remnants taking the name of
Israel in the north and Judah in the south. Israel fell to foreign
occupation first, with Judah following in 609 BC when the Babylonians swept in. Twelve years later King Jeconiah, grandfather to
the legendary Zerubbabel, was taken from Judah along with many
others in the first wave of the Babylonian captivity. In 586 BC the
second deportation completed this task of taking the Hebrew
people into exile, and the Temple of Solomon, having been sacked
many times by others, was now utterly destroyed and left in ruins.

Just as suddenly, it was Babylon's turn to suffer destruction.
This came at the hands of the Persians in 538 BC, and it was to this
new Persian king, Cyrus the Great, that Zerubbabel appealed for
his people to be allowed to return home. That appeal was granted
and Zerubbabel, as governor of Judah, returned home at the head
of thousands of his people. Two years later the foundation of the
Second Temple was established at the same place where Solomon's original Temple had stood. In 516 BC the Temple was finally completed and ruled again over Temple Mount. Upon its dedication the following year, it once more became the beating heart of
Jewish life.

To the north of Jerusalem on the Lebanese coast, the Phoenician merchant cities had also been required to acknowledge the Babylonians and Persians as overlords. Yet their policy of meeting oncoming armies with rich gifts and negotiations once again served them well. The descendants of Hiram retained a great amount of freedom in conducting their lives. They continued to live in their own cities throughout these years, and kept up their rich trade. Their penchant for secrecy is believed to have contributed greatly to the privileged status granted to them. The invaders from Babylon and Persia were well aware of the Phoenicians' lucrative trade, but were unable to learn from whence it came. Faced with the stark reality that if they destroyed the traders' cities, there would be no incoming wealth, those overlords allowed the Phoenicians to go about their business with little interference—provided annual payments of tribute were made. It proved to be a satisfactory arrangement all the way around. These experiences seemed to validate and strongly reinforce the Phoenicians' sworn resolve to keep their affairs carefully concealed from others.

Then came a new invader who struck the Phoenicians and Hebrews like no other had done before. This was Alexander the Great. At only twenty years of age Alexander became king of Macedonia upon the assassination of his father in 336 BC. The city-states his father had conquered all across Greece now revolted to see if they could break free of Macedonian control. Alexander's advisors recommended diplomacy, but instead he set out with 3,000 cavalrymen and imposed firm control over his small Greek empire. That done, he gathered about 42,000 men around him and began his campaign against Persia—and most of the rest of the known world—by crossing the Hellespont in 334 BC and entering the land of Anatolia, now known as Turkey.

Moving from victory to victory, Alexander reached Halicarnassus in the southwest corner of this vast peninsula, then swept northeastward into its heart. There he solved the riddle of the Gordian Knot in his usual, direct manner. He chopped it apart with his sword. Legend held that the person who solved the riddle would become king of Asia, and in this case it proved to be prophetic. Driving southward, Alexander reached the Mediterranean Sea at its most northeastern point, near the town of Issus. There he won a great victory over the Persian King Darius III, forcing the once-proud man from the field in a rout.

Alexander could have pursued Darius at that point, but it would have left the Eastern Seaboard of the Mediterranean exposed behind his back. So he chose instead to drive southward down the coast, expecting his greatest resistance in this direction would be from Egypt. He was mistaken. Alexander got no farther than the Phoenician city of Tyre, which refused to yield. The other Phoenician cities bent to the young Macedonian king because they stood on the mainland and could have been easily taken by force. But Tyre stood on its island half a mile from the coast, and in its 2400 years of existence had never been taken. Foreign armies on the shore had always become frustrated and negotiated for peace. But that was not Alexander's way—he began a siege against incredible odds.

The Phoenician masons had raised one of their greatest works at Tyre. Tall, massive walls encircled the city, reaching upward about 150 feet at their highest point, and tremendously thick. Undeterred, Alexander brought his own engineers and slowly built a causeway across the half-mile of sea using large stones and debris. All the while, defenders and attackers continued to fight from the battlements and construction site. The masons of Tyre had built well, and nothing could be done by the attackers until they finally gained a foothold on the edge of the island. Then Alexander's engineers went to work and were able to undermine the towering wall at one point, forming a breech. As his troops rushed in, many residents were killed and the city was put to the torch.

Yet even in the midst of all this mayhem, a Greek writer within Alexander's army reported a most unusual sight. Men from the Phoenician city of Sidon—who had previously surrendered to Alexander and been forced to serve in his army—engaged in a death-defying display of brotherhood.

> Young boys and girls [in Tyre] had filled the temples, but the men all stood in the vestibules of their own homes ready to face the fury of their enemy.

Many, however, found safety with the Sidonians among the Macedonian troops. Although these had entered the city with the conquerors, they remained aware that they were related to the Tyrians...and so they secretly gave many of them protection and took them to their boats, on which they were hidden and transported to Sidon. Fifteen thousand were rescued from a violent death by such subterfuge.[44]

Quintus Curtius Rufus
The History of Alexander 4.4

As noted earlier, to aid the enemy in the midst of battle has almost always been punished by execution under charge of treason. That the men of Sidon still came to the aid of their fellow Phoenicians suggested a bond of brotherhood in their society which had serious depth and strength.[45] One might say this was reminiscent of the practices by the Knights Templar and Freemasons—except that the Phoenicians clearly came first.

After the fall of Tyre, Alexander continued southward and captured Jerusalem, where he took Solomon's Temple into his hands. The conquest of Egypt was next, and it yielded to him quickly. Then like a row of dominoes, Alexander swept over the lands we now know as Iraq, Iran, Pakistan and parts of India. He returned victorious to Babylon, but any celebration was cut short by his mysterious, sudden death. Only nine short years after conquering the lands of the Phoenician and Hebrew people, he was gone.

Three of Alexander's successors divided all these conquered lands between them. One ruled over Greece, another over Egypt, and the third over the Near East and Asia. Being in this last group, the Phoenicians of Lebanon and the Hebrew people of Israel were required to pay tribute to a Greek king based in the city of Antioch. These Antioch kings were so preoccupied with ongoing rebellions in the vicinity of Pakistan that they left the quiet and relatively cooperative Phoenicians alone as long as the tribute was paid. The Hebrew people were less fortunate since both Antioch and Egypt claimed to be their overlord, causing their land to be a battlefield for more than a century.

Carthage and all the other Phoenician colonies continued to be free, which enabled their kinsmen in Lebanon to keep their identity alive. As the largest Phoenician colony, it was only natural that Carthage took over leadership of this widespread mercantile empire. That great city in North Africa became a sprawling metropolis of beautiful buildings and provincial villas, with a population variously estimated at between five hundred thousand and a million people.

Yet trouble was brewing in Italy. A new conqueror and tormentor of the Phoenician and Hebrew people was rising on the banks of the Tiber River, and this was Rome. Beginning as a small town near the Western Italian coast, Rome first defeated its Etruscan neighbors, then all the Gauls and Greeks in the Italian countryside. Eventually its rule expanded to the southern tip of the Italian peninsula, where it spied the large and fertile island of Sicily just off its coast.

At that time the western part of Sicily was controlled by Carthage, while the eastern part was in the hands of the Greeks encamped at Syracuse. Rome quickly brushed back the Greeks, then began the first Punic War with Carthage. When the dust from this conflict settled, Rome owned all of Sicily. After the war, an excuse was found to take from Carthage the islands of Sardinia and Corsica as well. Many people in Carthage, having drifted far from the Phoenician principle of living peacefully and negotiating with neighboring societies, wished to strike back against Rome and its legions. This counterattack was led by the Phoenician version of Alexander the Great, a gifted young man named Hannibal.

Hannibal Barca was the son of Carthaginian general Hamilcar, and only nine years old when he accompanied his father on a campaign to Spain. Hamilcar energetically expanded Carthage's colony to cover the southern part of the Iberian Peninsula, and raised a great army. There young Hannibal learned his lessons well. He rose to become an officer, and was still rising when his father and his brother-in-law died, leaving the command vacant. Hannibal was then twenty-six and—according to the Roman scholar Livy—a commanding presence.

There was no hesitation shown in filling his [father's] place. The soldiers led the way by bringing the young Hannibal forthwith to the palace and proclaiming him their commander-in-chief amidst universal applause....

The veterans thought they saw Hamilcar restored to them as he was in his youth; they saw the same determined expression, the same piercing eyes, the same cast of features...there was no leader in whom the soldiers placed more confidence or under whom they showed more daring. He was fearless in exposing himself to danger and perfectly self-possessed in the presence of danger. No amount of exertion could cause him either bodily or mental fatigue; he was equally indifferent to heat and cold; his eating and drinking were measured by the needs of nature, not by appetite; his hours of sleep were not determined by day or night, whatever time was not taken up with active duties was given to sleep and rest, but that rest was not wooed on a soft couch or in silence, men often saw him lying on the ground amongst the sentinels and outposts, wrapped in his military cloak. His dress was in no way superior to that of his comrades; what did make him conspicuous were his arms and horses. He was by far the foremost both of the cavalry and the infantry, the first to enter the fight and the last to leave the field. [46]

Livy
The History of Rome III:21

Two years after accepting this military command, Hannibal began the calling for which he had been groomed. Rome reached far into Carthage's Spanish territory to name itself protector of the city of Saguntum, to which Hannibal responded by going to Saguntum and tearing down the city walls. Rome angrily demanded justice from Carthage, but Hannibal argued for war. With little support from Carthage, Hannibal forced the issue by assembling

Fig. 10   Hannibal

his troops and marching them eastward from Spain in 218 BC. In a series of battles he moved quickly through what would become Southern France. Accompanied by his famous vanguard of powerful and intimidating elephants, Hannibal crossed the alps into Italy. With these bold moves, the Second Punic War began.

Now that he was in Italy, a series of remarkable events occurred. Hannibal's small army marched across the countryside and defeated the highly regarded Roman legions at every encounter. He brilliantly orchestrated his battles, and moved quickly to have the engagements be at the time and place of most benefit to his troops. The one limitation that held him back was the weak support he continued to receive from Carthage. The people there remained divided between waging war and seeking peace, so as a result Hannibal received little in terms of reinforcements or supplies. Then as the war dragged on, the tide began to turn.

Unable to defeat Hannibal in Italy, the Romans carried the battle to Spain. There the Roman legions won a series of impressive victories. Thus encouraged, they moved on to North Africa. Called home to defend Carthage, Hannibal was finally forced to fight on an unfavorable field at Zama. That battle was lost to the Romans. The result was a difficult treaty of peace that required Carthage to cede all its remaining colonies. It retained only the land immediately surrounding its metropolis in North Africa.

Before the Punic Wars, Rome controlled land only in Italy. During these two wars it managed to acquire from the Phoenicians ownership of Sicily, Sardinia, Corsica, Spain, Morocco, and almost all of North Africa. These were converted into Rome's first overseas provinces. In a single stroke the foundation for the Roman Empire was created.

Even so, the Roman people had been pressed almost to the point of extinction by Hannibal during this war. It proved to be an experience they could not forget. Prodded by angry leaders, Rome created a pretext for beginning the third and final Punic War. Carthage was presented with the demand that it move its entire city ten miles inland. With the city's whole life being based on sea trade, its people of course refused to move away from the sea. With that excuse in hand, Roman troops overran the metropolis of Carthage in 146 BC amid an appalling amount of slaughter. The city was completely destroyed, reportedly not leaving one stone upon another. This rage against the Phoenicians seemed to carry over into Roman literature, where these people became adorned with negative character flaws to justify the harsh treatment against them.

Strangely enough, Rome's near death experience at the hands of Hannibal created exactly the opposite reaction toward him personally. He was hailed as a worthy opponent, and described as one of the greatest generals who ever lived. Romans called him the father of military strategy. They used his techniques to hone their legions—making them an even more deadly force than before. However the glory accorded to Hannibal did not help his people.

In Lebanon the remaining Phoenicians living under Greek overlords took note of this ferocious punishment at Carthage and made a fateful decision. Throughout the centuries, many lands had appointed themselves overlords of the Phoenician cities and demanded tribute. Those cities in Lebanon paid the tribute and otherwise went about their sea trade and their society. They often flourished under these conditions, and easily survived oversight by the Egyptians, Assyrians, Babylonians, Persians, and finally Greeks. By continuing to pay tribute to the Antioch Greeks, there was no reason why the Phoenicians could not have carried on their life and society as before.

Yet the eastward-marching legions of Rome brought a unique danger. The hundreds of thousands of people killed at Carthage constituted what has been called the greatest slaughter of civilian population up to the events surrounding World War I. The utter destruction of this once-proud city sent a clear message to the Phoenicians. As a result, before the Roman troops under Pompey arrived in Lebanon during 63 BC, Phoenician society simply disappeared. One possibility was that it completely disbanded. Many casually-formed societies have done so. As we have seen, however, the Phoenicians were not casually-formed. For 3100 years at this point they had proved to be a particularly tight-knit society pledged to mutual support, secrecy, and preservation of their way of life.

So the other possibility open to the Phoenicians was to quietly continue their society out of sight. This was the same way they had once lived among the Minoans. And if some left the society at this crucial time, those who remained would have been the most committed. For their whole existence they had lived much like a secret society. The veil of protective secrecy around them had allowed only a small amount of their affairs to be seen. With the arrival of the Romans on Lebanese soil, the remaining Phoenicians drew the veil closed completely.

When Pompey led those Roman legions into Tyre, Sidon, Beirut, Byblos and other cities in Phoenicia, there were no visible reminders of Carthage or other ancient glories to be seen. He found only cooperative members of Greek society—albeit with some curious local customs. No perceived Phoenician "stain" fell upon them, and no repetition of Carthage's destruction was performed. It was closer to a re-enactment of Passover.

So Pompey and his legions continued south to Jerusalem where he joined the civil war being fought among the Hebrew people. Aristobulus II and the priestly group of the temple led one faction, known as the Sadducees.[47] They were opposed by Hyrcanus II and the Pharisees.[48] Pompey sided with Hyrcanus against the temple group, and together they laid siege to Jerusalem. When the city fell, Pompey entered the temple and—though it was forbidden—even entered the Holy of Holies. The Hebrew historian Josephus described those events this way.

> Of the Jews there fell twelve thousand, but of the Romans very few.... and no small enormities were committed about the temple itself, which, in former ages, had been inaccessible, and seen by none; for Pompey went into it, and not a few of those that were with him also, and saw all that which it was unlawful for any other men to see but only for the high priests. There were in that temple the golden table, the holy candlestick, and the pouring vessels, and a great quantity of spices; and besides these there were among the treasures two thousand talents of sacred money: yet did

Pompey touch nothing of all this, on account of his regard to religion; and in this point also he acted in a manner that was worthy of his virtue. The next day he gave order to those that had the charge of the temple to cleanse it, and to bring what offerings the law required to God; and restored the high priesthood to Hyrcanus, both because he had been useful to him in other respects, and because he hindered the Jews in the country from giving Aristobulus any assistance in his war against him. [49]

Josephus
Antiquitates Judaicae 14:4

Notable among the items *not* found in the Holy of Holies were the Ark of the Covenant, the tablets of Moses, nor any notable sacred writings. So either nothing of real value was kept in the temple at this time, or the things of greatest value were well concealed. Given the unequalled reverence and restricted access accorded to the temple, it is hard to imagine that it stood essentially bare of religious material. More reasonably, the greatest treasure was not accessible to the uninitiated.

As for the condition of the temple itself, 453 years had passed since Zerubbabel rebuilt the temple on its original foundation. This revered structure had greatly felt the weight of years. That caused the Roman-appointed king of Judea province, Herod the Great, to begin a major renovation of the temple in 20 BC. The restoration itself took only about eighteen months. But the surrounding structures were massively changed and this required another eighty years to complete.

The most striking of these other structures were the huge walls raised by Herod on all four sides of Temple Mount to create flat ground around the Temple. This allowed him to construct additional courtyards, which in turn permitted more people to participate in the offerings and observances. The most famous of these retaining walls is the one on the western side. Often called the Wailing Wall, it has become a place devoted to prayer, and one of the most holy sites in Judaism.

Yet the building and destruction that would take place on Temple Mount certainly did not end with King Herod. In the year 70 AD, Romans troops punished widespread Hebrew revolts in Judea by completely destroying the temple. It was consumed in fire and collapsed, never to be rebuilt after that time. Yet the whole area upon which it stood remains in place today. This includes many underground structures made of stone that may give clues to the Temple's foundations, a hidden crypt at that location, and other subterranean construction.

Many have sought to explore and examine the underground structures on Temple Mount in the hope of answering these questions. Unfortunately, the few recent attempts have resulted in passionate controversy, as shown by this event at the Western Wall.

> The underground tunnel at the center of the controversy was known officially in the 1980's as the "Western Wall Tunnel." Unofficially it was called the "Rabbi's Tunnel," because it was the project of Orthodox rabbis in Jerusalem....
>
> As they tunneled north along the Temple Mount's western wall in 1982, the rabbis found an ancient sealed underground gate. They broke through the gate and began to clear out chambers beneath the Temple Mount. Reports suggest they were looking for evidence of the Ark of the Covenant and the Holy of Holies from the ancient Jewish Temples. Palestinian workmen on top of the Temple Mount compound heard the sounds of their digging up through a cistern. They opened the cistern and rushed down. In an area where the cistern and gate complex came together, they found the Jews clearing out the gate room and passageways beneath the mount.
>
> A Palestinian riot resulted with numerous injuries. The Israeli government stopped the work beneath the mount and sealed the underground gate.[50]

Though it is not possible to do further physical exploration today, we are fortunate to have detailed maps produced by several earlier archaeological probes. Among these was an extensive engineering survey on and under Temple Mount by Charles Wilson and Charles Warren in 1864-1865 that was highly revealing. We will soon see what was available to the Knights Templar when they began their exploration on and under the Mount.

Chapter 6

Christ on Temple Mount

During the Roman occupation of Jerusalem, more happened than the final destruction of Solomon's Temple. There was an event of critical importance to the Knights Templar and to Freemasons: Jesus Christ was born in Bethlehem. His parents had gone to this small town five miles south of Jerusalem to take part in a census, and after his birth were forced to flee to Egypt to avoid the jealous wrath of King Herod. About a year later they returned to their home in Nazareth, where Jesus was raised. He grew up with his family in this modest town among the hills of Galilee in the northern part of Israel. He learned the carpenter's craft from Joseph, but little else was recorded about his early years other than a curious event that brought Jesus to the temple.

> Now his parents went to Jerusalem every year at the feast of the Passover. And when he was twelve years old, they went up to Jerusalem after the custom of the feast. And when they had fulfilled the days, as they returned, the child Jesus tarried behind in Jerusalem; and Joseph and his mother knew not of it. But they, supposing him to have been in the company, went a day's journey; and they sought him among their kins-

folk and acquaintance. And when they found him not, they turned back again to Jerusalem, seeking him.

And it came to pass, that after three days they found him in the temple, sitting in the midst of the doctors, both hearing them, and asking them questions. And all that heard him were astonished at his understanding and answers. And when they saw him, they were amazed: and his mother said unto him, Son, why hast thou thus dealt with us? Behold, thy father and I have sought thee sorrowing.

And he said unto them, How is it that ye sought me? Wist ye not that I must be about my Father's business? And they understood not the saying which he spake unto them. And he went down with them, and came to Nazareth, and was subject unto them: but his mother kept all these sayings in her heart.

Luke 2:41-51

Then, at thirty years of age, Jesus journeyed to see John the Baptist beside the Jordan River and was baptized. Having come into his calling, he gathered twelve disciples around him and began his ministry. Jesus returned to the temple in Jerusalem as an adult and famously drove out the moneychangers for plying their trade in the House of God.[51] He had a direct relationship with this temple, whose foundation was built for Solomon, and whose structure was raised by Zerubbabel, then enhanced by Herod.

Jesus began to perform what witnesses described as miracles, and developed a great following. These followers included Mary Magdalene, the woman often identified as his lover or wife. In *Holy Blood, Holy Grail* as well as in *The Da Vinci Code*, Jesus was said to have fathered a child by Mary Magdalene, which established a royal bloodline. This was offered as one of the secrets of Solomon's Temple, and of the Knights Templar. But if further proof exists for such a legacy, it still needs to be brought forward and has not yet fully come to light.

It seems true, however, that Jesus went to the city of Tyre where he delivered one of his sermons to the descendants of the Phoenician people. During the Crusades, a large stone upon which Jesus was said to have stood while preaching in Tyre was taken to Venice, where it has been preserved as a sacred relic in the Basilica di San Marco.[52]

The crucifixion of Jesus took place around the year 30 AD, on a hill known as Golgotha—the Place of the Skull—near Temple Mount in Jerusalem. A spear was used to pierce his side, giving rise to the legend of the Holy Lance. The ordeal of Jesus concluded with his body being taken down from the cross by his mother Mary, assisted by Joseph of Arimathea and Mary Magdalene, who placed it in a tomb cut from rock. When Mary Magdalene and another woman returned the following Sunday to anoint Jesus' body with spices, they found the huge stone that had covered the entrance to the sepulcher was rolled back and the tomb was empty. His disciples reported that Jesus then appeared to them in person, and described him as ascending into heaven.[53]

Thereafter his traveling disciples actively preached the sermons and teachings of Jesus, which came to be known as Christianity, to all parts of the Roman Empire. It coexisted alongside the many religious rites and gods of the Romans, and alongside Judaism. However all of that would change dramatically under Emperor Constantine, in a chain of events that led to the rise of powerful popes in Rome, launched the Crusades, and gave rise to the Knights Templar.

Flavius Valerius Constantinus, better known as Constantine the Great, was born around 272 AD in Serbia. He was the son of a highly skilled Roman military leader and diplomat named Constantius, who opened the way for his even more talented son. Constantine's mother Helena was a Greek of humble origin who was born just south of modern Istanbul. When the Roman Emperor Diocletian decided he needed help ruling his large empire, he appointed a junior emperor with the title of Caesar. This honor was given to Maximian who ruled in the West from Milan, while Diocletian ruled in the East from the city of Nicomedia, which is known today as Izmat in Turkey. Maximian rewarded Constantine's father for good service by giving him a high position in the West.

Constantius, the father, responded to his opportunity in less than gallant manner. He left his wife Helena, and married the stepdaughter of Maximian. This proved to be a judicious, if cold move on his part, because eight years later Diocletian elevated Maximian to equal rank with himself as senior or "Augustus" emperor. He also appointed a junior emperor or "Caesar" under himself, and one under Maximian. That meant the Roman Empire now had four emperors—a recipe for disaster, as events would soon prove.

Constantius, the father, was promptly named Caesar in the West. The cast-aside Helena remained at Diocletian's court in the East, where young Constantine, as the son of a Caesar was treated like minor royalty. Constantine came of age and served with distinction in several military campaigns.

Then in 305 AD failing health caused Diocletian to shuffle the Roman leadership again. He decreed that he and Maximian would step down as Augustus Emperors, and be replaced by the two Caesars. Thus Constantius became Augustus in the West, and Galerius was named Augustus in the East. In a surprising display of political strength, Galerius blocked the appointment of young Constantine to become Caesar in the West, putting his own man into that position. Fearing for his life in the court of Galerius, Constantine fled to the West, and took a position as tribune under his father.

Father and son then crossed the English Channel to deal with the restless Picts who were causing upheaval in Northern Britain. There Constantine found London was already the major city of England. The early Romans had built a bridge across the Thames in roughly the same place London Bridge stands today. The town of Londinium quickly sprang up on the river's northern shore, and a high stone wall was raised around the settlement for protection. That solidly built fortification continued to enclose the center of the city until the 1600's.[54] The location of Roman gates through the wall are still readily identified, marked as Aldgate, Bishop's Gate, Moorgate, Cripple Gate, Alders Gate, New Gate, and Lud Gate. Roman London held about 70,000 people, a surprisingly large number in that part of the world.[55]

The mission of Constantine and his father took them onward to York near the northern frontier.[56] It was already a walled city, though considerably smaller than London.[57] York mainly quartered military troops and included a large meeting hall or *basilica* which opened onto a courtyard surrounded by other buildings. Many years later York Minster was built on that exact spot. In the undercroft below the Minster, the foundations of this Roman basilica, courtyard and military housing can still be seen.

In 306 AD Constantius died and the Roman troops of York acclaimed Constantine to be the successor to his father as Augustus Emperor of the West. Britain quickly acknowledged Constantine, as did Gaul—the land known today as France. However when he notified Galerius that his men had forced the title of Augustus upon him, the older emperor in the East was furious. As a compromise, Constantine was given the position of Caesar in the West. That proved to be only a temporary solution.

When a falling-out occurred among the four emperors, they marched with their differences onto battlefields. Constantine confronted one of his opponents outside the city walls that protected Rome. Although he was not a Christian, Constantine was guided by a dream or vision to have all his men mark their shields with a new symbol: the Greek letters *chi* and *rho* which were the first two letters of the name *Christ*. The army he faced was at least twice as large as his own, but somehow Constantine's forces carried the day. The popular leader then entered Rome to a hero's welcome. Constantine's generous treatment of the weak Roman Senate and other prudent acts won the devotion of the city. Rome proclaimed him its Augustus Emperor.

Twelve years later the decisive confrontation came. Constantine faced his final opponent in a series of battles around the ancient Greek city of Byzantium, today called Istanbul. Bearing once again the Christian symbol on their shields, Constantine's forces emerged victorious.

After all these trials, Constantine became the sole Roman Emperor and exercised unlimited power.[58] He established his capital city in Byzantium, which became known as Constantinople in his honor.

Fig. 11 Emperor Constantine the Great

Christianity had sustained Constantine in his most difficult battles, and now he was in a position to return the favor. His mother Helena, who had long been a practicing Christian, was called to his side. Persecution of Christians became outlawed across the empire. Many years later Constantine finally converted to Christianity on his deathbed. His three sons became Christian before they inherited the Roman Empire from him. Christianity gradually replaced a diverse array of gods as the dominant religion of the Roman Empire. Of course all of this did not come about without a measure of opposition and bloodshed, but it came. The bishop of Rome was still rivaled at this time by the powerful bishops of Antioch and Alexandria, as well as by the Patriarch of Jerusalem—but his day was coming as well. Christianity spread throughout Europe and other parts of the world. The foundation for a force that would one day summon the Crusades was in place, and it proceeded to grow stronger year by year.

In launching all these things a role was played by Contantine's mother, Helena, whose adoption of Christianity early in her life undoubtedly influenced her son's movement in that direction. In 325 AD, shortly after her son became the sole Roman Emperor, Helena organized an expedition to Jerusalem to gather holy relics. On that trip she was also authorized by Constantine to decree the building of churches on sites important to the life of Jesus. At Jerusalem, Helena visited the site where Jesus was said to have been buried in the stone sepulcher, but found only a mound of earth with a temple of Venus upon it. Her son had previously approved the clearing of this site, and she stayed on to oversee that work. There she found what was believed to be pieces of the cross upon which Jesus had been crucified, as well as the stone sepulcher.

To preserve the site for future pilgrims, she began to build the Church of the Holy Sepulcher there. The resultant house of worship included a vast, impressive rotunda surrounding the place of Jesus' burial and resurrection. The round walls in that part of the church created a striking effect, particularly upon pilgrims already moved by being in the presence such a holy site. It clearly made a deep impression on the Knights Templar many years later, for they reproduced the rotunda of the Church of the Holy Sepulcher in many of their own churches—including the Temple Church in London.

After Helena's return from Jerusalem, Christianity spread far and wide across the Roman Empire. Antioch, in what is now Syria, had a strong Christian population ever since the time of Saint Peter. That venerable disciple apparently served as bishop in this city before going to Rome. Not far from Antioch lived a monk known as Saint Maron, who significantly assisted the spread of Christianity. He drew large numbers of followers to his ministry prior to his death in 410 AD. After that passing, some of his followers moved southward into the Lebanon Mountains, where they won many converts among the descendants of the Phoenicians. These conversions continued until the old Phoenician cities became predominantly Christian in their devotions.

This was also the time that the Western Roman Empire came under attack by Vandals, Visigoths and other Northern tribes. Upon the fall of Rome, the deteriorating western empire began to dissolve.

Yet the eastern portion of the empire continued to function as before, without interruption. Ruling from Christian Constantinople, this remnant of the Roman empire became known as the Byzantine Empire—derived from the old Greek name for that city—and controlled all the land around the Eastern Mediterranean from Greece to Egypt and North Africa.

Then came Muhammad. This charismatic leader arose in the land which would become known as Saudi Arabia. He lived and died in a fiery whirlwind that inspired energetic jihads across the land to spread his faith. As a result, Islam advanced on horseback and on the edge of a sword. It rolled northward to seize Damascus in 634 AD, only two years after Muhammad's death. Shocked, the Byzantine emperor Heraclius sent his armies to fight a series of battles in Syria with the Arab armies. After two years of unsuccessful encounters, however, the Byzantines were forced to withdraw. The resulting Arab Conquest swept over the lowlands of Lebanon, yet failed to dislodge the fervent Christians in the rugged mountains where they continued to hold dominion.

In 638 AD Jerusalem fell, followed by Gaza. The Conquest then swept over Northern Syria and into Mesopotamia. In 640 AD the Arab armies entered Egypt, leading to a two-year struggle in which Alexandria was lost and Byzantine control of that land came to an end. During the next hundred years, Arab-led armies of Islam took all of North Africa. It also spread eastward from Damascus to envelop what we now know as Iran and Pakistan.

This conquest caused drastic changes in Jerusalem, the city where Christianity had reigned since the time of Emperor Constantine. Churches and Christian edifices had multiplied throughout the city for hundreds of years. The Church of the Holy Sepulcher and other sites throughout the Holy Land had become places of pilgrimage for Christians from all over the Roman Empire. Somewhat surprisingly, all this religious activity bypassed Temple Mount, which became largely neglected. Other than one or two small shrines to individuals such as St. James the Less, the mount stood in an overgrown state of disrepair.

All of that activity changed dramatically in 638 AD when the Muslim conquerors arrived. Among the changes they made in Jerusalem was to build the Dome of the Rock on the highest point of Temple Mount. This was followed twenty years later by breaking ground for construction of the Al Aqsa Mosque on the southern end of the mount. Both of those structures would play a central role when the Knights Templar later arrived and the search for remnants of Solomon's Temple began.

The wave of Muslim conversions reached the far end of North Africa then burst into Europe by way of Spain and Portugal. That violent act unwittingly lit a fire under the pot from which the Crusades would boil over. By 732 AD the Arab Conquest had consumed most of the Iberian peninsula and churned into France, claiming land for Islam as far as Poitiers in Western France. An epic battle fought just north of that French town turned into a resounding victory for Charles Martel and his Christian armies. It stopped the inexorable Muslim advance and pushed the invaders back to the Pyrenees Mountains. Martel used those mountains as a protective barrier that extended from the Mediterranean in the south to the small surviving Christian kingdom of Asturias in Northern Spain.

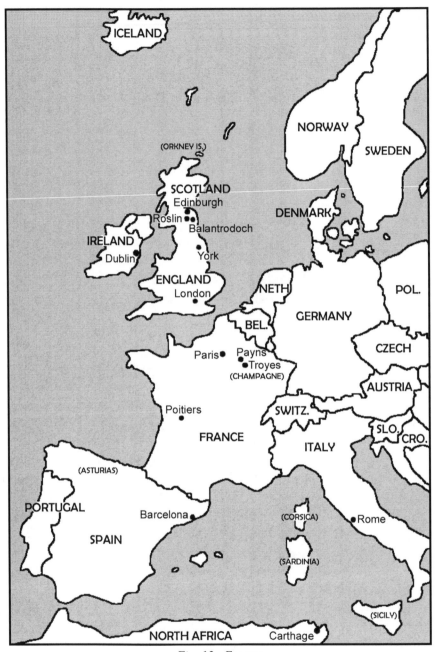

Fig. 12   Europe

Thirty-six years later Charlemagne rose to become king of France, bringing changes that transformed Europe and brought it a step closer to the Crusades. As the grandson of Charles Martel, Charlemagne inherited the substantial kingdom of the Franks, and immediately began to reassemble the scattered pieces of the Western Roman Empire. He extended the Frankish kingdom's borders eastward to include most of Germany and Austria. He led his troops southward to bring in Italy, as far as the city of Rome. In the West, he reached past the Pyrenees to take and hold Barcelona.

Yet Charlemagne did more than conquer. He established Christianity and the power of the pope, bringing them to a level never before seen or imagined. His successful campaigns brought Christianity to many new lands, and he gave the clergy important roles in the administration of his empire. Since they were also the writers of history at that time, the clergy responded to his unwavering support by naming him Charles the Great, which in its Latin form has come down to us as Charlemagne.

In conquering the part of Italy around Rome, he freed the pope from harassment by the Lombard kings who had ruled those territories. In gratitude, Pope Leo III conferred a considerable gift upon Charlemagne, crowning him as Emperor of the Romans in 800 AD. This act transformed the king's vast collection of conquered lands into the Holy Roman Empire. In reality, this revived only the *Western* Roman Empire, for the Roman empire in the East had continued without interruption as the Byzantine Empire, with its seat of power residing in Constantinople.

In return for crowning Charlemagne, the pope received a great gift of his own: the gift of power and authority over church and state. Jesus originally had twelve disciples, among whom Peter was acknowledged as the first among equals. After the crucifixion, these disciples and their successors functioned as bishops, establishing local priests and acting together to lead the church. The bishop of Rome, following the example of Peter, continued to be a leading voice among the Christian bishops, but had no commanding authority over them. The honorary title of pope only allowed the Roman bishop to be heard over the many differing voices within the church.

All of this changed when Pope Leo III placed oil on the forehead of Charlemagne and declared him to be the Holy Roman Emperor. This established a precedent and practice that no man could become emperor unless anointed or blessed by the pope. This concept rapidly expanded to give the pope religious authority over all Christian kings and the Catholic Church. It was a power jealously guarded by successive popes who sought to strengthen it and exercise it whenever possible.

Knighthood also took its place on the field of battle at this time. It grew out of the general state of warfare that existed across Europe's countless local lands and fiefdoms. Among these many confrontations, the deeds of the legendary paladins and officers of Charlemagne stood out. These men were mounted soldiers who took to the field heavily armed and played major roles in his victories. When not engaged in war, they also strove to maintain some semblance of peace. These early knights soon became a fixture throughout Europe. They embodied the leading image of the Middle Ages, arrayed in shining armor, seated upon a great warhorse, and charging across bloody battlefields in an age when kings fought kings for conquests.

One of the most popular fields across which they fought belonged to the kingdom of Asturias in Northern Spain. It had the distinction of being the last Christian enclave in the Iberian peninsula, and had successfully held out against the Muslim forces. From the fields of Asturias came the *Reconquista*, the slow and difficult reconquering of the lands of Spain and Portugal. Those clashes within the Iberian peninsula would continue until the 1400's—with the Knight Templar playing a significant role—but that was in the future.

In its early years, the powerful message of the *Reconquista* to all Europeans was that the fight between Christian and Muslim armies was not a distant, overseas problem. It was one that existed on their own doorstep. And the slow but sure Christian successes in Iberia instilled in Europeans the belief that this was a contest Christians would win. In 1099, when the Crusades finally came and Jerusalem was recaptured, this belief seemed to be completely validated.

Chapter 7

A Mantle of White, a Cross of Red

The Crusades in the Holy Land were marred by a particularly bloody massacre of Christian pilgrims during Easter observances in 1119. Roughly seven hundred pilgrims from several countries set out on the mountainous road from Jerusalem to the Jordan River where Jesus had been baptized. While passing through a particularly desolate area, they were attacked by Muslim raiders who killed three hundred of their number. Another sixty were taken captive. When some survivors managed to escape and return to Jerusalem, King Baldwin II sent out a party of knights to pursue the attackers. Unfortunately the marauders had already escaped.[59]

Driven by these and other killings across the Holy Land, nine knights led by Hugh de Payens[60] gathered on Temple Mount in Jerusalem and took a solemn obligation. They pledged to do everything possible to safeguard the pilgrims who traveled to Jerusalem and other holy sites. There was no way they could have known the full implication of what they were doing, for their sworn oaths marked the creation of the Knights Templar.

De Payens was a fitting choice to be the first Grand Master of the Templars, because he had been an intimate part of the gathering forces that swept across Europe and come to rest on the eastern shore of the Mediterranean.

Born into a small but well-established aristocratic family in France, the passing of his father made young Hugh the lord of Payns, a small town located seventy miles southeast of Paris. His lands were part of the sprawling province of Champagne, a region that produced the sparkling beverage of the same name. Since Champagne's capital city of Troyes was just seven miles away, Hugh was soon drawn into some of the major events taking place in France. One of those occurred in 1093, when Hugh was twenty-three years of age: a young man four years his junior became the Count of Champagne. The two men, both named Hugh, formed a close bond that would last through their lifetime and subtly shift the course of history. As lord of one of the largest provinces in France, the young Hugh de Champagne[61] took his place in society at a level just below the king.

This was also the time that France began to be affected by disasters ravaging the Byzantine Empire. Some years earlier, the Seljuk Turks had come westward from the lands around the Aral Sea in the middle of Asia. They intruded first into Persia then plunged into the Byzantine Empire during 1067. The Turks defeated the armies of Emperor Michael VII in an epic battle four years later, then kept pressing forward until they commanded almost all of Anatolia. As they began to settle the land with their own Turkish people the countryside came to be known as Turkey, and still bears that name today. Having lost more than half of his empire, the Byzantine Emperor put up a strenuous defense to avoid losing more. Yet when the dust settled, his principal city of Constantinople stood only a few miles from the new Turkish border.

The Seljuk Turks then gathered their strength and drove southward to seize the lands of other Muslim rulers. By adding Syria, Lebanon and Israel to their holdings in Turkey, they created a substantial empire of their own. Unfortunately, the Turks were more aggressive and stringent followers of Islam than the people they replaced. The treatment of Christian pilgrims in the Holy Land deteriorated drastically.

In March of 1095, Byzantine Emperor Alexius I appealed to Pope Urban II in Rome to help him deal with these Turkish invaders. The idea of unifying all the Christians of Europe on a mission spiritually led by the pope strongly appealed to Urban. As a result he called an immense conference at Clermont-Ferrand with the hope of arousing support for such a mission. Those attending the council quickly embraced the idea of recapturing the Holy Land and stopping the vandalization of churches there. Urban delivered an impassioned speech to the assembled lords and clergy in which he promised immediate admission to heaven for any who died in the course of this Crusade. The appeal resonated with the assembled throng, and whipped them into a religious frenzy. This passion was soon transmitted across the length of Europe. Lords and kings pledged contingents to crusade on their behalf, or even decided to lead the men themselves.

In Europe, the main force of fighting men finally came together by August of 1096. Known as the Prince's Crusade due to the nobility of its leaders, this force constituted about 35,000 fighting men, including 5,000 knights. One of those knights was Hugh de Payens from the province of Champagne. When de Payens enlisted in the First Crusade, his close friend Hugh de Champagne could only watch events unfold from France. This difference in their participation was not unusual in those days. The nobility who went on that Crusade tended to be from the lower aristocracy, or were the junior sons of great families—sons who would not inherit the family title. The kings of Europe were urged not to go by the pope, lest the loss of high leaders throw Europe into tumultuous battles over succession. Thus William II, king of England and Normandy, was dissuaded from going, while his brother Robert of Normandy was welcomed as a leader of the campaign.

The duchy of Lorraine was near Champagne, and it provided Godfrey of Bouillon to be one of the leaders of the Crusade. Hugh de Payens was believed to have gone on crusade in the service of Godfrey, since the lord of his own province was not enlisted.

The several armies of this Crusade took different routes to Constantinople and arrived there between November of 1096 and May of 1097. These Crusaders fully expected to receive food, supplies and a hero's welcome in the Byzantine capital. Instead they found a nervous Alexius I confronted by many more armed Europeans than he had expected. A sign of the constant games within games during the Crusades—on both the Christian and Muslim sides—was that the emperor made these new arrivals swear fealty to him and promise to turn over all lands they conquered. After many arguments, the Crusaders, seriously in need of food, gave their agreement.

The provisioned Crusaders then marched south into Turkey where they engaged in a series of battles. Near the southern coast they were welcomed at the Armenian Christian kingdom of Cilicia. Refreshed by provisions from the local people, they were guided through the mountains to the beginning of the Eastern Seaboard of the Mediterranean. There the warfare resumed at the Muslim-held city of Antioch in what is today Syria. The Crusaders promptly put the city under siege, but given its large size they were unable to surround it completely. This caused an agonizing siege of eight months until victory finally came in 1098. The leaders of the Crusade then argued for the better part of a year over who would rule this valuable city. Bohemond of Taranto won that privilege and was left in Antioch while the others marched southward.

Thus it was 1099 when the Crusaders entered Lebanon with its mixed population of Muslims in the coastal cities and Christians occupying all the highlands along the Lebanon Mountains. The local people had learned to live with each other by this time, and seemed to be less fanatical than the heavily armed Crusader and Muslim armies. The Muslim cities sought no battles with the Crusaders, and the Christian highlanders sought no Crusader help to attack the cities. They simply let the European armies pass through their land on the way to Jerusalem. Later they would indeed choose sides, but at first there was patient waiting and avoidance of bloodshed.

Continuing south, the patchwork of Western armies finally reached Israel and the Holy Land. Widespread confusion among the Muslim defenders led to little resistance until the Christians reached Jerusalem, where the ultimate siege began. The Crusaders who stood before the walls of Jerusalem had with less than half

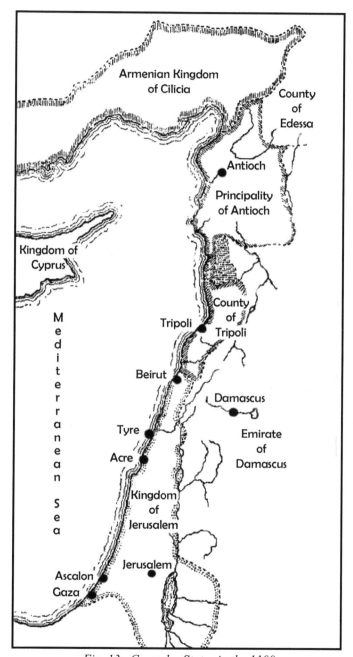

Fig. 13   Crusader States in the 1100s

the force that left Europe three years earlier, having been whittled down by battles, starvation and lack of water. They numbered now only 12,000 men, which included a bare 1200 knights.

The siege continued for five difficult weeks until the city wall was successfully breached and the Crusaders poured into Jerusalem. Whether it was the three years of privation or the perceived mistreatment of pilgrims which fueled them, the entering troops killed almost every inhabitant of the city. The knight Tancred was said to have to have offered protection to some of the Muslims in the Temple Quarter, but unfortunately those people were killed anyway. Some Crusaders must have successfully spared a few inhabitants, however, for there were accounts of survivors being tasked with hauling bodies of the less fortunate from the city streets. Even so, it was a poor commentary on the conduct of a religious war.

When occupation of the city was complete, Godfrey of Bouillon became its ruler. He was followed in this role by his brother, Baldwin of Edessa, and life settled down into a normal pattern. With this, many of the knights and fighting men felt their mission was completed. They packed their few belongings and returned home to lives and loves in Europe, to celebrate and be celebrated. That left barely enough fighting men to hold the land. Hugh de Payens was among those who stayed.[62]

While talking with his fellow knights about how they could be of service in the Holy Land, de Payens had to be aware of a group of local brothers in Jerusalem who provided hospital care for sick and weary pilgrims. These were the Hospitallers.

With the capture of the Holy Land, the door was thrown open to a large influx of pilgrims from Europe and the Byzantine Empire. Yet the long and arduous pilgrimage took a severe toll on many whose spirits were stronger than their bodies. To their aid came this obscure group of Benedictine monks attached to the monastery of Saint John, who provided shelter and medical care for the afflicted. By 1100 AD a man named Gerard Thom became provost of this group and organized them into a formal religious order known as Hospitallers. Under his guidance the new order began to receive rich grants of property to support their much-needed work. The highest validation of his group's efforts came in

1113, when Pope Paschal II formally recognized it as the Order of Saint John of Jerusalem. The official garb granted to them was the black robe of the Benedictines, but with a white cross added. They had no military role at that time. They simply served as monks providing shelter and medical care.

Meanwhile in France, an assassination attempt on the life of Hugh de Champagne in 1104 AD[63] apparently caused him to contemplate his mortality and consider living a more religious life. This prompted him to undertake his own journey to Jerusalem, which reunited him with Hugh de Payens. In the Holy Land, de Champagne lived the demanding but rewarding life of a knight amid the dangers of the countryside. He was also able to renew his relationship with Baldwin of Boulogne, a member of the ruling family from the province north of his own. At that time Baldwin was the reigning King of Jerusalem, having been elevated upon the death of his brother Godfrey four years earlier. Hugh de Champagne returned to France in 1107 to tend to the affairs of his province, with his friend Hugh de Payens accompanying him or following shortly thereafter.

In France, de Champagne became active supporting the Cistercian monks, even to the point of contemplating the taking of religious vows. This reformed branch of the Benedictine Order distinguished itself from the black-robed Benedictines by choosing white robes to identify their Cistercian Order, and by being more ardent in adhering to their religious vows. This no doubt had a strong influence on Hugh de Payens and other members of the nobility in the province of Champagne, for a remarkable series of events began to happen in 1114.

In that year Hugh de Champagne returned to the Holy Land accompanied by de Payens and possibly other knights from their province. While living in Jerusalem, de Champagne made a grant of lands to a young Cistercian monk named Bernard, allowing the monk to establish a new monastery at Clairvaux just east of Troyes. This newly-made abbot would become known as St. Bernard.[64] He also would play a role in the rise of the Knights Templar, a moment that was growing closer. In 1116 the Count of Champagne left the affairs of Jerusalem in the hands of de Payens and returned to France.

When Baldwin II ascended the throne in Jerusalem, it was noted that he was from Rethel in France, another neighbor of Champagne. That there seemed to be a firm hold on power in Jerusalem
by the people from this region was much in evidence. This was
this same Baldwin II who a year later[65] would embrace and support the Knights Templar.

As we have seen, the humble beginning of the Templars came
in response to an urgent need by Christians in the Holy Land. The
small number of knights in that land could barely defend the major cities of Jerusalem, Jaffa, Beirut and Antioch. Those cities were
surrounded on all sides by large numbers of Muslims who could
call on many more fighting men than could the Christians. Fortunately for the outnumbered few, the Muslims were not able to
unite, and continued to fight among themselves. Although Islamic
leaders were unable to raise a sufficient force to regain those cities,
they could—and did—put countless small raiding parties on the
highways and byways of the Holy Land. An abbot noted these
dangers on his pilgrimage during 1106 and 1107.

> And there are many springs here; travellers rest by the
> water but with great fear, for it is a deserted place and
> nearby is the town of Ascalon from which Saracens
> [Muslims] sally forth and kill travellers on these roads.
> There is a great fear too going up from that place into
> the hills.[66]

The particularly bloody massacre of pilgrims in 1119 finally
pushed de Payens and eight other knights to unite as the Knights
Templar. When they met with King Baldwin to tell him of the solemn obligation they had taken, the monarch was overjoyed. These
bloody attacks on pilgrims had been a thorn in his side, and a
blemish on his reign. In gratitude he gave this new order of
knights a wing of his palace on Temple Mount. This they were
permitted to use as their residence and meeting place. As mentioned earlier, this building previously served as the Al Aqsa
Mosque. The great hall and its many adjoining rooms seemed a
proper venue for the king, but it had much more space than he
needed. Keeping the new defenders of the pilgrims close to him

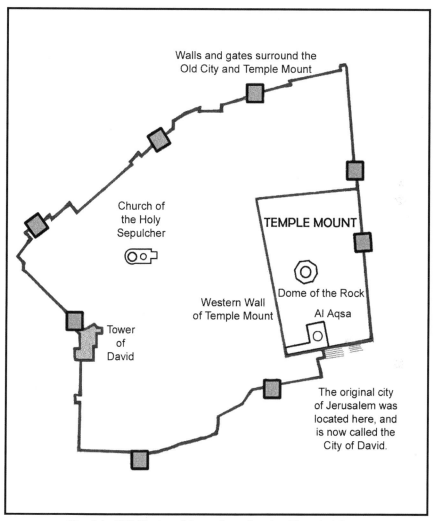

*Fig. 14   "Old" city of Jerusalem showing Temple Mount,
the location of Solomon's Temple*

was as much a benefit for the king's image as it was a welcome gift for the nine knights. The Crusaders believed this great hall stood on, or near, the site of Solomon's Temple. To commemorate that hallowed place's association with their Order, these men began to call themselves the Knights Templar.

Their official name, confirmed later by the pope, was *Pauperes commilitones Christi Templique Solomonici*, or the Poor Fellow-Soldiers of Christ and the Temple of Solomon. The reference to poverty reflected the other vows taken by these knights, in addition to protecting pilgrims. They swore to act in a more holy manner than many of their rough-hewn fellow Crusaders, and took vows of poverty, chastity, and obedience. Their first oaths of obedience were given to Patriarch Warmund, the spiritual leader of Jerusalem, and to King Baldwin, the civil leader. By these vows, the Knights Templar assumed the lives of monks, just as one might find in an abbey or monastery. But instead of remaining isolated behind abbey walls their mission required them to be active in the world with sword in hand, fighting against any who attacked Christians in the Holy Land. This combination of religious peace and military action was relatively new in the West, but not in the East. For many years Muslim warriors had already managed to combine devotions with annihilations to a significant degree. Even farther east—in China—the Shaolin religious order of fighting monks had maintained similar practices in their monastery since 477 AD.

With the launching of their new order in Jerusalem, the Templars immediately began to perform their protective duties. The men who joined de Payens in this original circle of Knights Templar were Godfrey de Saint-Omer,[67] Payen de Montdidier, Andre de Montbard[68], Archambaud de St. Agnan, Geoffrey Bison, two men known only as Rossal and Gondamer, and a ninth knight who was not named. Unfortunately, only a few details of these men are known, yet it is noteworthy that they all lived in or near the province of Champagne before coming to the Holy Land. Apparently this was a close group of men whom Hugh de Payens came to know well, and in whom he put complete trust.

The Templars gradually began to adopt a uniform similar to the white robes of the Cistercian monks, but marked by a distinctive red cross. Though they would later add other forms of dress within their order, this was the distinctive image by which they came to be known on the battlefield, and in the imagination of people in all parts of Europe. Knights in those days were admired for their power. Yet they were also feared because some used that power to enrich themselves at the expense of others. All the knights who went to the Holy Land were accorded some measure of respect in Europe, but those who also took vows of poverty, chastity, and obedience to God were raised to a higher level. Their vows did not allow them to enrich themselves personally. Nor could they establish a dynasty for their heirs, as others had done across the continent. These men used their formidable power only in the service of pilgrims and God. This endeared them to lords and commons alike.

The Knights Templar soon began to have an impact on battles across the Holy Land. And if imitation is the sincerest form of flattery, then the Hospitallers now paid the Templars the ultimate compliment. When the founder of the Hospitallers, Gerard Thom, died in 1120, this order of monks elected Raymond du Puy to lead them. Being a knight himself, and having seen the honors heaped upon the Knights Templar when they were formed the previous year, du Puy resolved to add a knightly dimension to his own monastic order. He actively recruited a number of knights and formed a separate group alongside the monks who still provided shelter and care for pilgrims. These then took to the battlefields of the Holy Land with their knightly armor covered by distinctive black robes marked with a white cross. They served alongside— and sometimes in competition with—the Knights Templar, whose shining armor was covered by white robes and a bright red cross.

As de Payens and his Templars established themselves in their knightly duties, they were awarded another benefit by Baldwin II. The king decided to move to the Tower of David in the western part of the city, leaving the Templars in sole possession of the building they knew as Solomon's Temple. It also caused the knights to "secure their perimeter" by intensely searching the buildings and passageways on or under Temple Mount. In the process of doing this, they were said to have acquired secrets and powers that enabled them to quickly rise to a position of tremendous authority and wealth in Europe and the East.

These secrets and powers have traditionally been attributed to discoveries involving Solomon's Temple, and covered a wide range of possibilities. A Holy Grail or cup that held the blood of Jesus and retained tremendous powers was preserved in many legends. These included King Arthur and the Knights of the Round Table, which some have interpreted as being based on the Knights Templar and their round churches.

One of the deep secrets suggested in the book *Holy Blood, Holy Grail* in 1982 and made popular by *The Da Vinci Code* was that the Templars discovered and protected the bloodline of Jesus, who was thought to have fathered a child by Mary Magdalene. This reportedly began a dynasty of secret descendants of Jesus, with serious repercussions for the Catholic Church. Other explanations of the Templars' quick rise to power included discoveries involving the Ark of the Covenant, Hebrew religious writings containing mysteries such as Kabbalah, encrypted number systems allowing secret messages to be interpreted from the Bible, or the stone tablets of Moses which contained the sacred writing of God and transmitted divine power. All of these possibilities have their advocates, and in some cases the arguments presented on their behalf have been quite compelling.

The Ark of the Covenant or the tablets of Moses might have been recovered, but we would only know this if they eventually surfaced in a private or public collection. That has not happened, so there is no indication that these objects were the valuables from Solomon's Temple found by the Knights Templar.

In the area of Hebrew religious writings and mystical number systems, however, something intriguing has appeared, and that is the practice of Kabbalah. Arcane Kabbalah knowledge is thought to have formed part of the original oral law of Judaism given to Moses by God on Mount Sinai around the 13th century BC, though some traditions assert that it goes back to Adam in the Garden of Eden. In any event, by the time of Solomon the mysteries of Kabbalah were said to have been openly and widely practiced. Then as more foreign conquests happened in Israel and Judah—leading up to and including the Babylonian Captivity—there was thought to be a great deal of concern that this esoteric knowledge would fall into the wrong hands. So the teachings of Kabbalah became tightly-held secrets shared with only a few, and virtually disappeared from sight.

We next see Kabbalah being taught after the temple was destroyed for the last time in 70 AD. The teachings of Rabbi Shim'on son of Yohai were particularly prominent around that time. This special knowledge included a way to study the books that came to appear in the Old Testament, using methodologies which were clearly mystical in nature.

So here we have religious teachings being practiced in the time of Solomon, then disappearing into secrecy, only to reappear after the temple fell. Of all the things that were rolled up and stored among the temple's most valuable possessions—and might be understood to confer special powers or abilities to its possessor—Kabbalah would have to be considered a serious candidate to be among them.

That the Templars were later accused of following mystical Eastern practices only adds to the evidence pointing in this direction.

Yet it would be appropriate to ask if it is even possible for secret writings and objects to have gone undiscovered for almost a thousand years on Temple Mount. With people constantly occupying that holy place and raising new buildings, surely anything of value would have long since been discovered. That objection would be quite reasonable, were it not for a number of discoveries that have been made there, even as recently as 2007. Virtually no archaeological work has taken place on Temple Mount in recent years, due to the conflicting authority and ideology of Jewish and Muslim factions. As a result, a unique opportunity arose in October of 2007 when Palestinian workers dug a trench about 300 yards in length across the top of the Mount to lay an electrical cable. Members of the Israeli Antiquities Authority were allowed to examine the trench, and found a number of ancient fragments. Those finds were later identified as being ceramic table vessels and animal bones which scientists have dated to the eighth century BC—a time when the original Temple of Solomon still stood upon the mount.[69] These pieces had remained undiscovered on Temple Mount for 2700 years, even though they lay close to the surface. It would therefore seem fairly clear that artifacts could have remained undiscovered from that same early date until the arrival of the Templars, which was a much shorter period of time.

Earlier probes, made specifically for the purpose of discovery, show that there are actual passageways under the mount filled with debris that have still not been explored to this day. One of these was the Rabbi's tunnel in the lower part of the Western Wall that was mentioned earlier, where digging was shut down by Muslim protesters in 1982. Going farther back, the engineering excavations in 1864-1865 by Charles Wilson and Charles Warren located and documented so many tunnels under the mount that they could only remove debris from a few to see what they contained and where they led. The others were left for future exploration that never came. The existence of unexplored underground passageways in not just a possibility, it is a documented certainty, as clearly shown in these engineering survey drawings.

So what does this mean for Solomon's Temple and its ancient contents? We are told that in 362 AD[70] an attempt by Jewish workers to rebuild the destroyed temple resulted in the last remaining foundation stones being removed, just before they were forced to abandon their project. It is clear that no foundation stones have been found since that time. With the complete destruction of the Temple down to the ground, the only part of it that could have remained would have been an underground structure such as the crypt mentioned earlier.

If an underground structure had survived, where would we look for it? Making a deposit in the open courtyard would have been seen by many people and therefore not been "secret." And if the temple was under attack, as happened many times, soldiers in the courtyard could kill the bearer and take possession of the valuables before they were deposited. So it is most reasonable that such a crypt or vault would need to have been located under the temple itself rather than outside in the courtyard. Indirect evidence also points to burial under the temple, since the great churches and cathedrals built using those same masonry techniques often placed their crypts under the massive structure.

Within the building, the part of Solomon's Temple that was most protected stood farthest from the great front doors. It remained off limits to all but a select few, and that was the Holy of Holies. This would certainly have been the most secure place to locate such a crypt or vault.

But where was Solomon's Temple located on Temple Mount? This has been one of the great mysteries over which people have argued for many years. The mount is an extensive walled enclosure that is roughly rectangular in shape. It averages just under 1000 feet in the east-west direction, and just over 1500 feet north-and-south. The mount currently contains two large buildings along with open courtyards, a number of trees, and a few run-down minor structures along some of the walls—particularly in the south, where the Templars built additional quarters for themselves. The two prominent buildings are the Dome of the Rock, located close to the center of the compound, and Al Aqsa Mosque at the southern end.

Both of those two major sites have been proposed as the location of Solomon's Temple, along with several other sites. The southern location was advocated by some of the Crusaders themselves. The building that had once been a mosque before it became the Knights Templar headquarters was identified as the Temple of Solomon. Given that fact, it is reasonable to consider this location first. As mentioned earlier, King Herod's expansion of the mount added retaining walls on all four sides, and filled the additional space thus created by adding underground structures and many tons of earth. When completed, the flat area of Temple Mount had been extended to the north, south and west, forming the large rectangle we see today.

Detailed topographic maps made in 1864-1865 by Wilson and Warren showed the rocky mount had a continuous upward slope on the south flank of Mount Moriah. On this slope was built Herod's immense structure. And as it turns out, the line of that ancient hillside was preserved for us by Herod's workmen, and for good reason. When David and Solomon lived in Jerusalem, the city did not lie to the west of Temple Mount, the way we see it

today. The city was much smaller and lay to the south of the
mount, in the area known as the City of David. This location of the
city was described in the Bible and has been confirmed by archaeological excavations. That meant the main route to the temple in
Solomon's day was a path up the south side of the hill, possibly
reinforced with stone steps for part of the distance. Retracing that
route today, we come to the southern retaining wall of the Mount,
where a large double-gate entrance was built. Although this passageway is blocked today, a number of writers in earlier years
noted they were able to walk up the long flight of stairs there,
finally emerging just in front of the Al Aqsa Mosque. When I
checked the area in front of Al Aqsa, there was indeed a flight of
stairs emerging there. In building the retaining wall, Herod's
workers seem to have preserved the original walkway up the side
of the hill—the long flight of stairs that is still there today. The
topographic maps show the only digression from the hillside
slope might come at the northern end of the stairs, where they rise
quickly to the current surface. The fact that these stairs emerged in
front of Al Aqsa Mosque meant that the entire building stood upon the landfill added by Herod at the south end of the mount.
Being built on landfill, it could not have been the original site of
Solomon's Temple.

Having said that, the Knights Templar lived in the large building at the head of those stairs, so they had easy access to the structures under Temple Mount. The extensive work by Wilson and
Warren mapped out thirty-four cisterns and other underground
structures there, including the famous "Solomon's stables." Additional tunnels and rooms have been found since that time. All of
this meant the Templars could easily have made their way forward into those passageways and possibly come to a crypt under
the original Temple. But if the Temple was not at the Al Aqsa site,
where was it?

Just north of that mosque stands a water well known as the El Kas
fountain, and this is another favored location. The well shaft clearly gives access below the surface, so locating a crypt in this place
would have been quite feasible. Much farther north in the area of
the Dome of the Tablets, also called the Dome of the Spirits, is

another suggested location, where access below the surface is again clearly in evidence. Yet there is one more site, favored by many scholars such as Leen Ritmeyer, that holds particularly strong promise.

This last location is on a summit of the mount, where the Dome of the Rock now stands. It was on or near this place that Abraham was said to have brought his son for sacrifice, as directed by God. Abraham had agonized over this duty, only to be spared at the last minute when God provided a ram for sacrifice instead.[71] Although there is still some energetic discussion, the largest number of experts now seem to feel this was the site of Solomon's Temple. Proponents of this location generally place the Holy of Holies at the highest point, with the rest of the gold-filled Temple laid out eastward. This would have made its entrance face the Mount of Olives across the deep valley. In the annual Red Heifer ceremony held at dawn on the Mount of Olives, it was said that one could see in the distance rays of sunlight entering the open doors of the Temple and reaching all the way to the veil shielding the Holy of Holies.

For this site we do not have to guess if there was an underground crypt or passageway. It is still there today. I know because I have been inside it.

When you walk into the building called the Dome of the Rock, the stone summit of the mount stands exposed in the center of the large room. It is surrounded by pillars that hold up the ornate roof. Stepping forward, you are able to approach the rock itself, where the Ark of the Covenant would have rested during official ceremonies in the Holy of Holies. At the southeastern edge of this rocky summit, stairs lead down to a cave below. Whether the cave was natural or was carved by hand I could not determine, since so much of it has been modified by usage and decoration. Yet when one knocked gently upon the man-made walls there was a hollow sound, which suggested the underground passage continued in several directions. Even one of the stone slabs on the floor gave off a hollow sound, where it seemed to cover a shaft leading downward.

Entry into this crypt from the Holy of Holies would not necessarily have been by these stairs, however, since we are told that the Crusaders built or widened the stairs during their occupation of the mount. The ancient entry into this crypt appears instead to have been by way of a hole cut through the surface of the rock and down into the cave below. This opening, measuring about three feet (one meter) in width, bears no rope marks, which meant it was not an accessway to a cistern like most of the other cuttings under the Mount. Nor can this opening that pierced the rock be attributed to the Crusaders, since long before they arrived a pilgrim saw it in 333 AD.

> There is a perforated stone, to which the Jews come every year and anoint it, bewail themselves with groans, rend their garments, and so depart.[72]

This journal kept by the Pilgrim of Bordeaux is one of the most persuasive pieces of evidence confirming the location of Solomon's Temple. Some remains of the temple were said to still be visible at that time, before the final removal of foundation stones in 362 AD. And the perforation through the stone that the local Jewish people anointed is still visible today.

Coming down into the crypt via the shaft or a narrow flight of stairs would be consistent with the concept of having a secret accessway to the crypt that was small enough to be concealed easily. The main chamber of this crypt provided enough room to store many artifacts, even some of significant size. In addition, the small hollows burrowed into the rock would have been ideal for secreting things of great value, where the hollow might then be plugged with a stone of suitable size and shape to conceal its location from viewers using the murky candlelight of that day.

Re-emerging upward into to the Holy of Holies, thick stone tiles could then be dropped back into place to cover the accessway. If there were floor boards covering the stone, they likewise would have been fitted back into place. With those pieces being the same as the flooring around them, the access place would have been nearly invisible.

*Fig. 15   Perforated stone leading to the crypt below Solomon's Temple
is shown at upper left in this view from above.*

This identical design exists at Rosslyn Chapel, and no doubt at many other churches as well. At Rosslyn, countless people have entered through the northern doorway, turned left and walked across smooth stone slabs—completely unaware that they just walked on the entryway to an underground crypt where the lords and ladies of the land were laid to rest. Such an arrangement in the floor of Solomon's Temple would have been quite secure.

If indeed the Knights Templar found something of value in the crypt or passageways under Temple Mount, that means later archaeologists would have opened the secret place only to find it devoid of those objects of value. Those later visitors would have found only pieces from ancient documents, chips from a wooden ark, remnants of divine writing, or bits of stone from the tablets of Moses. And perhaps some of those traces still exist. That has traditionally been the challenge facing archaeologists. They often find only broken pieces of ancient pottery and buildings, yet are able to piece together a persuasive picture of what once was there. In a sense, that is our task as well.

If such valuable items were found by the Templars, those should have been reflected in their actions and practices thereafter. So we will watch for those indicators. However available evidence already suggests that in addition to whatever relics and documents the Templars may have found under the mount, they found something else involved with Solomon's Temple that may have been even more valuable. Among the Lebanese people they found the descendants of the Phoenicians who had helped build Solomon's Temple.

Chapter 8

A Mantle of Green, Christians in Lebanon

When the numerous Christians in Lebanon saw heavily armed Crusaders pass through their land in 1099 on their way to Jerusalem, their welcome to these fellow Christians was tempered by the worry that these Europeans might just sail away again. After Jerusalem was taken and the Crusaders returned to Lebanon to attack and sack the Muslim coastal cities, everything changed. The Christians in Lebanon—who had once been pushed out of those coastal cities and taken refuge in the Lebanon Mountains—now poured down from the hills into those cities again. They rebuilt their churches there, and many began to earn a good living by providing whatever services and supplies the Crusaders needed.

One after another the former Phoenician cities fell to the Crusaders, including Tripoli, Byblos, Beirut, Sidon and Tyre. Each capture brought more Christian descendants of the Phoenicians back to the cities and into relationships with the Crusaders. Then in 1119 the Knights Templar came into being.

We usually think of the Templars as knights on horseback who rode off to battle, as indeed many of them were. Yet the Templars were also far more complex than that. At their height, they reportedly had up to 900 knights and 6300 support people in their Order.[73] This ratio of roughly seven support people for each knight seemed to be maintained to greater or lesser degree throughout the life of their Order. When they first became Templars on that mount in Jerusalem, the knights began to fill these positions with the few members of their personal staff who had not returned to Europe. But as the Templars received gifts of estates to support them, and added more knights, they needed to recruit additional serving men. About ten years after their formation, when the Templars had thirty knights, their support people would have numbered about 200. Charles Addison gave us a look inside that early Templar society.

> The order of the Temple was at this period divided into the three great classes of knights, priests, and serving brethren, all bound together by their vow of obedience to the Master of the Temple at Jerusalem, the chief of the entire fraternity. Every candidate for admission into the first class must have received the honour of knighthood in due form, according to the laws of chivalry, before he could be admitted to the vows; and as no person of low degree could be advanced to the honours of knighthood, the brethren of the first class, i.e. the *Knights* Templars, were all men of noble birth and of high courage. Previous to the council of Troyes, the order consisted of knights only, but the rule framed by the holy fathers enjoins the admission of esquires and retainers to the vows, in the following terms.
>
> "[Section] LXI.[74] We have known many out of divers provinces, as well retainers as esquires, fervently desiring for the salvation of their souls to be admitted for life into our house. It is expedient, therefore, that you admit them to the vows, lest perchance the old enemy should suggest something to them whilst in God's service by stealth or unbecomingly, and should suddenly drive them from the right path." Hence arose the great class of serving brethren (*fratres servientes,*) who attended the knights into the field both on

foot and on horseback, and added vastly to the power and military reputation of the order. The serving brethren were armed with bows, bills, and swords; it was their duty to be always near the person of the knight, to supply him with fresh weapons or a fresh horse in case of need, and to render him every succour in the affray.[75]

The most visible of these supporting brothers had direct battle-related duties, while less-seen but equally necessary brothers performed the myriad non-military responsibilities. They acquired armor and horses, procured and prepared the daily food, maintained the living quarters and performed other needed services. They also could be assigned to work at one of the estates donated to the Templars, raising a building or laboring to produce the crops that augmented the knights' revenue. Collectively, all these people were called sergeants or serving men, and were commanded to wear a simple black or brown robe, surmounted by the red cross of the Templars.[76]

The third group of brothers within the Order were clerics who had a unique and intriguing collection of responsibilities. They were literate, highly skilled in business matters, and eventually became recognized by their distinct appearance and influence.

The early mark that distinguished these brothers was the simple ability to read and write. In those early days, literacy and further education were primarily reserved for priests and other clerics. Europe's Medieval Dark Age was dimly lit by a few religious scribes who copied ancient writings by the Greeks and Romans—thereby preserving those insights and teachings at a time when a good sword was usually regarded as more important than a good book. Europeans had only slowly begun to emerge from that rustic state by the time of the Crusades. Some members of nobility were taught the rudiments of reading, but primarily the task of writing and recording was left to the religious clerics retained for that purpose. Originally the word *cleric* meant a person who was ordained into the priesthood. However it descended in common usage to the word *clerk*, which meant a person who could read, write, and keep records. The white-clad Knights Templar from noble families—following the custom of their peers—seem to have left the writing and record-keeping to their literate clerks.

This created a problem. In their early days, the Templars were not allowed to have ordained clerics among their number, being limited to lay brothers only. This made them dependent on outside clerics, and exposed all their private affairs, written communications and financial dealings to others. As may be gleaned from the fact that almost all the original Templar knights came from lands in or adjacent to Champagne in France, they were a tightly-knit group. The coming years would clearly delineate the intense secrecy in which they preferred to shroud their affairs. So one can imagine how being forced to depend on outsiders would have galled them.

The solution proved to be a simple one. They secretly ignored this restriction and cultivated their own group of literate brothers. In the meantime, they lobbied heavily to have the restriction lifted. In order to conceal these people, the Templars gave them the title of chaplain, and charged them with reading prayers and Bible verses to the knights and other brothers. Twenty years after their founding in Jerusalem, the Knights Templar finally won the pope's permission to have ordained clerics among them.[77] With that dispensation, this third suborder of the Knights Templar—known as the clerics or "green robes" was born.

> Third came the clerics—priests who acted as chaplains to the order and, because they were the only group of the three with any claim to literacy, frequently acted as scribes and record keepers and were responsible for other duties of a nonmilitary character. The clerics also wore the Templar cross, on a green mantle. The *clerics wore gloves* [78] at all times, to keep their hands clean for "when they touch God" in serving mass. The clerics were clean-shaven, according to the custom of the time, while the knights were required to keep their hair cut short but to let their beards grow.[79]

In recruiting the large number of people required to support their knights, the Templars discovered that the few Europeans who stayed in the Holy Land after the fall of Jerusalem were spread far too thinly over the many Crusader cities being occupied and protected. Fortunately there was a source of help.

In Lebanon, the Templars were already employing the local Christians for many services. And a large number of those individuals were more than common laborers. Just like their Phoenician ancestors, these Lebanese people were well known for their remarkable business skills—an excellent reputation that has continued to the present day. Foraging for food and other supplies in the Middle East was a daunting task for Europeans, yet it was a normal day's work for those raised in this land. Local Christians caused the needed goods to flow and were able to perform many of the labors required of serving men in the Order. It was a match made in heaven. Nor were they limited to handling household matters.

A pressing need for the Templars was the rebuilding of walls they had destroyed while capturing these cities in the Holy Land. They also needed to add strong castles for use in battles that were certain to come. In short, they needed skilled masons.

It turned out that these Lebanese people were heirs to the masonry tradition that we saw begin around 3200 BC. This was visible in the raising of their temple to Our Lady of Byblos and the construction of their first city walls, civic buildings, and other temples. The Phoenicians traded goods and services with the skilled masons of Malta and the people of Egypt when the Great Pyramid was built around 2575 BC. Building with ashlar-cut stones became a Phoenician hallmark after that date, a skill they brought to Santorini, Crete, Solomon's Temple, Carthage, Cyprus and many other harbors and buildings across the Mediterranean. They had used their skills to build walls and defenses at Tyre that slowed the conquests of Alexander the Great. Now those abilities and technology were put to use on behalf of the Templars—at Tyre and many other cities—to build the fortifications that were needed. The masons among the Lebanese Christians proved to be of considerable value.

Europeans had likewise refined their stoneworking skills ever since the Romans introduced them to aqueducts, massive walls, fortresses and finally churches. The merging of European and

*Fig. 16   Knights Templar masons built the central arches in front
of Al Aqsa Mosque, including this one, while they resided there*

Phoenician traditions in the Holy Land produced outstanding results. One of the identifying signs of this work was the use of the mason's mark to verify each stone was perfectly finished and ready to be placed into the structure at hand. On Temple Mount in Jerusalem, I had the opportunity to see some of the masonry buildings erected there by the Knights Templar. The perfectly-cut ashlar blocks in these structures still bear the distinctive diagonal tooling on the face of the stones that was traditional for Templar work in the Holy Land. An architect who was privileged to examine them further verified that they still bore their mason's marks as well.[80] Given the life-or-death need for fortifications in the Holy Land, the ability of Lebanese Christians to provide masons would have been a valued service.

There was one other particularly significant skill found among the Lebanese people, and that was their fluency with languages. This had been essential to the Phoenicians in their international trade, and continued to be a staple in Lebanese society. Even today a large part of the Lebanese population is fluent in three languages or more, with Lebanese-Arabic, French and English leading the list. Most of the Crusaders were from French-speaking lands, with the next largest contingent being English-speaking. After that were contingents speaking German, Italian and other tongues. This meant the Crusaders needed to have fluency in at least French, English and Arabic to communicate with other troops and to obtain food, supplies and support in the Holy Land. The Lebanese people were able to provide that service.

Hiring local Christians had one other benefit, especially since "local" meant Lebanon. The early Phoenicians had been highly literate people, who brought the Phoenician alphabet and public literacy to many lands.[81] They were also staunch record-keepers, as Wenamun saw when he was shown books recording transactions between Phoenician Byblos and Egypt, and as other observers likewise attested.[82] This literacy is still reflected today in the large number of universities that blanket Lebanon. When the Templars needed people to keep their records, write contracts for supplies, and handle correspondence between the Holy Land and Europe, they no doubt found the Lebanese Christians were better able to perform these tasks than the knights themselves.

Of course, not all local Christians would have been literate, which meant many of them would have come to wear the brown and black robes of serving men. But those among them who had the necessary writing skills would have been among the first hired to do those tasks. And to one day wear the green robes.

The Knights Templar seemed to make more use of this local talent than did the other Crusaders scattered between the northern city of Antioch in Syria and the southern city of Gaza on the Egyptian border. This could be due to most of the European "kings" in these different areas having so much of their attention riveted on daily battles and petty squabbles. Or perhaps it was due to exceptional vision by Hugh de Payens at the head of the Templars. His creation went on to achieve fame that long outlived him, while the small local kingdoms turned to dust.

That Hugh de Payens and the Templar Order took a special interest in the Lebanese people was manifested many times. After the Lebanese city of Tripoli was captured by the Crusaders it eventually found its way into the hands of the Templars for protection. Beirut also became a Crusader town, with Guy of Brisbarre being named Lord of Beirut in 1127. In time its protection was also assigned to the Templars. At Sidon, the Crusader Castle-by-the Sea still holds its strategic position beside the harbor, and on a nearby hillside the fortress of St. Louis stands in ruins. The Templars purchased the rights to hold Sidon, consolidating their control of Lebanese lands. Farther inland, they assumed the rights to the castle of Beaufort. After the city of Tyre finally fell into Christian hands in 1124, the Templars gained a share of its control as well.[83]

The Templar knights yielded to other Europeans most of the land of Syria in the north and Israel in the south. Yet they blanketed all of Lebanon and kept most of it for themselves. This was an odd choice. The lands to the south were closer to Jerusalem and the Crusaders' seat of power, so its ports were correspondingly more important. The lands to the far north in Syria were away from the concentration of Crusaders, offering more privacy and autonomy. Yet for some reason the Templars chose to concentrate their holdings in Lebanon. Apparently they valued what they obtained from the Lebanese people, and wanted to keep as much of it as possible for their own use.

You may have noticed some correlation between the services provided by Lebanese Christians and the duties of the green-robed brothers among the Knights Templar. That is not necessarily a coincidence. To import people with these talents from Europe would have been a prohibitively expensive proposition. And even then they would have to learn the local Arabic language. The Templars seem to have taken the easy way out by drawing from among the local Christians in Lebanon for these clerical services.

Realistically, one difficulty in doing that would have been the need to develop some level of trust between the local people and the invading Europeans. This would have been particularly challenging due to the strong tradition of secrecy among these Lebanese descendants of the Phoenicians. The fact that the Westerners and locals practiced Christianity—and were beset by ardent Muslim opponents on all sides—would have been a strong step in the direction of trust-building. The old mantra "the enemy of my enemy is my friend" seemed to apply. The beginnings of trust came.

Another step in this process would have been the cautiously-taken vows and obligations required of new members in the Templar Order. These oaths were taken by all the brothers, from highest to lowest, creating the beginning of a bond between them. As the years passed and those vows were kept, even in life-and-death situations, trust would have deepened. By all accounts the Templars were notoriously firm about living up to their obligations. They did not leave a wounded brother upon the field, nor retreat while the battle was still being fought. They were known for fighting to the death, rather than break the vow made to their brothers. This seems to have engendered a tremendously close bond of brotherhood among the Templars.

When the Knights Templar went searching under Temple Mount, apparently looking for things of value from Solomon's Temple, we have often been told that they searched blindly and were fortunate to make their discoveries. Yet how likely would it be for that to have happened? Hebrews, Romans, Byzantines and Arabs had been back and forth over and under the Mount while clearing away rubble and raising their own structures over the centuries. It would reasonably have required more than walking down a dark passage to find hidden materials—whether they were scrolls with exotic mysteries or the stone tablets of Moses.

So it is fair to ask if the Templars might have had help. Lebanese Christians have always been proud of their role in the events of the Bible—including the building of Solomon's Temple. One sees books counting the number of times Lebanon was mentioned in the Bible.[84] Lebanese Christians have also conscientiously preserved elements of their society from generation to generation, as we have seen. In doing this they may or may not have retained specific knowledge about crypts and storage places beneath Solomon's Temple. Perhaps they had only hints, clues and memorized phrases, similar to those that fueled the *Da Vinci Code* search. But now that a stronger bond of trust had been established with their new brothers, whatever they had would reasonably have been shared.

Yet that brings up a puzzle. If Lebanese Christians were aware of this special knowledge or other valuable material, why give it up at all? Had something changed?

Before 1099, Muslim rule over the Holy Land would have made the rescue of any such valuables from Solomon's Temple not only difficult but virtually impossible, much like the situation on Temple Mount today. But then the Crusaders came and took control of Jerusalem and the surrounding lands. With them came a brief window of opportunity to recover any treasured writings and objects that may have been preserved, and take them to a more secure place. There was no guarantee these vastly outnumbered Crusaders would be able to hold the Holy Land forever. In fact, the overwhelming number of Muslim forces on all sides almost guaranteed the opposite would happen.

If the contents of a secret crypt were ever to be taken to a place Christians would regard as safer, it would have had to be done while Crusader control was in place. And if there was going to be a group among the European Christians to whom a secret location was entrusted, it would reasonably have been the brothers with whom they shared vows, obligations and trust—the Knights Templar. And those contents were not leaving their hands in any event, because Lebanese Christians were among the Templars.

They would still be there to protect the secrets, along with their Western brothers in the Order.

In the year 1125 the Count of Champagne did a most remarkable thing. We saw that almost all the people involved in the creation of the Knights Templar, including Hugh de Payens, came from within and around his province of Champagne, so it would seem that the Count might have had some role in its formation. He now made his participation more explicit. Handing over the hereditary rights of Champagne to another, he came to the Holy Land and took the vows of the Order, placing his hands in those of his life-long friend, the Grand Master. By so doing, the Count agreed to serve the rest of his life as a Templar. And though he no longer personally appeared on the world stage, the newly-raised knight who became known as Sir Hugh continued to work behind the scenes during a pivotal moment for the young Templars. To be more than a minor cult of knights in Jerusalem, they needed to obtain the pope's approval of their order. They also needed to seek from the nobility of Europe significant financial support for their efforts.

According to popular legend, King Baldwin II of Jerusalem decided one day in 1126 to send a request to the influential St. Bernard, Abbot of Clairvaux, asking the abbot to seek the pope's blessing for the Knights Templar. Bernard was said to have accepted this mission, and things progressed from there. The reality, as we have seen, was somewhat different. The saintly Bernard had received the lands for his monastery at Clairvaux from the hands of the Count of Champagne, and owed him a profound debt of gratitude. Bernard confirmed this in a letter to the Count written on the occasion of Hugh's leaving France to become a Knight Templar. This letter avowed the deep thanks Bernard owed to his benefactor.[85] It was never in doubt that Bernard would be passionate advocate for the Templars whenever it was needed. The public request for his support clearly came from Sir Hugh and Grand Master de Payens, with King Baldwin II signing the letter to give it appropriate weight when St. Bernard presented it to the pope.

Bernard began his work immediately and arranged for Pope Honorarius to grant an audience with Hugh de Payens and four of his brother knights. With the pontiff's invitation in hand, de Payens set out for Rome in 1127. The pope received him, warmly approved the cause of the Knights Templar, and let his opinion be known.[86] In addition, a great Council of the church was summoned for the following year in the city of Troyes, at which the Templars' elevation to a formal Order of the Church would be discussed and offered for approval. It is noted in passing that Troyes was the family seat of the Count of Champagne.

With that critical council arranged and the clock ticking, de Payens had to move quickly. He desperately needed to recruit more knights into the Templars for two essential reasons. If he wanted the Templars to be taken seriously as a substantial group, worthy of being made a formal monastic order, he needed to come before the Council with more than the nine-to-thirty knights variously estimated to be in his chivalric brotherhood at that time. Equally important, he needed to put more knights into the field in the Holy Land against the overwhelming Muslim forces—not just to achieve victories, but to survive. This recruitment was one of his most pressing needs and—as a leader of knights—he was eminently qualified to assess, inspire and enlist these people.

Yet he had another need as well, without which the service of these knights would be rendered virtually useless. He needed rich gifts from the kings and nobility of Europe to support and equip those knights, along with their sergeants, in the Holy Land. More than gold and silver, he needed lands and estates. Gold could be spent only once, but land and estates could be farmed to produce revenues year after year—and those streams of revenue could be spent forever. Unfortunately, fundraising was an area Hugh de Payens was ill equipped to handle.

His lands and manor of Payns had come to him by right as his father's son. He had no need to seek it, negotiate rights, define boundaries, or draw new contracts with peasants to farm the land and pay appropriate rents. Moreover, begging for gifts of land was beneath the dignity of a member of French nobility. Not that such begging was not done, but disrepute often fell upon those who did it. He lacked experience in determining the suitable amount to seek from a prospective donor, and how to tender the request appropriately to obtain a good response. Fortunately, he had people with him who were past masters at this enterprise: the brothers he had recruited in Lebanon.

These Lebanese brothers were descended from the people widely regarded as the master sea traders and businessmen of the Mediterranean world. The extent to which this Phoenician heritage was deeply imbued in their society was demonstrated as late as 1975 in Beirut, which was the financial capital of the Middle East until regional wars began. The ability of Lebanese entrepreneurs to charm a customer, negotiate an agreement, attend to appropriate details, and write a durable charter conveying property to its new owner was among the best in the East or in the West.

The role of these "clerical" men—who later wore green robes within this Order—has regularly been overlooked in describing the activities of the Templars. Most assessments dutifully acknowledge that the knights made up only ten-to-fifteen percent of the Templar brethren. Then those assessments tend to ignore the other brothers and focus on the deeds of those dashing men on horseback. That would be like acknowledging the Master and Wardens of a Freemason lodge, but forgetting all the other officers and brothers. And so it was with the Templars.

When Hugh and his four accompanying knights came to Europe to solidly establish the foundation of their organization, they would have brought roughly thirty-five servingmen as well, if they kept to the normal ratio among the Templars. Some of these brothers would have been retainers to ensure the knights were properly outfitted and fed, but the rest would have been the administrators and scribes needed for a successful diplomatic mission of this nature. To this latter group fell the task of accompanying the Grand Master and handling details of the contracts and diplomacy that were required. Vague promises of support had to be gently nudged into formal commitments and signed documents. What the Grand Master could not do without seeming *déclassé* or lacking honor, his enterprising serving brothers from the Holy Land could do effortlessly, with a certain grace, and with the confidence born of experience.

Not surprisingly, one of the first visits paid by the Master of the Temple and his quiet associates was to the new Count of Champagne, Theobald de Blois. From that man came a generous donation of lands at Barbonne, twenty-five miles northwest of Troyes. Numerous other visits followed in the north of France, each time accompanied by a donation of land, gold, or revenue rights in some form. To assure the proper transfer of title and flow of income from the lands, the Templars developed a practice of leaving behind a few brothers to manage the estates and rights. Over time this was formed into a network of preceptories[87] and estates that became one of their hallmarks. A few of these men-left-behind were knights, but most were drawn from among the clerical brothers and serving brothers, due to the nature of the work and the need to have most of the knights serve in the Holy Land.

While in Northern France, de Payens paid a critical visit to King Henry I of England, who was also the Duke of Normandy. Henry was apparently in residence at his Norman estates at the time. The *Anglo-Saxon Chronicle*, written by English scribes during those days, reported the encounter this way.

> This same year (1128 AD), Hugh of the Temple came from Jerusalem to the king in Normandy, and the king received him with much honour, and gave him much treasure in gold and silver, and afterwards he sent him into England, and there he was well received by all good men, and all gave him treasure, and in Scotland also, and they sent in all a great sum in gold and silver by him to Jerusalem, and there went with him and after him so great a number as never before since the days of Pope Urban.[88]

Going onward to England as the king urged, de Payens and his men were gifted with a number of rich manors by different lords and ladies, including the Old Temple grounds in London. Those Old Temple lands were just south of High Holborn along Chancery Lane, and gradually became the primary preceptory or headquarters for the Templars in England. The knight they left behind served as the Prior—later called Master—of the Temple in England. With him were a number of administrative brothers who began to draw revenue from the English estates and forward it to the Holy Land. The building of a round Templar Church commenced shortly thereafter.

Meanwhile, the Grand Master and his remaining brothers continued northward into Scotland. There they received additional gifts of land that included the fair property of Balantrodoch south of Edinburgh. At that place they established their preceptory in Scotland, and commissioned a more modest church. Their local headquarters was similarly on a more modest scale, perhaps beginning to reflect how much their administrative resources were being stretched by that point.

De Payens then returned to France in time to attend the Council of Troyes that had been promised to him by the pope. At Troyes, where he and the Count had begun their close relationship many years earlier, Hugh discovered that Bernard of Clairvaux had prepared the stage well. De Payens was asked to describe for this distinguished council of church leaders the existing organization of the Knights Templar, as well as its current religious vows and practices. The strictness of their voluntary obligations was apparently quite pleasing to the assembled religious leaders. As a result, the council asked Bernard to draw up a formal religious "Rule" to guide the Templars.[89] This was a traditional step in officially forming a monastic order, and generally was based on an existing Rule, with modifications added to meet the specific needs of the order. Bernard was a "friend in court" for the Templars, so the Rule for them strongly resembled the practices they were already performing.

It should be noted that the clerical administrators who had shown their value to the Templars during the fundraising expedition were already being distinguished with the title of chaplain. They now began to receive additional rewards alongside the knights, such as this part of the Templar Rule.

[Section] X.   Let a repast of flesh three times a week suffice you, excepting at Christmas, or Easter, or the feast of the Blessed Mary, or of All Saints.... On Sun-

Fig. 17   Templar church at Balantrodoch, Scotland

day we think it clearly fitting and expedient that two messes of flesh should be served up to the knights and the chaplains. But let the rest, to wit, the esquires and retainers, remain contented with one, and be thankful therefor.[90]

Having received the blessing of the council and the pope, the Templars prepared for their return to the Holy Land. Hugh set sail at the head of many newly-recruited knights, aboard ships laden with heavy quantities of gold and silver. He left behind in

France, England and Scotland small contingents of men to oversee the many scattered manors and lands. Those brothers were charged with turning the properties into productive estates, and sending more boatloads of gold and silver to Jerusalem for support of the growing phenomenon that was the Knights Templar.

Ten years after the Council of Troyes, the pope recognized the escalating prominence of the Knights Templar by yielding additional concessions to them in his official letter *Omne datum optimum*. In this remarkable document he made the Templars exempt from the laws and rulers of every country, owing their allegiance only to the pope. Their properties in different lands became part of an international domain that could not be touched.

The papal letter also granted a special reward for the clerical brothers in recognition of their critical role within the Templar Order. In addition to their previous title of chaplain, they were given all the rights and authorities of priests. They now put on their green robes and became a distinct third group among the Templars.

In further recognition of their contribution, the dean of the chaplains was granted extraordinary privileges. These included being seated immediately beside the Master at table, being served first, and other favored considerations.[91] The quiet clerical men had made substantial contributions, and still had more to give.

This proved to be a critical milestone for the Templars and the secrecy in which they began to wrap themselves. We saw how secrecy was an essential part of Phoenician society, enabling those people to survive life-threatening challenges for many centuries. It had also served their heirs well. Now it began to play a greater role among the Templars.

This granting of priestly rights to the green-clad brothers finally allowed the Templars to eliminate outsiders from any role in their affairs. This included writing their private correspondence, recording their finances, or the hearing of their confessions in which all manner of things might be unburdened. They were at last able to draw the veil of secrecy firmly around their society.[92]

Chapter 9

Templars, the Lionheart and Saladin

Richard the Lionheart arrived on the shore of the Holy Land in 1191 to join the labors of the Crusades, and chose to do so in the fellowship of the Knights Templar. This suggested how far the knights of the Temple had come by that time, and the almost mystical aura that was beginning to surround their name and deeds. Accounts written during the Crusades recorded these stirring events.

> The English and French monarchs laid aside their private animosities, and agreed to fight under the same banner against the infidels, and towards the close of the month of May, in the second year of the siege of Acre, the royal fleets of Philip Augustus and Richard Coeur de Lion floated in triumph in the bay of Acre. At the period of the arrival of king Richard the Templars had again lost their Grand Master, and Brother Robert de Sablé or Sabloil, a valiant knight of the order, who had commanded a division of the English fleet on the voyage out, was placed at the head of the fraternity. The proudest of the nobility, and the most

valiant of the chivalry of Europe, on their arrival in Palestine, manifested an eager desire to fight under the banner of the Temple. Many secular knights were permitted by the Grand Master to take their station by the side of the military friars, and even to wear the red cross on their breasts whilst fighting in the ranks.

The Templars performed prodigies of valour; "The name of their reputation, and the fame of their sanctity," says James of Vitry, bishop of Acre, "like a chamber of perfume sending forth a sweet odour, was diffused throughout the entire world, and all the congregation of the saints will recount their battles and glorious triumph over the enemies of Christ, knights indeed from all parts of the earth, dukes, and princes, after their example, casting off the shackles of the world, and renouncing the pomps and vanities of this life and all the lusts of the flesh for Christ's sake, hastened to join them, and to participate in their holy profession and religion."

On the morning of the twelfth of July, six weeks after the arrival of the British fleet, the kings of England and France, the christian chieftains, and the Turkish emirs with their green banners, assembled in the tent of the Grand Master of the Temple, to treat of the surrender of Acre, and on the following day the gates were thrown open to the exulting warriors of the cross. The Templars took possession of three localities within the city by the side of the sea, where they established their famous Temple, which became from thenceforth the chief house of the order. Richard Coeur de Lion, we are told, took up his abode with the Templars, whilst Philip resided in the citadel.[93]

Much had happened since the early grants by kings and popes set the Templars on their way. Hugh de Payens had assembled and led the first glittering array of knights into battle across the hills and plains around Jerusalem. His successors then led similar clashes of arms on countless fields. Among those confrontations was the memorable siege of 1153 at Ascalon, on the Mediterranean shore north of Gaza. It revealed the fierceness of the fighting, and the dedication of the Templars.

> The same year, at the siege of Ascalon, the Master of the Temple and his knights attempted alone and unaided to take that important city by storm. At the dawn of day they rushed through a breach made in the walls, and penetrated to the centre of the town. There they were surrounded by the infidels and overpowered, and, according to the testimony of an eyewitness, who was in the campaign from its commencement to its close, not a single Templar escaped: they were slain to a man, and the dead bodies of the Master and his ill-fated knights were exposed in triumph from the walls.[94]

Upon the passing of a Master of the Temple, whether in the bloody manner that happened at Ascalon or through natural causes, a new Master was chosen by the brothers from among their number. This was true at the passing of Hugh de Payens on or about 1136, and with each succeeding Master. The eighth Master of the Temple, Odo de St. Amand, fared better in 1170 than his predecessor had at Ascalon.

> Saladin besieged the fortified city of Gaza, which belonged to the Knights Templars, and was considered to be the key of Palestine towards Egypt. The luxuriant gardens, the palm and olive groves of this city of the wilderness, were destroyed by the wild cavalry of the desert, and the innumerable tents of the Arab host were thickly clustered on the neighboring sand-hills. The warlike monks of the Temple fasted and prayed, and invoked the aid of the God of battles; the gates of the city were thrown open, and in an unexpected sally upon the enemy's camp they performed such prodigies of valour, that Saladin, despairing of being able to

take the place, abandoned the siege, and retired into Egypt.[95]

Given the Order's "bravest in battle" dedication and accompanying mortality rate, recruitment of fighting knights and sergeants was a serious challenge. Yet the steadily growing reputation and glory earned by the Knights Templar aided their cause. The mystique of the Templars became compelling, and new recruits were there to be found. Even though their recruiting missions in Europe were less dangerous than service in the East, they were no less daunting—for that was not the only challenge the Templars faced.

The expenses incurred to support each knight were staggering, given the need to provide horses, armor, retainers and ongoing provisions in a distant land. This created a growing need for acres of land to produce these essential revenues, pushing the white-clad knights and their green-robed brethren in Europe to mount an ongoing "recruitment" of real estate as well as men. Ingeniously weaving themselves into the social fabric, the knights and administrators positioned their Order as an extremely popular recipient of gifts and bequests.

> An astonishing enthusiasm was excited throughout Christendom in behalf of the Templars; princes and nobles, sovereigns and their subjects, vied with each other in heaping gifts and benefits upon them, and scarce a will of importance was made without an article in it in their favour. Many illustrious persons on their deathbeds took the vows, that they might be buried in the habit of the order; and sovereigns, quitting the government of their kingdoms, enrolled themselves amongst the holy fraternity, and bequeathed even their dominions to the Master and the brethren of the Temple.
>
> Thus, Raymond Berenger, Count of Barcelona and Provence, at a very advanced age, abdicating his throne, and shaking off the ensigns of royal authority, retired to the house of the Templars at Barcelona, and pronounced his vows (A.D. 1130) before brother Hugh

de Rigauld, the Prior. His infirmities not allowing him to proceed in person to the chief house of the order at Jerusalem, he sent vast sums of money thither, and immuring himself in a small cell in the Temple at Barcelona, he there remained in the constant exercise of the religious duties of his profession until the day of his death. At the same period, the Emperor Lothaire bestowed on the order a large portion of his patrimony of Supplinburg; and the year following (A.D. 1131) Alphonso the First, king of Navarre and Arragon, also styled Emperor of Spain, one of the greatest warriors of the age, by his will declared the Knights of the Temple his heirs and successors in the crowns of Navarre and Arragon, and a few hours before his death he caused this will to be ratified and signed by most of the barons of both kingdoms. The validity of this document, however, was disputed, and the claims of the Templars were successfully resisted by the nobles of Navarre; but in Arragon they obtained, by way of compromise, lands, and castles, and considerable dependencies, a portion of the customs and duties levied throughout the kingdom, and of the contributions raised from the Moors.[96]

The resulting Templar empire came to extend over the full length of Europe, from Ireland to the Mediterranean. The Irish contribution increased in 1170 when King Henry II became implicated in the murder of Saint Thomas Becket, the Archbishop of Canterbury. One of the ways this remorseful king made amends to the pope was to donate Clontarf Castle in Dublin to the Knights Templar. That prime property north of the Liffey River became the Templar preceptory in Ireland. As such, it took on the role of administering the other Irish properties that came to the Templars as well.

Surprisingly enough, Clontarf Castle not only still exists, it has been made into an elegant hotel in which one can sleep where the Templars slept—albeit in markedly better beds.[97] It is easily

Fig. 18   Clontarf Castle, the Templar preceptory at Dublin, Ireland

reached in Dublin by local bus. The old Templar church still stands behind the castle, tucked away in a walled-off graveyard. The chapel no longer has a roof, but otherwise remains in reasonably good repair. Behind the church and castle rests part of the old jousting and exercise field, now converted into a public park. Standing among the few trees of the park, it is almost possible to hear the pounding of horses' hooves, the clash of metal on armor, and the chiming of the church bell, calling Templars to afternoon prayers.

Similarly in Scotland, the grant of land Hugh de Payens received at Balantrodoch a few miles from Rosslyn Chapel served as the Templar headquarters for that country. The ancient church there is remarkably similar to the one at Clontarf, reflecting their shared heritage. Balantrodoch apparently enjoyed spacious grounds, since the church was located at some remove from the manor house. When approaching the town of Temple on this old preceptory property, one comes to a fork in the road today. If taken to the right, the paved lane comes to the roofless church still standing guard over a well-populated graveyard. Doubling back to the fork and taking the branch to the left, one looks for a long driveway on the left that passes between the houses of the village to an open field beyond. There, standing alone, is an archway made of old, carefully-cut stones. Local lore holds that this archway marked the gatehouse to the Templar manor, which stood among the stately trees just beyond.

Scotland had other Templar properties as well, including the Maryculter and Aboyne lands on the River Dee in Aberdeenshire. There were also lands outside the towns of Nairn and Ardersier in Nairnshire, and numerous smaller properties, some of which still bear the Temple name.

Far to the south in London, near the palaces of remorseful Henry II, the Templars completed their expansion from the relatively small property at High Holborn to the more commodious estate on the banks of the Thames. Passage from the old site to the new was an easy five minute walk down Chancery Lane to Fleet Street—which formed the northern boundary of the Templar estate. At the corner of Chancery and Fleet a pedestrian gateway opens today to Inner Temple Lane, where a short walk down the lane reveals the prize of the preceptory, the Temple Church. In 1185, Patriarch Heraclius traveled from Jerusalem to preside over the dedication ceremony for this remarkable place of worship. The resultant pageantry and great social stir was believed to have included King Henry and possibly his son Richard, who would become known as the Lionheart.

This church—like several other Templar chapels—was built with a round tower in imitation of the Church of the Holy Sepulcher in Jerusalem. It reflected the circular enclosure around the tomb of Jesus and the place of his resurrection. As such, this part of Temple Church became much in demand among Christian nobility and kings as a place to be buried. Adjacent to the round tower, just as in Jerusalem, was a long, rectangular chancel, with an altar dedicated to the Virgin Mary. Later the chancel was enlarged by gift of another English king,[98] resulting in the final appearance of Temple Church as seen today.

From this grand estate beside the Thames, the Templars administered manors and properties spread across the length and breadth of England. These included Ewell in Kent, Daney and Dokesworth in Cambridgeshire, Getinges in Gloucestershire, Cumbe in Somersetshire, Schepeley in Surrey, Samford and Bistelesham in Oxfordshire, Garwy in Herefordshire, and Cressing in Essex.[99]

Meanwhile the land of France contained several kingdoms at that time and therefore had several Templar preceptories. If one encampment had primacy of place, indications are that the honor first went to the Templar estates at Bar-sur-Seine in the province of Champagne. This manor stood between two of the most important early Templar sites: the city of Troyes and the abbey of Saint Bernard at Clairvaux.

As the kings of Isle de France—meaning the area around Paris—expanded their holdings by acquiring territories owned by other kings, they began to create a France similar to the one we know today. Responding to that shift, the Templars accepted a suitable property in Paris around the year 1240 and raised a great fortress there. This site in the heart of the city then became the leading preceptory for the Knights Templar in France. Its impressive grounds and buildings stood near today's Temple subway station in the 3rd arrondissement, just north of Notre Dame Cathedral. It was bordered by the streets Rue du Temple, Rue de Bretagne, Rue Charlot, and Rue Béranger. From this grand edifice, the Templar estates in France were administered, including Sommereux, Oisement, Abbeville and Gombermond in the north; Civray, Nantes, La Guerche and Baugy in the west; Hyères, Marseille, Roaix, and Richerenches in the south; and Troyes, Coulours, Epailly and Bure-les-Templiers in the west.[100]

Preceptories in other countries likewise oversaw estates contributing to the rich flow of funds supporting the Templars. In Spain were the estates of Zaragoza and Tortosa among others. In Portugal were Tomar, Pombal and Soure. Germany and Poland had Tempelhof, Bamberg, Mala Olesnica and Wielka Weis. Italy added Taranto, Brindisi, Perugia and Siena. Sicily contributed estates at Syracuse and Messina. In Greece were Fuste, Paleopolis and Lamia. The parade of estates continued eastward to Cyprus and all across the Holy Land.

As impressive as their extensive holdings were—exceeding that of many kings—the Templars continued to be drained by the ongoing war in the Holy Land. They found themselves in need of still more sources of gold and silver.

So they adopted and modified some Near Eastern financial practices for their own use, creating the equivalent of traveler's cheques in that early day and age. For most people in Europe this was a radically new concept, and it was made possible by these many Templar preceptories scattered across the continent and all the way to Jerusalem. One of the great risks of travel in those days was that thieves preyed on people who carried enough gold and other valuables to finance long journeys through foreign lands. The Templars took that risk upon themselves, granting travelers the right to deposit their small fortunes at a preceptory near their home, and receive encrypted notes in return. These notes could then be presented at any Templar preceptory in any country along their journey—and the equivalent in silver coin or other money would be given to them. For this service the men of the Temple charged a reasonable fee that was gladly paid. The service became immensely popular, and this concept of bank checks became well established.

The enterprising Templars combined this with a multitude of other financial services, including lending money to kings and noblemen to live their luxurious lifestyles and fight their wars. They also managed estates for people who were absentee owners, and offered their well-guarded Templar strongholds as safe places to deposit valuable assets. These financial services became a massive business operation that was said to have eventually rivaled the Templars' main activity of fighting in the Holy Land.

Historians have frequently noted this unusual financial activity, but virtually never look deeper and wonder how it came about. In truth, the knights among the Templars could not have done it. As pointed out by a scribe who recorded the minutes of the Council of Troyes in 1129, the two noble Counts who were present were illiterate—they apparently could not read the proceedings of the Council. And a skill level far higher than simple literacy was required to accurately keep all the written and financial records necessary for these services. This included the ability to draft cryptic documents that allowed funds to be transferred and reissued only under appropriate conditions, and release them to the right person. Priests could read and write, but were prohibited by the Church from engaging in moneylending. So who could possibly have done this?

The often-overlooked clerics among the Templars of course come to mind. These green-robed men had the proper roots to restore and improve upon this ancient financial practice. The Lebanese Christians among the Templar clerics belonged to a society whose international financial skills had been developed for many generations. Their penchant for secrecy and numbers made the cryptic workings of these financial instruments a reasonable outcome of their work. They caused the far-flung Templar empire to flourish.

How good was the internal security and secrecy of the Knights Templar? Consider that this third suborder of clerics among the Templars was created by the pope, its members accompanied the Master of the Temple in his non-military work, and the dean of their group sat immediately beside the Master at the meals of the Order. Yet these clerics were largely invisible to the people of that time, and in subsequent years remained nearly invisible to historians. Fascination with armed knights on horseback would account for part of this. The covering title of "chaplain" did much of the rest, since it would lead people to believe these men were Bible-readers at daily prayers and little else. The essential roles they played among the brothers of the Temple were better performed out of public view. And so it was done in that manner.

Richard Plantagenet, known as the Lionheart, was crowned king of England on 23 September 1189. At that time his court and all of Europe was still reeling from the fall of Jerusalem to the Muslim leader Saladin, and Crusade fever was in the air. Richard threw himself immediately into preparing for the Third Crusade, and ten months later set sail with his French ally, King Philip Augustus.

As fate would have it, the boat carrying Richard's fiancée, Berengaria of Navarre, became shipwrecked on the island of Cyprus, only 100 miles from the Holy Land. The treasure aboard that ship was appropriated by King Isaac of Cyprus, who cast the English survivors into prison until he could decide what to do with them. Richard solved that problem for him by coming ashore in full rage with all his troops, and quickly conquered the island. Reunited with Berengaria, he married her on the spot.

Finally able to join the other Crusaders in the Holy Land, Richard arrived at the port city of Acre where its Muslim leaders were under siege. Alongside the French, German, and Templar forces he marched victoriously into the city six weeks later.

After the fall of Acre, however, the French and German leaders decided they had done enough crusading. They boarded their ships and returned home. Undeterred, Richard and his troops stayed on to continue fighting alongside the Knights Templar. Together they campaigned across the land and recorded a number of stirring victories.

> The Templars took part in the attack upon the great Egyptian convoy, wherein four thousand and seventy camels, five hundred horses, provisions, tents, arms, and clothing, and a great quantity of gold and silver, were captured, and then fell back upon Acre; they

were followed by Saladin, who immediately commenced offensive operations, and laid siege to Jaffa.
The Templars marched by land to the relief of the
place, and Coeur de Lion hurried by sea. Many valiant
exploits were performed, the town was relieved, and
the campaign was concluded....[101]

Despite his many victories, Richard lacked the greatest one of
all. The city of Jerusalem did not fall, even after two arduous
campaigns. The most Richard could accomplish was to sign an
agreement with Saladin that enabled Christians to have access to
Jerusalem. He also gained confirmation of Christian control in the
cities they had captured.

His last act in the Crusade was to prepare for departure by
dressing himself in the guise of a Templar knight to avoid detec-
tion by his enemies. Richard then set sail for home late in the year
of 1192.

This left the Templars in possession of several individual cities,
all ruled from the port city of Acre, but surrounded by unfriendly
territory on all sides. That meant they were now dependent upon
the sea to obtain their much-needed supplies from Cyprus and
Europe. Those seaways were frequently their only means of communication with the equally isolated cities of Tyre and Tripoli
farther up the Lebanese coast. Their solution was a simple one:
they became expert seamen and amassed a large fleet of ships. Yet
that posed something of a mystery in itself. How exactly do military men who make their living on horseback become seamen
with naval skills?

This turned out to be another area where their Lebanese brothers were able to help. Their relatives up the coast were heirs to the
most skilled boatmakers and seamen in the East.

The continuation of these boatmaking and seamanship talents
in Lebanon was amply demonstrated as recently as 2004, when I
met the boatmaster at Tyre. He was just completing the building
of a cedar boat at that time, made completely in the Phoenician
manner. Not a single nail was used in constructing it. Each piece
was handcrafted with mortise and tenon joints, then held fast with
stout wooden pegs. After he showed me this exquisitely detailed

*Fig. 19   Richard the Lionheart leaving the Holy Land
wearing the uniform of a Knight Templar.*

workmanship, I witnessed her maiden voyage and saw she was completely seaworthy. He explained that he had been shown how to do this when he was young, and was now showing his son how to do the same. Clearly these skills were being passed down from father to son during the time of the Lionheart, because they are still being handed down today.

Before long, a significant fleet of ships was assembled for the Templars, and sailed under their control. Having this force upon the sea also contributed to keeping the Templar headquarters in the seaport of Acre, even after inland cities became available.

The fortunes of war changed for the better in 1228 when Emperor Frederick II—the ruler of Germany and Italy—brought the Sixth Crusade. His attacks on Egypt resulted in the leader of that land yielding the city of Jerusalem to Christian control. Only the Temple Mount area was held back. The mount, which contained the Dome of the Rock and Al Aqsa Mosque, remained under Muslim control. Finally, and joyfully, Christian pilgrims returned to Jerusalem in large numbers. Unfortunately that joy was short lived. In 1244 Jerusalem fell once more to Muslim forces. It would not return again to Christian control until it was taken by the British in 1917.

Despite many difficulties, the Knights Templar, Hospitallers and a scattering of other groups maintained their presence in the Holy Land during the years that followed. They held fast to their key cities and fortresses, sending out frequent forays along the normal pilgrim routes. Depending upon the strength or weakness of their adversaries over the years, there was an ebb and flow of control over the adjacent countryside.

Finally, however, the Muslim leaders gathered together a large force of soldiers and horsemen then set out to rid themselves of the infidels in their midst. One by one they began to extinguish the Christian strongholds. In the far north, Antioch fell in 1268. In Northern Lebanon they took Tripoli in 1289. Then they approached the critical lynchpin in the Crusader strongholds, the city of Acre, site of the Templar headquarters. The ensuing battle was epic in scale, with everything placed at risk. As the fighting became ever more desperate, the defenders' acts of valor bordered on the legendary.

In the spring of the year 1291, the sultan Khalil marched against Acre at the head of sixty thousand horse and a hundred and forty thousand foot....

William de Beaujeu, the Grand Master of the Temple, a veteran warrior of a hundred fights, took the command of the garrison, which amounted to about twelve thousand men, exclusive of the forces of the Temple and the Hospital, and a body of five hundred foot and two hundred horse, under the command of the king of Cyprus. These forces were distributed along the walls in four divisions, the first of which was commanded by Hugh de Grandison, an English knight. The old and the feeble, women and children, were sent away by sea to the christian island of Cyprus, and none remained in the devoted city but those who were prepared to fight in its defense, or to suffer martyrdom at the hands of the infidels. The siege lasted six weeks, during the whole of which period the sallies and the attacks were incessant.... On the 15th [of May] the double wall was forced, and the king of Cyprus, panic-stricken, fled in the night to his ships, and made sail for the island of Cyprus, with all his followers, and with near three thousand of the best men of the garrison. On the morrow the Saracens attacked the post he had deserted; they filled up the ditch with the bodies of dead men and horses, piles of wood, stones, and earth, and their trumpets then sounded to the assault. Ranged under the yellow banner of Mahomet, the Mamlooks forced the breach, and penetrated sword in hand to the very centre of the city....

Three hundred Templars, the sole survivors of their illustrious order in Acre, were now left alone to withstand the shock of the victorious Mamlooks....

The following morning very favorable terms were offered to the Templars by the victorious sultan, and they agreed to evacuate the Temple on condition that a galley should be placed at their disposal, and that they should be allowed to retire in safety with the christian fugitives under their protection, and to carry away as much of their effects as each person could load himself with. The Mussulman conqueror pledged himself to the fulfilment of these conditions, and sent a standard to the Templars, which was mounted on one of the towers of the Temple. A guard of three hundred Moslem soldiers, charged to see the articles of capitulation properly carried into effect, was afterwards admitted within the walls of the convent. Some christian women of Acre, who had refused to quit their fathers, brothers, and husbands, the brave defenders of the place, were amongst the fugitives, and the Moslem soldiers, attracted by their beauty, broke through all restraint, and violated the terms of the surrender. The enraged Templars closed and barricaded the gates of the Temple; they set upon the treacherous infidels, and put every one of them, "from the greatest to the smallest," to death.... The residue of the Templars retired into the large tower of the Temple, called "The Tower of the Master," which they defended with desperate energy. The bravest of the Mamlooks were driven back in repeated assaults, and the little fortress was everywhere surrounded with heaps of the slain. The sultan, at last, despairing of taking the place by assault, ordered it to be undermined. As the workmen advanced, they propped the foundations with beams of wood, and when the excavation was completed, these wooden supports were consumed by fire; the huge tower then fell with a tremendous crash, and buried the brave Templars in its ruins. The sultan set fire to the town in four places, and the last stronghold of the christian power in Palestine was speedily reduced to a smoking solitude.[102]

Just before the walls of Acre fell, some Templars led by Thibaud Gaudin saved a few of the people and what fortune of the Order remained in the city by spiriting them away to Sidon in Lebanon. Shortly after Acre's demise the final remaining strongholds at Sidon, Tortosa and Atlit were evacuated and left to the Saracens.[103] The repercussions of this devastating loss of the Holy Land reverberated throughout the Knights Templar brotherhood and all of Europe.

Chapter
10

A River of Gold
and Friday the 13th

When Jacques de Molay became Grand Master of the Knights Templar, he did not know that he was about to preside over the dispersal of his Order—nor that he would face death in flames, tied to a stake. Fate may have had some hand in what was to come, for his life was intertwined with the Templars from the beginning. Jacques was born in rural France about eighty miles southeast of Troyes, in the region that produced so many founding members of this knightly brotherhood. Around his twenty-first birthday he was received into the Templar Order at the nearby town of Beaune. After serving in France for about ten years he was sent to the Holy Land in the 1270s. There he became immersed in combat service and experienced the full rigors of a soldier's life on the dusty fields of the Mediterranean coast. Having distinguishing himself in the field, Jacques apparently won assignment to Britain in the honored position of Preceptor of England, and Master of the Temple in London.[104] Then came the news in 1291 that the Templars had lost their last foothold in the Holy Land.

Couriers announced the fall of Acre and the last three fortresses, which forced the battered remains of the Templar fighting corps to regroup on the island of Cyprus. There the Templars established a new headquarters at Limassol, the port where Richard the Lionheart had landed when he conquered that island. Before Richard quit the Holy Land and returned home, he had sold Cyprus to the wealthy Crusader Guy of Lusignan, with the provision that the Knights Templar be allowed to keep the castles and settlements they had established there during his brief reign over the island. As a result the Templars were a force on Cyprus throughout the hundred years since Richard's departure, entrenched at Limassol, Famagusta, Gastria, Khirokitia, and Yermasoyia.[105]

Jacques de Molay returned to the East and arrived on the island of Cyprus just before or after the death of Grand Master Theobald Gaudin in 1292. First elected Grand Commander on an interim basis, de Molay was then chosen by his brethren to serve as the new Grand Master.

Surrounded by the battered and scattered pieces of this once-proud Templar force, he immediately set about regrouping his fighting men. Having lost the Holy Land, whose protection was their sole mission, he redirected the surviving Templars to renew their discipline, and prepared them for retaking what had been lost. He set an example for his men in strict observance of the articles of their Rule, and began to root out many of the shadowy practices that had crept into the Order during its long exposure to mysticism in the East.

A number of accusations were made against The Templars for having unorthodox forms of secret worship, but these tended to be contradictory allegations of worshiping cats, idols, the devil, or heads. Of these, the only one borne out by any hint of evidence seemed to be the reverence shown to a particular head. During this time there was a great emphasis in virtually all parts of the Catholic Church on the collection of relics from saints. Altars were thought to be more holy if they contained a finger or fragment of bone recovered from a person who had been elevated to sainthood. Many Christian churches proudly displayed a severed hand, foot or head of a saint, making them instantly a place of local pilgrimage.

Fig. 20 Jacques DeMolay

In keeping with that tradition, the Templars were known to have collected many relics in their forays across the Holy Land, some of which eventually found their way into the hands of others. One of their most prized possessions was said to be the skull and crossed leg bones of the virgin and martyr Saint Euphemia.[106]

> ...the Order, with its extensive eastern connections, built up a large collection of relics.... Relics were also used to strengthen links with potential patrons in the west and to maintain interest in the affairs of the Holy Land...in 1272 Thomas Bérard [the Templar Grand Master] sent to London pieces of the True Cross, together with relics of saints Philip, Helena, Stephen, Laurence, Euphemia, and Barbara.[107]

It is unfortunate that the Templars did not communicate what actual practices they pursued behind closed doors, but that was quite understandable. Prior to their trials in the early 1300s, strict rules of Templar secrecy kept them from divulging any such information. And once those trials got under way, any statements with respect to practices not strictly endorsed by the Catholic Church would only have confirmed them as deviants from doctrine. It was often remarked, however, that Crusaders who lived in the Holy Land for any length of time frequently began to adopt aspects of local dress, customs and practices. However the written record gave little documentation of the extent to which individual Templars may have become adherents of Kabbalah or other mystic Eastern practices.

De Molay's call for strict conformance with the rules of the Templar Order seemed to have met with some success in the East, where virtually all the Templars in that region were gathered together on the island of Cyprus. It proved a much more daunting challenge in the West, yet he pressed on.

The main mission that he set for himself, however, was to seek from the pope and the kings of Europe new support for another Crusade to retake the Holy Land. The long series of dispiriting failures in the later Crusades worked against him in this, and his first mission to Europe in 1294 fell flat. Yet he was a determined man, and the initial rejection only strengthened his resolve.

The Templars were not the only military order struggling through these dark days. The Knights Hospitaller of St. John had been evicted from the Holy Land alongside the other Crusaders, and now occupied their own cities on Cyprus. From the time they became a military order in 1120, the Hospitallers had fought alongside the Templars—and sometimes in direct competition with them. Across the Holy Land, the major Christian cities had been protected either by the Templars, the Hospitallers, or by an individual European lord who amassed a sufficient force to see to that military duty himself. While the Knights Templar cast their mantle of protection primarily over cities in Lebanon and Israel, the Hospitallers mainly established themselves farther north, in the land known today as Syria. The order of black knights with the white cross developed a powerful center for their Order at Krak des Chevaliers, just north of the Lebanon border. Their second major fortification was farther north at Magat on the seacoast between Tripoli and Latakia.

The Hospitaller leaders in Europe allied themselves with the Templars in consistently advocating Crusades over the years. Yet they also stood in brusque confrontation with the white knights over scarce resources in gold, silver and estates needed to fund their work in the East. In each European country the Hospitallers established their own priories, similar to the Templar preceptories. In England, the priory house of the Hospitallers was in the London suburb of Clerkenwell, just east of Old Temple, the original Templar property. In Scotland, the Hospitaller priory stood to the west of Edinburgh at Torphichen. In France, the black knights established several priories, similar to the custom of the Templars.

Despite these many similarities, a growing divergence in the direction of the two orders now began to manifest itself. Templar Grand Master de Molay focused all his attention on returning to the Holy Land at the head of a powerful force. Meanwhile Hospitaller Grand Master Guillaume de Villaret believed the re-taking of Jerusalem had become a hopeless cause, a pessimistic view shared by many leaders in Europe. Accordingly, de Villaret cast about for some new opportunity to fight on behalf of Christian pilgrims—some new way to continue making his Order relevant and useful.

The mainlands of the East were teeming with Moslem forces, so de Villaret astutely identified the island of Rhodes as a potential prize and base for his Hospitallers. This was the easternmost island in the Aegean Sea, the body of water that stood as a buffer between the Christian West and the increasingly Muslim East. Although Rhodes was occupied by enemy forces, de Villaret hoped to concentrate all his fighting men on this single objective and, with a bit of luck, possibly capture it. For the moment, it was only a dream, just as de Molay dreamed of Jerusalem. Yet they were both men of action, and began to vigorously plan, solicit, and organize toward their objectives.

Other powerful men were at work in Europe, most notably Philip IV of France who was engaged in manipulating the popes and the battlefields of the continent. King Philip was surnamed "the Fair" because of his handsome appearance—certainly not for any deference to justice on his part. Twenty-four years younger than de Molay, Philip inherited two things upon his father's untimely death during a failed war in Spain: a crushing war debt, and a lavish lifestyle. To make matters worse, Philip began a new war of his own with England. As his debt mushroomed, the heavy-handed monarch sought a measure of relief by aggressively taxing his people and the Christian clergy in France.

Objecting to this taxation of the clergy, Pope Boniface VIII ordered that no such levy could be made without the consent of the pope. He followed this with an official letter asserting that the pope had higher authority than any king. Philip responded by having the Pope captured and so severely beaten that he died a month later in October of 1303.

The successor to Boniface was Benedict XI, who lived only eight months in office before dying under conditions often described as suspicious.

Philip then arranged to have a French archbishop chosen as pope. This was Clement V. The new pontiff apparently decided dying young was not appealing, and proceeded to give King Philip almost everything he wanted. This would work to the severe detriment of the Templars. As a sign of his loyalty, Clement moved the seat of the Church from Rome to France, eventually settling at Avignon near Marseille.

Pope Clement was Jacques de Molay's direct superior. For that reason it put the Templar Grand Master in an extremely difficult position when the pontiff proposed merging the Templars and Hospitallers into a single order. To be fair, this idea was not original with Clement. Moreover, with no ongoing victories in the Holy Land, there was little justification to maintain two large military orders. Even so, it was another cross for de Molay to bear.

Not to be outdone by the pope, the French king also began to cast a desirous eye upon the Knights Templar. Philip's finances, already depleted by the war with England, now suffered further losses from a war with Flanders. The Templars were involved in helping to finance these ventures because they were authorized by Philip to collect various taxes owed to him. Those amounts were then stored in the Templar treasury at Paris until the funds were disbursed as he directed.[108] In a dark foreshadowing of events to come, Philip fed his need for funds by seizing the property and persons of Italian bankers from Lombardy in 1291. He applied the same harsh measures to Jews in France in 1306, pressing their assets into his treasury.

That same year Philip admitted to having reduced the weight of silver coins in his realm, which ruined their value, and overnight the French currency was worth only a third of what it was before. Violent riots broke out in Paris, forcing the king to take refuge in the fortress of the Templar preceptory.[109] The Templars of Paris took Philip in and protected him without complaint. Unfortunately, the king's manipulation of the coinage of the realm had created an immediate need for more gold and silver—and he had several days to sit in the richly appointed Templar buildings while thinking about where he might obtain it.

Since Philip's coveting of Templar riches would soon bring a tragic day of reckoning, we need to take a peek behind the curtain of the knightly order's financial affairs. The foundation of Templar wealth was the many estates accumulated from noble

Fig. 21   Knights Templar preceptory in Paris

benefactors over the years, and these were scattered across most of the countries of Europe. Those estates produced the goods and revenues that met the Templars' needs on a consistent basis. Additional bounty in the form of gold and silver, as well as the occasional new estate, had also been endowed upon the military brothers from time to time, though this was waning due to the lack of success in the Holy Land.

The third leg upon which their financial powerhouse stood was the banking services that we saw them offer to pilgrims, kings, and wealthy clients. Unfortunately the flow of pilgrims had largely dried up since the eviction of Crusaders from the Holy Land in 1291. That left the Templars with their banking and check-writing services limited largely to Europe. It also put more of their resources into the up-and-down market of kings and lords who took out loans or deposited tax revenues into the Templar vaults for safekeeping.

It was this last usage that probably gave outsiders the impression of Templar preceptory vaults overflowing with money. Those making deposits, such as the King of France, could come visit their piles of gold and silver in the vaults and make sure their bullion was still there. This no doubt gave the impression that all the other storage rooms were likewise piled high with riches. However that was rarely the case.

The Templars had never demonstrated a desire to stockpile their riches in the West, even in the early days of the Order. Their declared purpose was to raise every gold or silver coin they could find in Europe, then send it East in the form of horses, armor, and supplies, or as gold and silver bullion to buy whatever they could not send. What they had was a flowing river of gold. It coursed from West to East, where the mouth of that gilded river sustained the body of the Order.

The need for these funds in the East was intense, as illustrated by a disagreement between Jacques de Molay and his treasurer in Paris. The Parisian administrator made a decision to lend 400,000 gold florins to King Philip.[110] The Grand Master became furious and upbraided the man—because he needed those funds in Cyprus and could not afford to have his golden river dammed up to create this reservoir for the king's benefit.

The headlands for this river of gold was the more than 870 estates collected by the Templars over the two centuries of their existence.[111] To the greatest extent possible, each of these estates was required to produce as much value as possible in crops or other goods, then sell them in towns and markets to convert them into gold and silver coin. Each small bag of precious coins then needed to be picked up and brought to central collection points such as the Templar preceptories, where the modest, trickling streams became the river of gold that was needed.

The difficulty with this system was the same one encountered by the pilgrims. People traveling with significant sums in those days were ready targets for highway robbery. The Templars had been able to solve that problem for others, and now they solved it for themselves. Two basic remedies were available to prevent robbery at that time: strength and concealment. For the first, providing a body of knights to make the rounds was simple and effective in the Templars' early days, when the estates were few and the knights were plentiful. As the number of estates grew and the knights became desperately needed in the East, the use of concealment became the more reasonable answer. This involved using unmarked couriers and unheralded country houses or city residences where the couriers could stay as they made their rounds. This invisible network required no knights to attend to it, and could be handled by the literate brethren who also managed the cryptic financial instruments offered to the pilgrims.

All these small streams were gathered and quickly forwarded to the East, where the proceeds were consumed by Templars in the performance of their duties.

There was another reason why large sums were not left in Templar treasuries, being sent to the safe houses forming this river of gold instead. King Philip's attack on the Templars in October of 1307 was not the first time the Order's vaults were raided. In 1285 their treasury at Perpignan, France was broken into by Spanish King Peter III, who seized the funds left by his brother. King Peter seemed to feel justified in this act because he and his brother were at war.[112] In July of 1307, King Edward II of England broke into the London Temple and took money, jewels and precious stones worth about £50,000. In short, the Templars were well aware that their treasuries were highly visible targets for powerful men, so they did not let funds collect in stationary places but kept the river flowing.

In June of 1306, at the same time that Philip IV was devaluing the coinage of his realm, Pope Clement V sent tremors through the Knights Templar and the Hospitallers by delivering official letters to Grand Masters de Molay and de Villaret. In these missives he announced a desire to receive their consultation and advice on the proper steps for recovering the Holy Land! Both men were ordered to meet with the pope in France for this purpose. For Jacques de Molay, this was a moment of joy and elation, the opportunity for which he had hoped and prayed. Finally someone was willing to listen to his thoughts on a Crusade that would breathe new life into his Templar Order. That he would agree to meet with Clement was never in doubt. On the other hand de Villaret, the Grand Master of the Hospitallers, declined the pope's offer.[113] The leader of the black knights was able to offer the excuse that his campaign to take Rhodes was about to get under way, and in fact the siege of that island did begin the following year as promised. Yet it was also possible that he had accelerated his war plans to avoid putting his life in the hands of Philip and the king's new pope, especially given the strange wording of the papal letter.

> We order you to come hither without delay, with as much secrecy as possible, and with a *very little retinue*, since you will find on this side the sea a sufficient number of your knights to attend upon you.[114]

De Molay's elation over his potential Crusade may have clouded his judgment, for he set forth by boat with great excitement in early 1307 to plead his case to Clement. Traveling with sixty knights, he first went to Paris to deposit into his preceptory vaults the money he brought to cover his expenses. Consistent with the Templars' "river of gold" approach, the preceptories were apparently forwarding their funds to Cyprus so quickly that there was not enough in Paris to cover his living expenses. In any event "he was received with distinction by the king,"[115] then set off to Poitiers for meetings with the pope. There de Molay vigorously defended the Templars' right to remain independent of the Hospitallers,[116] and participated in seemingly endless conferences planning the details of a maddeningly vague Crusade.

Meanwhile, Philip continued to weave his web around de Molay. The king's men aggressively gathered accusations against the Templars, and he used them to issue orders for their arrest.

> According to some writers, Squin de Florian, a citizen of Bezieres, who had been condemned to death or perpetual imprisonment in one of the royal castles for his iniquities, was brought before Philip, and received a free pardon, and was well rewarded in return, for an accusation on oath, charging the Templars with heresy, and with the commission of the most horrible crimes. According to others, Nosso de Florentin, an apostate Templar, who had been condemned by the Grand Preceptor and chapter of France to perpetual imprisonment for impiety and crime, made in his dungeon a voluntary confession of the sins and abominations charged against the order. Be this as it may, upon the strength of an information sworn to by a condemned criminal, king Philip, on the 14th of September, despatched secret orders to all the baillis of the different provinces in France, couched in the following extravagant and absurd terms....
>
> "We being charged with the maintenance of the faith; after having conferred with the pope, the prelates, and the barons of the kingdom, at the instance of the inquisitor, from the informations already laid, from violent suspicions, from probable conjectures, from legitimate presumptions, conceived against the enemies of heaven and earth; and because the matter is important, and it is expedient to prove the just like gold in the furnace by a rigorous examination, have decreed that the members of the order who are our subjects shall be arrested and detained to be judged by

the church, and that all their real and personal property shall be seized into our hands...."[117]

The warrant from Philip then ordered secret preparations be made prior to springing the trap on the Templars on 13 October 1307.

On that Friday the 13th all of the Templars who could be found in France were suddenly arrested. The vast majority of men escaped, but enough were seized to set Philip's plan in motion. The imprisoned knights and retainers of course denied at first the terrible charges against their Order. Then on the 19th of October they were turned over to the grand inquisitor of the Church, who put to work the most expert torturers of that day upon the hapless Templars. It is worthy of note that the Templars were subject only to the pope. They gave their service to him, and looked to him for protection. Yet it was not the king's soldiers who inflicted the great damage upon the Templars, but rather the inquisitors provided by the pope. It has been recorded that one hundred and forty were subjected to extremities of torture in Paris by these inquisitors. Brother Bernarde de Vado, when later examined by the commissary of police, explained part of his ordeal this way.

> They held me so long before a fierce fire that the flesh was burnt off my heels, two pieces of bone came away, which I present to you.[118]

Thirty-six of those men died declaring their innocence and that of the Knights Templar. The rest not only suffered painful physical damage, but also seem to have been shown forged letters from Grand Master de Molay urging them to confess to guilt and end their ordeal. As a result, large numbers of the Templars gave confessions to the charges made against them and the Order. Later, away from the torture, many revoked their confessions; but the immediate effect was that they had given the king what he wanted.

With these forced confessions in hand, Philip went back to Pope Clement V and forced further action. Philip demanded the Church support the French crown's actions by issuing a papal bull[119] to the other kings of Europe, ordering them to follow France's example and arrest all the Templars in their realms. Clement complied and sent that order a month later, requiring all Templars be held for trial. By the time those kings and rulers finally acted, however, only a handful of Templars could be found. The rest had disappeared.

Those are the things we know, but puzzling questions remain. Where did the surviving Templars go, and what did they do? And to the extent that there was Templar treasure, where did it go?

Chapter 11

Vanished into Thin Air

The central mystery surrounding the precipitous fall of the Knights Templar in 1307 was "How did they escape, and where did they go?" This was more than a passing curiosity, for these were powerful and influential men, and some of them came from the leading families of that age. Given that there were approximately 4000 brothers[120] in the Templar Order before the sudden arrests on the 13th of October—and only about 500 of those men appeared in the official records of arrests and trials in the East and West—what happened to the 3500 others? And how was it possible for so many people to disappear from under the noses of the police and papal authorities?

The possibility that the Templars were given word of the coming attack has been raised by several writers including Baigent and Leigh.[121] That was a definite possibility. Yet if there was a warning, that raised a difficult and perplexing question: why were roughly 232 Templars arrested in France at their normal places of work, including the Grand Master? The Templar brotherhood was extremely close and known for never leaving a brother on the field of battle. That injunction was not only contained in the Rule of their Order, it had been their practice on countless battlefields. If they knew of the impending arrests, how could they have left those men behind? Moreover, if a tipster had given warning, the horrendous torture inflicted on the captured brothers should have given some hint that this was the case. The king of France was described as being outraged over the poor results of his raid on the Templars, and would not have been lenient or quiet if there was even a hint of such betrayal. Yet no such hue and cry went up among the French officers, and no traitor was brought forth.

Either way, warned or not, the vast majority of the Templars suddenly and completely disappeared. If there was no warning given, that would make the puzzle of their disappearance even more difficult to solve, but let us see where it leads.

The Knights Templar practiced two modes of operation. They boldly and publicly wore their tunics of white with the blood-red Templar cross, appeared at public functions with their green-robed clerics, and were attended by a surrounding sea of brown-and-black clad servingmen, all of whom also bore the red Templar cross. There was no missing these men when they went down a public street, or charged across a battlefield in a mass of armor, uniforms and weapons. Their other mode of operation was the quiet and secretive manner in which they conducted their clandestine meetings, lived their personal life, and handled their financial affairs. No one knew what they were doing, or when they were doing it. Their finances were wrapped in the tightest possible security by their clerical people so that not even the king of France—who displayed an intense interest in their financial affairs—knew how they were moving their funds nor how much they held in their treasuries. His disappointment after the 13th of October raids netted him so little monetary gain was strong proof of the Templars' security and their ability to control their life-giving flow of funds in secret.

Integral to Templar security was the requirement that as few people as possible knew any particular secret. Even the Rules of their Order, the guidelines by which they lived, were not revealed to new members beyond what they needed to know. Only by living in the Order for many years was more of the Rule gradually told and learned. Their meetings were not only off limits to outsiders, there were different levels of meetings. In some of these the servingmen could not participate, while other meetings were even more restricted. In their financial affairs, the "need to know" rule would have limited the number of brothers who were told which nondescript houses were in the invisible network through which their river of gold and silver flowed. Ideally, only the green-robed clerics who directly administered these finances would have known. When disaster struck on Friday the 13th, this financial network was part of the strong Templar fabric that had to answer the call of brothers in distress. Following the strict regimen of the Templar Order, they owed their highest duty to God and to their brothers in distress, whether on the battlefield or any other place. Those were the hallmarks of their Order, and took precedence over all other considerations.

When that disaster came, the few financial administrators who knew the locations of these houses were obliged to tell the brothers immediately around them. Yet this overriding obligation to help brothers in distress was not limited to those few—it was borne by every brother. That meant that as one discovered the location of such a safe house, he was required by the sacred obligations that constituted the core of his life to tell others whom he knew positively to be brothers. The presence of severe danger would have caused the word of a secure place to cascade quickly to every branch and tendril of the Order.

Yet just as surely as they had a sworn obligation to tell their fugitive brother of a safe place, the Templar injunction against telling such a secret to anyone who was not a brother was equally strict. This was ingrained in every facet of the Templar Order, from the legendary secrecy of their initiation rituals, to their chapter meetings where an armed guard stood at the door with a drawn sword. They believed that the lives of their brethren and the life of their Order hinged on keeping their secrets, even unto death. A leaked word about battle plans could kill a brother just as surely as leaving them alone on the battlefield. Neither of those was imaginable or acceptable in their tightly-knit society.

The Grand Master and brothers of the red cross showed on the battlefields of the Holy Land that they were prepared to fight to the last man and die in battle. It was the nature of their chosen path in life, and they accepted it. It permeated their entire brotherhood, even down to the person who only saddled the knight's horse. They seemed to feel they could do no less than their brothers who had already died keeping their vows. This was part of the Templar mystique that cast a spell on members of the public. There was the feeling that Templars were part of something worthy, something greater than themselves, and it was addictive.

Only in a society such as this could the life-saving secret of an underground "railroad" of secure houses be passed quickly to thousands of people, allowing them to safely step inside. Then be followed just as quickly by the sudden closing of that door behind them. The men simply disappeared.

In all the other countries of Europe and the East, there was no question that the Templars had clear warning of their impending fate. This was due to the kings in those lands at first refusing to follow Philip's outrageous example. King Edward II of England went so far as to send letters to the kings of Portugal, Castile, Aragon and Sicily urging them not to give credence to those charges against the Templars.

> Verily, a certain clerk, (Bernard Peletin,) drawing nigh unto our presence, applied himself, with all his might, to the destruction of the order of the brethren of the Temple of Jerusalem. He dared to publish before us and our council certain horrible and detestable enormities repugnant to the Catholic faith, to the prejudice of the aforesaid brothers, endeavouring to persuade us, through his own allegations, as well as through certain letters which he had caused to be addressed to us for that purpose, that by reason of the premises, and without a due examination of the matter, we ought to imprison all the brethren of the aforesaid order abiding in our dominions. But, considering that the order, which hath been renowned for its religion and its honour, and in times long since passed away was instituted, as we have learned, by the Catholic Fathers, exhibits, and hath from the period of its founda-

tion exhibited, a becoming devotion to God and his holy church, and also, up to this time, hath afforded succour and protection to the Catholic faith in parts beyond the sea, it appeared to us that a ready belief in an accusation of this kind, hitherto altogether unheard of against the fraternity, was scarcely to be expected. We affectionately ask, and require of your royal majesty, that ye, with due dilligence, consider of the premises, and turn a deaf ear to the slanders of ill-natured men, who are animated, as we believe, not with the zeal of rectitude, but with a spirit of *cupidity* and envy, permitting no injury unadvisedly to be done to the persons or property of the brethren of the aforesaid order, dwelling within your kingdom, until they have been legally convicted of the crimes laid to their charge, or it shall happen to be otherwise ordered concerning them in these parts.[122]

Philip, having gone too far to withdraw, needed to justify his actions by impelling the other monarchs to do the same. So he turned to the pope over whom he had great influence and demanded the necessary papal letter requiring the heads of the Christian nations in Europe to arrest all Templars in their lands. Clement V complied, and on the 22nd of November issued the papal bull *Pastoralis praeemenentiae* requiring those arrests and directing that the Templars be turned over to Church authorities for inquisition and trial. The traditional hint of excommunication left those kings with little choice but to take action against the Templars, even if done reluctantly.

As a result, England began its belated arrest of Templars on 8 January of 1308 [123] with similar actions taking place in Scotland and Ireland. By then almost three months had passed since the arrest of Templars in France, so their British brethren had ample warning of what would befall them. In large groups or one-by-one, most of the Templars disappeared into the underground railroad carrying brothers to safety.

This underground railroad concept was not a new creation by the Templars. There already existed in Europe a long-standing practice of "sanctuary asylum" performed by many churches. Harboring fugitives from authorities in this manner was actually enshrined in English law from at least the 600s AD onward. The innovation brought by the Templars was that their fugitives were being protected *from* the Church, as well as from the State. Therefore the Templars could not flee to churches, but had to provide their own places of sanctuary and asylum.

Having reached their clandestine places of safety, the Templars were momentarily protected. But then where did they go?

The pope had wanted all Templars to join the Hospitallers so he could merge the two orders. This would have kept all of their combined manpower and properties under his control. In 1312, five years after the surprise attack on the Templars, the pope directly instructed the remaining men in that order to join the Hospitallers.[124] Unfortunately his word did not carry much weight with the Templars by that time. Perhaps it had something to do with the tortures applied by the pope's inquisitors. In any event, relatively few in Europe seem to have followed that path.

In fairness to the pope, however, his preferred path suffered a number of difficulties from the start. Not the least of these was that the Hospitallers had been nose-to-nose rivals of the Templars for almost two hundred years. Across the battlefields of the Holy Land and the courts of Europe the two orders had struggled on an almost daily basis trying to out-do the other.

> The Knights Templars and Hospitallers…two Orders who even in the face of their common foe could not restrain their own bitter rivalry and dissensions.[125]
>
> Albert Mackey

The thought of casting aside Templar white and donning Hospitaller black would have been almost unimaginable even in the best of times, and these were not the best of times. Still, in a season of difficult choices, this was a possibility.

One of the indicators of what happened during those days was seen in the execution of the pope's order that all Templar lands likewise be given to the Hospitallers. This did not go well at all.

Despite aggressive pursuit of these lands by the Hospitallers and papal authorities, there seemed to be considerable confusion. Secular authorities laid claim to many of these properties, such as the exceedingly valuable Templar preceptory grounds in central London. Those lands never did pass to the Hospitallers. Many smaller cases were disputed all across Europe. So few Templars came to the Hospitaller standard that there seemed to be minimal support or records on hand for the men in black as they tried to claim ownership of these prizes.

The situation in Cyprus, however, was somewhat different. Minor skirmishes between the Templars and Hospitallers had driven the King of Cyprus to distraction, and only became worse when Pope Clement's orders to arrest the Templars arrived on the 6th of May in 1308. [126] By that time there were only eighty-three Templar knights, thirty-three retainers, one non-military serving brother, and one chaplain on the island.[127] That was strange, since Cyprus served as the headquarters of the Knights Templar at that time, and had been the gathering place for all troops withdrawn from the Holy Land. In the seven months since Philip's arrest of the Templars in France, the overwhelming number of Templars apparently shed their Templar robes and disappeared into a more clandestine existence.

The properties of the Templars at Nicosia, Paphos, Famagusta and Limassol were quickly seized and inventoried. The lack of funds in the main treasury at Nicosia led to the belief that those funds had somehow been moved to Limassol. Yet when their encampment at Limassol was raided only 120,000 white *besants* were found, with the rest having been secretly moved to some other place.[128]

It is notable that among the thousands of Templars who had once been based at Cyprus, only one green-robed clerical brother remained. These administrative people had managed the Templars' financial system and the network of safe locations through which it passed. They seem to have been among the first to disappear, taking what remained of the Templar funds with them. In keeping with their long-standing Lebanese Christian connections, this last Templar cleric on Cyprus was Stephen of Safad, who was from a town in the borderlands between Lebanon and Israel.[129]

When the Templars on Cyprus were finally brought to trial in 1310, their testimony—as well as that from non-Templars on the island—clearly repudiated the charges against them. As a result, no actions were taken against the Order in Cyprus.

> The Templars were followed by thirty-five non-Templar witnesses, who appeared between 1 and 5 June. These included a wide sector of society, taking in priests, canons, friars, monks, knights and burghers. Many of them had known or even lived with the Templars for years and had seen nothing wrong: they had always celebrated the divine offices properly, they gave large quantities of alms in the form of bread, meat and money, they provided alms and hospitality, and many of them had been decapitated by the Saracens rather than renounce Christ.[130]

When the papal bull *Vox in excelso* disbanded the Knights Templar in 1312 great pressure was brought to bear on these men in Cyprus to convert to the Hospitallers. For those who had come East and dedicated their lives to the religious war, failing to convert would have meant giving up that dream, in addition to the difficulties of going underground. While some almost certainly left this theater of operations in the East, the temptation for many others to stay would have been strong. Helping to push them in this direction was the success of the long Hospitaller siege of Rhodes. That island fell to the black knights on 15 August 1309, allowing them to build encampments in a land where they faced no competition from other lords, and every inch was theirs. The offer for Templars to start a new life in a new place must have been a compelling one. No doubt more than a few of those 118 men remaining on Cyprus swallowed the bitter pill and chose to begin again in a new uniform and a new home.

For the battered Knights Templar in Europe, however, there were more appealing choices. One of those beckoned from the west in Spain and Portugal, where the Templars had long maintained close relationships with the local rulers.

We saw that after the Muslim conquest swept those lands, only the small Christian country of Asturias was left in the north. From there a crusade slowly drove southward, recovering bits of land one battle at a time. By 1128 the small but determined Christian forces had recovered about half of the land that makes up present-day Portugal and Spain. Given the name *Reconquista*, this crusade had as its goal the reconquering of the whole peninsula.

In that year, when Hugh de Payens was in Europe seeking knights and lands for his new order, Queen Theresa of Portugal made a gift to the Knights Templar of the town of Fonte Arcada and other lands. In return she asked that the Templars attempt to conquer more territory from the Muslim forces, or Moors as they were called at that time and place. The Templars dutifully participated in a number of campaigns on that peninsula, and were rewarded in 1159 with the lands of Ceras and Tomar in central Portugal, roughly halfway between the cities of Lisbon and Porto. There they built the Castle of Tomar with its famous round church, the *Convento de Cristo*. This Templar church and castle still stand today and are remarkably well preserved.

Anxious to obtain even more assistance in 1169, the Portuguese monarch granted to the Templars the right to keep one-third of all lands they could conquer south of the Tagus River, which flowed westward into the city of Lisbon. This generous offer kept the Templars active on the battlefields of Portugal for another hundred years.

When Philip of France leveled his accusations of heresy against the Knights Templar in 1307, King Dinis of Portugal gave it no credence whatsoever and took no action against them. This prompted Pope Clement to issue the papal bull *Regnas in coelis* the following year, in which he ordered Dinis to investigate the Templars in his lands. The king's response came in 1310 when he joined with Castile in Spain to declare the Templars innocent in the Iberian peninsula.

Undeterred, Clement sent to them copies of his papal bull in 1312, *Vox in excelso,* that suppressed the Templar Order in all Christian lands. This was followed a few months later by the papal bull *Ad providam* that ordered all Templar property be turned over to the Hospitallers. Determined not to let anyone outside Portugal

*Fig. 22   Tomar Castle of the Knights Templar in Portugal,
including their round Convento de Cristo church*

take control of these prized lands, Dinis argued that the Templars had only been granted *use* of those properties in Portugal, while ownership had remained with the king. To solidify his claims to the land he created a new military brotherhood, the Order of Christ, into which he accepted all of the Portuguese Templars. He then invested this new order with all the Templar lands in Portugal. In other words, the Knights Templar continued to operate in Portugal just as before. The only change was in the name carved over the doors of their estates.

With this warm embrace from King Dinis, the conversion of Templars in Portugal to the Order of Christ was a smooth change. As to the number of brothers who might have joined them from other parts of Europe or the East, there was no record preserved. It is known, however, that this new Order stayed fairly modest in size. This was perhaps due to the Order of Christ being created more than eleven years after King Philip's attack, so most of the Templars in other lands had already moved on and found some acceptable alternate course for their life.

One of those alternatives appeared nearby in Spain. Castile was the largest of the Spanish kingdoms, and had already established its own knightly Order of Calatrava in 1164. The smaller kingdoms in Spain had similar orders, which were likewise open to the Templars. But since those were well-established groups, a Templar entering one of them would have been required to give up the white mantle and red Templar cross, take new vows, live under new rules, and submit to new traditions.

If this Spanish reception might not have been quite as welcoming to the Templars as the one accorded to them in Portugal, it did come with one small attraction. Spain was still in active battles with the Moors across the southern part of its traditional lands, and would remain so until 1492. For Templars returning from the battlefields of the East, that might have been quite appealing. For the European Templars who had grown used to their duties managing estates and financial houses, the attraction was not as great.

Another intriguing possibility has been raised so many times that it deserves some consideration. After the Templars were outlawed in 1312, it has been suggested that some of them were driven to piracy. Surprisingly enough, there are several facts that point in this direction.

The Templars were in possession of a significant navy ever since their Grand Master's headquarters was moved to the city of Acre in 1191. Their ships became frequently seen in European ports, as well as Eastern ports and North Africa. Once the order went out from Philip IV to arrest the Templars in France and seize their possessions, the Templar ships put out to sea and were never heard from again. At that point each Templar captain was master of his ship and crew, and had the option of sailing to any port where arrest warrants had not yet gone out. That list became shorter when the pope ordered their arrest in all Christian countries. With his men and himself running risk of imprisonment each time he put into port, the captain could have sold his ship at the next port and retired to a comfortable house on the shore. No doubt some did. On the other hand, if they continued to sail with a writ out against them, they were outlaws with limited options, to wit smuggling contraband or other forms of outright piracy.

The havens for such piracy would largely have had to be in non-Christian ports, where the pope's orders of arrest had no standing. The increase of piracy in the ports of Tunis, Tripoli and Algiers along the Muslim-occupied shores of North Africa may have been related to this. Known as the Barbary Coast, this stretch of land eventually gave rise to the Barbary pirates. The account of a Spanish Templar who reappeared in a different guise is intriguing in this regard.

> For many there must have been a powerful temptation to embark upon another career, an ambition which could be most easily achieved outside Christian lands. Channels of communication with the north African powers were, in fact, well established, and it would not have been all that surprising to the Aragonese, when, in September 1313, Bernard of Fuentes, former Preceptor of Corbins, turned up at the court of James II in Barcelona as the ambassador of the Muslim ruler of Tunis.[131]

Although not proven to be directly connected, there was a striking resemblance between one of the most popular pirate flags and the Templar flag, as well as with one of their more esoteric practices. The "Jolly Roger" banner of these pirates became famous as a black flag bearing a white skull and two crossbones. The flag that Templar knights carried into battle was called the *Beauceant*, and consisted of two panels, one black and one white. As we have seen, the Templars were also known for collecting relics—primarily bones—of Christian saints while they were in the Holy Land. One of their most treasured relics was said to be the skull of St. Euphemia, which was displayed in ceremonies with her two crossed leg bones. Some have argued that the bones were not those of St. Euphemia, but it is now widely accepted that the Templars revered the skull and crossed bones of some deceased donor during their private ceremonies.

There was one other possible motive for choosing a life of piracy: a sea captain's ability to retaliate for the brutal torture and murder of his brothers. Preying on European ships, especially French ships, may have seemed not only fair but obligatory. Coming from a religious order, it would be a bit of a stretch to think very many captains took this path. But some might easily have done it—enough to establish a legend and a flag, which was then revived from time to time.

Meanwhile, a much larger number of men were in England, Scotland and Ireland, finding their own way forward.

Chapter 12

Underground Railroad, Lodges and Inns

$\mathcal{T}$he other avenue open to the Knights Templar after the shock of October 13th was to escape northward from France into Scotland and England. Since no action was taken against the Templars in Britain at that time, this path certainly made sense. For those who took such a route, they found their hosts among the British Templars to be in an unsettled state. While some members of the regional preceptories stayed at their posts, hoping for the best, many of the knights, clerics and servingmen had already started to disappear into the Templars' underground of secure locations.

King Edward II of England and Ireland—who was also a claimant of the Scottish throne—held out against the pressures of Philip IV and the pope as long as he could. But his will finally broke, and on the 8th of January in 1308 he ordered the arrest of all Templars in his realms. Just as Philip had done before him, Edward's labors produced only a few hundred captives.

> The total number of Templars in custody was two hundred and twenty-nine. Many, however, were still at large, having successfully evaded capture by obliterating all marks of their previous profession, and

some had escaped in disguise to the wild and mountainous parts of Wales, Scotland, and Ireland. Among the prisoners confined in the Tower [of London] were brother William de la More, Knight, Grand Preceptor of England, otherwise Master of the Temple; Brother Himbert Blanke, Knight, Grand Preceptor of Auvergne [in France] one of the veteran warriors who had fought to the last in defense of Palestine, had escaped the slaughter at Acre, and had accompanied the Grand Master from Cyprus to France, from whence he crossed over to England, and was rewarded for his meritorious and memorable services, in defense of the christian faith, with a dungeon in the Tower.[132]

During those three months of calm before the storm began in Britain, the primary concern of the Templar brothers would have been the concealment of arriving French brethren, and hastening to expand those secret locations, against their own possible need of refuge. The forced conversion of their covert financial system to support fleeing Templars put every brother into the game of survival, whether threatened immediately themselves or entrusted with the protection of another. And survival meant something different to Templars than it did to most people. We saw that several times while peering inside this Order during its two hundred years of existence.

Faced with death on the battlefield, on the open road, or in quiet towns that might suddenly explode into fighting, Templars clung to the strong bonds they shared with their brothers. Death would come sooner or later. But when it came, they wanted it to be with honor, knowing they had stood by their brothers, just as their brothers had stood by them. Even their Rule charged them to not go forward alone, requiring them to eat with their brothers, to pray with their brothers, and to stay with their brothers on the battlefield.

In one common hall, or refectory, we will that you take meat together....

Section VIII of the Templar Rule[133]

Fig. 23   Seal of the Knights Templar

When the sun leaveth the eastern region, and descends into the west, at the ringing of the bell, or other customary signal, ye must all go to *compline* (evening prayer)....

Section XVI of the Templar Rule

We will briefly display the mode of life of the Knights of Christ, such as it is in the field and in the convent.... The soldiers of Christ live together in common in an agreeable but frugal manner...in one house, under one rule, careful to preserve the unity of the spirit in the bond of peace. You may say, that to the whole multitude there is but one heart and one soul.... Among them there is no distinction of persons; respect is paid to the best and most virtuous, not the most noble. They participate in each other's honor, they bear one another's burthens, that they may fulfil the law of Christ.[134]

Saint Bernard
De Laude Novae Militiae

Even the unusual and widely-recognized symbol of the Knights Templar—two knights upon a single horse, reflected this ultimate commitment to brotherhood. The usual explanation offered for this unique symbol—that it signified them as being the poor soldiers of Christ—makes no sense, of course. Even in their earliest and poorest days, the Rule of the Templars allotted to each knight several horses.

To each one of the knights let there be allotted three horses. The noted poverty of the House of God, and of the Temple of Solomon, does not at present permit an increase of the number, unless it be with the license of the Master....

Section XXX of the Templar Rule

Another clue that the symbol proudly displayed by the Templars did not denote poverty was that the Templars were one of the richest societies that ever existed. Their wealth and properties extended from the Middle East to Western Europe. Individual knights could not own personal property of any value, such as gold chains or silver dishes. But as members of their Order they had castles, armor, horses and the like in great profusion, and wanted for nothing. Poverty was not what made them exceptional.

The only time one could have seen two Templar knights on a single horse would have been when they were returning from the battlefield. If one knight's horse died in battle, and he faced imminent death on foot with the enemy on every side, no other knight was allowed to leave the field of battle. The nearest knight was obliged by stubborn honor to fly to the aid of his brother, no matter the cost. I believe it is that loyal knight, having rescued his brother, whom we see returning after battle with his fellow knight seated behind. That was the symbol of the Templars. To them, it embodied their pride, their honor, and lifelong bonds of brotherhood.

The Templar Rule and culture seems to have so strongly permeated every aspect of their life that it imbued each white knight, green cleric, and brown-clad servingman with this indelible sense of brotherhood. Among the Templars. the punishment for failing to live up to those standards was swift and clear.

Suffice it to say that the average person of that day seemed unable to understand the Templar response to mortal danger. Danger was an old and expected enemy that had come to visit again. Some retreat might be necessary. Haste could be required. But running off by oneself was not possible. All the brothers with you had to be given aid. If you arrived first and others came later, you sheltered them, and shared what you had. For all of their adult life the Templars had been trained in this manner, and lived it each day they wore the red cross of their Order—surrounded by men who did the same.

The Templars clearly acted in haste, but not by running down the highway or country roads, which would have resulted in many of them being caught as they fled. Instead they seem to have retreated quickly to secure places of safety, for they vanished without a trace.

The Knights Templar have been customarily described as holding large estates that were well-known to the people of their day. Certainly there were many such estates. However it was also true that many of their holdings were much smaller and less well-known. These latter properties also changed hands frequently, making ownership unclear even to their neighbors. Malcolm Barber, a well-respected chronicler of the Templars, noted that:

> ...the Order was not simply a passive recipient of donations, but an active agent in the land market, buying, selling and exchanging property on a considerable scale.[135]

This atmosphere would have made it difficult for anyone other than a Templar scribe to know exactly which properties belonged to their Order. Desired properties and buildings could be purchased, and then passed through the hands of several people who may or may not have actually existed. After that, they were available for use in the Templars' clandestine financial system. Such properties were not on the Templars' books, and any tracks that might have been left behind were soon lost in the flurries of transactions.

During the Templars' hour of great need in late 1307, the treasuries of their northern preceptories might have been as bare as those of the French, but their river of gold still flowed. Collections from every estate would have gone on as before. But now that the Grand Master resided in a French prison and the survival of their Order was in doubt, there was no reason to send the funds forward. Like an army foraging for supplies before a battle, the systematic stripping of estates by Templar officers—removing anything of value—would also have been appropriate under the circumstances. Judging by later reports of Templar manors having been found in extremely poor condition, that may well be what happened.

All available funds were needed immediately to lodge, conceal and feed the brothers already in hiding, and to make preparations for the remaining brothers' expected needs. Adding rooms onto covert houses would have been a reasonable task, along with storing extra money and the laying in of supplies. Purchasing additional houses or inns near cities would also have been prudent, since they would be necessary if the dreaded order to arrest all Templars came down in Britain and immediate lodging was needed for all brothers.

In this regard, it should be noted that one of the most famous of all English inns, known as the Tabard, was built that same year in Southwark, just across the Thames River from London. It stood near the south end of London Bridge. This was the inn Geoffrey Chaucer described among the opening lines of *The Canterbury Tales*, when he told of people gathering there for their pilgrimage to Canterbury.

> *Befelle that in that season, on a day,*
> *In Southwerk, at the Tabard as I lay*
> *Redy to wenden on my pilgrimage*
> *To Canterbury, with devoute couràge....*[136]

The Tabard was not a Templar inn, since it was built for religious brothers at the Abbey of Hyde. Yet it does indicate that religious brothers owned inns during those days without being out of the ordinary. The popularity of building inns at that time was further attested by antiquary John Stow in 1598, who wrote in his *Survey* that Southwark had "many fair inns, for receipt of travellers, by these signs: the Spurre, Christopher, Bull, Queen's Head, Tabard, George, Hart, King's Head...."[137] Even better, it was customary at that time for each inn to actually be a collection of buildings completely encircling a private yard. This gave privacy to their guests, who never need be seen by the people in neighboring establishments.

Of course, all of these things could not have been done by men still in Templar uniform. It would have been necessary for many of them to take leave of their preceptories and estates to join the underground railroad that was being extended and provisioned. Yet no matter how serious the need for people to work on these places of safety, some Templars had to stay behind in the nearly empty preceptory buildings to assert continued Templar owner-

Fig. 24   Tabard Inn, south of London

ship of the major estates and keep the Order's place in society. If somehow the angel of death were to pass over them and the Order were to miraculously survive, the few who remained would welcome back the many who had left.

Unfortunately, there was no passover that year. The arrests in Britain began during January of 1308. A few hundred Templars were roughly seized and locked into prisons, while the great majority of brothers remained at large. Trials dragged on year after year while the seized Templars suffered in prison. Meanwhile the brothers who had taken the underground railroad lived quietly in the lodging houses they had appropriated, still eating together, and meeting in secret to see what aid could be given to their captured brothers.

In Scotland the Templar trials were held in Edinburgh's once proud Holyrood Abbey. Today it stands in regal ruins on the grounds of Holyrood Palace, at the lower end of Miracle Mile near Canongate. As we noted earlier, in all of Scotland only two Templars were caught, Walter de Clifton and William de Middleton. The proceedings against them began on 17 November 1309.

> After the examination of the above two Templars, forty-one witnesses, chiefly abbots, priors, monks, priests, and serving men, and retainers of the order in Scotland, were examined upon various interrogatories, but nothing of a criminatory nature was elicited. The monks observed that the receptions of other orders were public, and were celebrated as great religious solemnities, and the friends, parents, and neighbours of the party about to take the vows were invited to attend; that the Templars, on the other hand, shrouded their proceedings in mystery and secrecy, and therefore they *suspected* the worst....
>
> The serving men and the tillers of the lands of the order stated that the chapters were held sometimes by night and sometimes by day, with extraordinary secrecy.[138]

When the trial in Scotland was concluded, there was no record of any charges or punishments lodged against the two Templars or the knightly Order to which they belonged. It is generally believed that they were released due to lack of sufficiently incriminating evidence.[139]

In London the trials finally began on 20 October 1309, after the English Templars had languished in prison for a year and nine months. Forty-three Templars and seven witnesses from outside the order were called to testify, and it took a month for them to appear one by one. All denied the charges against their Order. Not having achieved the goal of finding damning evidence, the church leaders conducting the trial petitioned the king to let their inquisitors have greater freedom to extract the "truth" from the reluctant Templars. King Edward gave his authorization for this to be done, and on the 16th of December those orders went out to the sheriffs holding the Templars at London, as well as to the concentration centers in Lincoln and York. Even so, the methods used must not have been too excessive, since the trials continued into the following year without much progress.

In frustration Pope Clement wrote to King Edward and chastized him for not allowing the inquisitors to use the rack and similar tortures in performance of their duties. With that, Edward capitulated completely. His order on 26 August 1310 directed the constable of the Tower and all the sheriffs to turn their Templars over to the inquisitors, and permit those men to do to the bodies of the Templars whatever they should feel was necessary. To their credit, the English jailers seem to have been reluctant to follow such grisly instructions, for the king had to send his orders twice more, each time more sharply than the last, requiring they turn the Templars over for torture.

Despite the agonies thus inflicted, the next set of trials still produced no confessions. After each such occurrence, the level of punishment and privation was raised higher. Almost a year later, in June and July of 1311, breakthroughs were achieved. Two serving men of the order as well as a chaplain finally buckled under the inquisition and gave their confessions. After four years of fruitless efforts in England, the church leaders conducting the inquisition were willing to accept those three confessions as all they were going to get. Accordingly, they arranged a compromise whereby any Templar could simply attest that the Master in their order might have given absolution for sins, admit that he had no right to do so, and ask forgiveness for this and any other heresy. Since this vague statement amounted to virtually no confession at all, most of the brothers immediately agreed to it, received absolution from the church, and were set free. After that they were able to simply disappear like their brothers. Only a few men, including William de la More, Master of the Temple in England, refused even that minor statement. He finally died in solitary confinement in the Tower. That ended the Templar trials in England.

In France, the ordeal of the Templars took a nasty turn. Since the goal of the French king was the destruction of the Order and the subsequent acquisition of the Templars' property, their original confessions were all he needed to achieve his desires. After that, he had been content to let the shattered and disgraced men receive absolution from the church for their "crimes," and be released from prison to fend for themselves. However by 1310, many of those men were regaining their health. They would reasonably have also heard about their brethren in England and other lands steadfastly refusing to give credence to the charges against them. As a result, many in France who had given up their confession under torture now renounced those statements and proclaimed their innocence. Once they did that, they could no longer be shielded by their hidden brothers. The entire concept of being hidden required that one not make public statements or be publicly visible. Yet clearly these men regretted having given in to the torture and felt compelled to go public.

Their new declarations undercut everything Philip was trying to accomplish in France. Furious, he ordered the arrest of those Templars who recanted their confessions. Philip then arranged for the Archbishop of Sens to pass death sentences on them, which the prelate did in this manner.

> "You have avowed that the brethren who are re-
> ceived into the order of the Temple are compelled to

renounce Christ and spit upon the cross, and that you yourselves have participated in that crime: you have thus acknowledged that you have fallen into the sin of *heresy*. By your confession and repentance you had merited absolution, and had once more become reconciled to the church. As you have revoked your confession, the church no longer regards you as reconciled, but having fallen back to your first errors. You are, therefore, *relapsed heretics* and as such, we condemn you to the fire."[140]

The next day, on May 12, 1310, fifty-four Templars were taken to the Porte St. Antoine des Champs at Paris, and were burned to death. Over the months that followed, dozens of other Templars were rounded up and forced to reaffirm their confession under penalty of life in prison or death. Many, perhaps shamed by their earlier weakness, accepted the penalty. Altogether, a total of a hundred and thirteen Templars were reported as being burned at the stake in Paris, with others being burned in Lorraine, Normandy, Carcassone and Senlis.

With no real evidence against the Templars, save what had been procured in France, Pope Clement still proceeded to abolish the Templar Order on the 22nd of March, 1312, in his papal bull *Vox in excelso*. He closed the door on the Templar Order and cast out its brothers to make their own way in the world as best they could.

Even then, Jacques de Molay and a handful of other brothers remained in prison. From time to time they were trotted out to publicly confess again in futile efforts by King Philip and Pope Clement to justify their actions. At one such display on 18 March 1314, everything went horribly wrong.

A public scaffold was erected before the cathedral church of Notre Dame, at Paris, and the citizens were summoned to hear the Order of the Temple convicted by the mouths of its chief officers, of the sins and iniquities charged against it. The four knights, loaded with chains and surrounded by guards, were then brought upon the scaffold by the provost, and the bishop of Alba read their confessions aloud in the presence of the assembled populace. The papal legate then, turning towards the Grand Master and his companions, called upon them to renew, in the hearing of the people, the avowals which they had previously made of the guilt of their order. Hugh de Peralt, the Visitor-General, and the Preceptor of the Temple of Aquitaine, signified their assent to whatever was demanded of them, but the Grand Master raising his arms bound with chains towards heaven, and advancing to the edge of the scaffold, declared in a loud voice, that to say that which was untrue was a crime, both in the sight of God and man. "I do," said he, "confess my guilt, which consists in having, to my shame and dishonour, suffered myself, through the pain of torture and the fear of death, to give utterance to falsehoods, imputing scandalous sins and iniquities to an illustrious order, which hath nobly served the cause of Christianity. I disdain to seek a wretched and disgraceful existence by engrafting another lie upon the original falsehood." He was here interrupted by the provost and his officers, and Guy, the Grand Preceptor, having commenced with strong asseverations of his innocence, they were both hurried back to prison.

King Philip was no sooner informed of the result of this strange proceeding, than, upon the first impulse of his indignation, without consulting either pope, or bishop, or ecclesiastical council, he commanded the instant execution of both these gallant noblemen. The same day at dusk they were led out of their dungeons, and were burned to death in a slow and lingering manner upon small fires of charcoal which were kindled on the little island in the Seine, between the king's garden and the convent of St. Augustine, close to the spot where now stands the equestrian statue of Henry IV.[141]

In this manner the official existence of the Knights Templar came to an end. Several hundred of the brethren had died, some agonizingly and in flames.

Yet many thousands of their brothers had survived in places of hiding. Those survivors had been shaped by the Templar Order to live in a world based on brotherhood, initiations, taking of obligations, meeting in secret, and being part of something greater than themselves. Now they had to adapt, and join their old life to a new one.

In what world did they find that new life? Though the Middle Ages seem to have taken place long ago, people lived normal lives with similar cares for family, survival and prosperity that we feel today. Few families illustrate those times as well as the St. Clairs of Roslin, who went from being soldiers of fortune to peers of the realm. It was into this world that the fugitive Templars fled.

The St. Clair Barons of Roslin

The St. Clairs of Roslin were real people who, through coincidence or unspoken purpose, walked in and out of the affairs of the Knights Templar and Freemasons for many generations. They were involved from the time the first Templar Grand Master rode his horse into Scotland in the twelfth century. And they remained so until the Masonic Grand Lodge of Scotland was formed in 1736 with a St. Clair as its first Grand Master. They also consecrated Rosslyn Chapel with the approval of the Vatican and contributed to the swirl of mysteries surrounding all these guarded societies.

The patriarch of the St. Clairs came to England from Normandy in France, riding alongside William the Conqueror and his armies in 1066. This was Walderne, Comte de St. Clair, who was distantly related to the new King William.[142] This Norman Conquest was scarcely accomplished when the king of Scotland—mindful of that southern invasion in Great Britain and faced with his own ongoing wars in the north—decided to seek capable Norman knights to help him protect his kingdom. Among those answering the Scottish king's call was Walderne's second son, William de St. Clair.

The young and aspiring William arrived in Scotland around 1070,[143] where he was promptly accepted into service. Though he was the son of a battle-tested knight, William's first duty in Scotland was far less arduous. Known as "The Seemly St. Clair" for his strikingly handsome appearance, he caught the attention of King Malcolm's new queen, Margaret, and became her cup-bearer or steward. Since William was apparently not yet fully seasoned in military matters, his ability to win Margaret's favor with service and gifts was believed to have influenced the king's decision to confer upon him the Barony of Roslin.

William discovered his new estate to be strategically located on the southern approach to Edinburgh, just nine miles from the heart of the city. That ideal location made it distant enough from the bustle of civic life to insure privacy and tranquility for his future family, yet close enough that the high promontory in the center of Edinburgh, called Arthur's Seat, could be easily seen from Roslin. He then had the good sense to marry Dorothy, a daughter of the earl of Dunbar, who bore him a son named Henry.[144]

Almost two decades passed before tragedy struck.

> William the Conqueror, offended att King Malcolm . . . sent about this time the Duke of Glocestre, with a great army, to invade the Scots. King Malcolm, hearing therof, sent the Earles of Marche and Monteith with a company of men of warre, to aid and assist the Sinclair's forces; wherupon Sir William Sinclair rushed forward, with a design to put the enimie out of ordre, but being enclosed by the contrary party, he was slain by the multitude of his enimies.... He left three childring, two daughters, who died infants, and one sone, Sir HENRY SAINTCLAIR, who succeeded his father, and was entirely beloved of the King and Queen, who gave him Roslin in free heretadge, and made him Knight.[145]
>
> *Genealogie of the Saintclaires of Rosslyn*

Young Henry was at most sixteen years of age when he thus became the 2nd Baron of Roslin, but he was an experienced knight nine years later when the First Crusade was mounted amid great pomp and circumstance in 1096 by Pope Urban II. Minor knights such as himself did not receive prominent billing in the historic records of the Crusades, so we do not know much about his service in the Holy Land other than that he may have fought in the siege of Antioch. However it is worthy of note that these were the same campaigns in which Hugh de Payens and other founders of the Knights Templar fought. It is therefore possible that he could have known them or even served alongside the knights who would one day wear the white robe and large red cross of the Templars. Yet in terms of actual record of such contact, there is none.

In any event, young Henry, like most of the knights who went on the Crusades, did not stay in the Holy Land after the three long and bloody years of battle that finally won the walled city of Jerusalem. He returned home to the green hills of Roslin, and to the service of Scotland.[146]

Then in 1128, Hugh de Payens came to Scotland seeking knights and support for his newly formed order of Knights Templar. Among the grants he received was the land of Balantrodoch, to be used as the Templar Preceptory headquarters in Scotland. Some sources have suggested this land was granted to de Payens by Henry St. Clair, but it does not appear that the St. Clair properties extended quite that far. The more widely credited source for this grant of land was King David I of Scotland. It was true, however, that the Templar land at Balantrodoch—today known as the town of Temple—rested only four miles to the east of Roslin Castle. Given that St. Clair and de Payens had both served in the Crusades and now owned neighboring estates, they could easily have gotten together for camaraderie. De Payens was on a mission to ask everyone to contribute and surely would have asked St. Clair for financial support towards Balantrodoch's expenses, or the courtesy of providing aid to the Preceptory in time of need. The same request would reasonably have been made to other landed gentry in the region as well. At a time when strangers were giving generously to the Templars, it would have been impossible for a former companion in arms to refuse.

To discover how difficult it might be to communicate between encampments in Roslin and Balantrodoch, I walked that distance during an exploratory trip to Roslin. It was possible to hike comfortably from the still impressive walls of Roslin Castle to the roofless remains of the Templar church at Balantrodoch in a couple of hours—a distance that could easily have been covered on horseback in about thirty minutes. The St. Clairs and the newly-created Knights Templar could have come to each other's dinner table in a half-hour's time, and would be able to do so for the next 184 years.

Henry married Rosabelle Forteith of Strathearn, and when their first son came along he was named Henry after his father. In 1153, Henry the elder passed away, and Henry the younger became the 3rd Baron of Roslin. The new Sir Henry married Elizabeth Gartnay, then made an important contribution to the St. Clair legacy by building the first St. Clair castle. He chose a place just below the flat farmlands in the northern part of the Roslin estate, where the land began to slope downward among undulating hills and forestland. As the masons he employed began to lay their stones, he had no way of knowing that this would one day be the site of Rosslyn Chapel. He simply wanted a respectable manor house of durable stone for his family. The size and design of this first castle are not known, since so much was stripped away later. But it did include a small chapel downstairs, simply adorned with ashlar-cut stones and a rounded ceiling. We know this because it is still there. Inside Rosslyn Chapel today are old steps leading down to this modest but ancient place of prayer, now known as the Lower Chapel. This first stone manor was raised during the time of 1205 to 1210.[147]

Shortly after the castle was completed, Henry was succeeded by his son William[148] in 1214, who became the 4th Baron of Roslin. William married Katherine Forteith, the daughter of Robert, 4th Earl of Strathearn, continuing the links to that family which were begun by his grandfather.

The customary tracing of lineage by focusing on the inheriting son often overlooked the fact that families among the nobility usually included other children as well. This sometimes caused a serious problem, since the splintering of an estate among many children would—in a few generations—reduce nobles to commoners in all but name. As a result the heads of families felt a strong motivation to have the whole of their estate pass to a single heir whenever possible, to preserve the family's status and possessions. Lineage records are strewn with cases where lesser claimants objected to being left out by such an arrangement, and took recourse to military confrontation or appealed to the crown for conversion of rights to other heirs.

This led to the common practice whereby noble families pushed non-inheriting sons into religious orders such as the Benedictines or Franciscans. The vows of chastity that normally accompanied this monkhood or priesthood also meant those sons would live out their lives without having children—an additional boon in terms of avoiding future claimants. This led to one of the strongest attractions of the Knights Templar among the younger nobility. The Templars were a religious order that had the same difficult vows of chastity and obedience. But for the young man being prodded into religious service by his family, it was a colorful and exciting military alternative to drab monkhood in some quiet abbey.

Lineage records show quite clearly that the St. Clair family had many younger sons who did not inherit the family's titles and estates. In the years after 1300, when records were better kept, a number of those younger sons were seen becoming monks, bishops or abbots. For example in 1309, the younger brother of the Baron of Roslin was made Bishop of Dunkeld, a cathedral town located just north of Perth.[149] During these tumultuous 1200s it is entirely possible that some of their younger sons could have been attracted by the nearby Templars at the Balantrodoch Preceptory, and entered that military religious order. Unfortunately, all we have for most of these younger sons is their name, rather than the course they took in life, so there is no way to know for certain if some of them joined the Templars.

Sir William and his wife Katherine had a son whom they named Henry, and the lad became the 5th Baron in 1243. Twenty-one years later Henry became Sheriff of the three counties of Edinburgh, Haddington and Linlithgow, which also gave him the title of a Lord of Parliament.

His son William became the 6th Baron of Roslin in 1270. William also succeeded his father in the valued position of Sheriff for those three counties, and a Lord in Parliament. It was at this time that a crisis in the succession to the Scottish crown occurred and plunged the country into a devastating war. When all the children of King Alexander III died before him, the king called upon William St. Clair who stood high in the king's favor. The Scottish monarch asked St. Clair to pledge loyalty to his granddaughter Margaret as the royal heir, if he should die without male issue. Then the king perished in an accident, and Margaret died a few years later in 1290. This generated a fierce struggle between rival claimants to the throne, one of whom was Robert the Bruce. During the conflicts that followed, there occurred the event that has been most often presented as the missing link between the Knights Templar and Freemasonry.

The infighting among Scottish nobility opened the door for English King Edward I to advance his own claim on the Scottish throne. As English armies arrayed themselves across the land, the St. Clair family joined the fighting on Scotland's battlefields, taking the side of Robert the Bruce.

During these struggles the well-respected William St. Clair passed away in 1297. His position in the conflicts was taken by his son, Henry, who became the 7th Baron of Roslin. The clashes between English and Scottish forces even came to Roslin on the 24th of February in 1303. Known as the Battle of Roslin, it was described as taking place over the course of several sharp engagements on the nearby fields and hills.

After that battle St. Clair brought a respected English prisoner home and treated him so well that the man was willing to give some valuable advice. He noted the modest family castle which existed at that time was highly vulnerable to attack. A nearby promontory overlooking the North Esk River, only a few hundred yards away, would be a vastly superior location. Following that prudent advice, a new Roslin Castle—the one that still stands today—was built on the proposed location.[150] Three sides of the rocky site fell away steeply to the glen and river below. These became crowned by a series of thick stone walls. On the side facing the narrow landed approach, massive towers were built, with a

Fig. 25 Roslin Castle

gatehouse in front. When those walls were complete, the narrow approach was torn away and a drawbridge placed in its stead. The result was a virtually impregnable fortress in its day, highly suitable for protecting the family and household staff of the St. Clairs in times of necessity and conflict.

While that fortification was still under construction, another climactic event occurred. The Knights Templar who had risen to great prominence and high esteem all across Europe were suddenly attacked on the 13th of October in 1307. Though the first attacks came in France, it sent shudders of shock and disbelief as far north as the highlands of Scotland. The Templar Preceptory at Balantrodoch became abandoned except for a caretaker, whose testimony we heard during the trials in Edinburgh.

> Being asked concerning the other brothers in Scotland, he stated that John de Hueflete was Preceptor of Blancradok [Balantrodoch], the chief house of the order in that country, and that he and the other brethren, having heard of the arrest of the Templars, threw off their habits and fled, and that he had not since heard aught concerning them.[151]

Henry St. Clair, living four miles west of Balantrodoch, would reasonably have been sympathetic to the plight of his knightly neighbors. In the first month after the Templars were attacked, there was little question that he could have given these men shelter. But then an order came from Pope Clement V to all Christians in Europe that no aid be given to Templars under pain of excommunication. That papal directive might have had more force in other days, but by this time Robert the Bruce and Scotland had already been excommunicated by the pope. Even so, after the first few weeks, whatever generosity could be given by St. Clair or others in Scotland would have had to be judicious and covert.

Returning to the battles over Scotland's crown, Robert the Bruce's primary Scottish rival for the throne was the tenacious John Comyn. Robert resolved this difficult situation much like Alexander the Great, who untangled the Gordian knot by cutting it in two with his sword. On the 10th of February in 1306, Robert

invited Comyn to a meeting in Dumfries, then killed him in front
of the altar in the local church. That was the offense for which the
pope excommunicated Robert, and then did the same for the
whole of Scotland. Unfazed, Robert exercised his dominant claim
to the throne, and was crowned King of Scotland on the 25th of
March.

The English immediately began a dogged pursuit of the new
King Robert, driving him steadily backward. Yet fortune was with
him, for the battle-hardened King Edward I of England died the
next year, leaving his weak son Edward II in command. Robert
was fighting at Aberdeenshire in the north of Scotland when the
Knights Templar were attacked in France and he gave the event
scant attention. Clinging to the breath of life and hope he had
been given, Robert fought almost daily to place bits of Scotland in
Scottish hands. He recorded major victories at Dumbarton in 1311,
at Perth in 1312, and ventured into English territory to capture the
strategic Isle of Man in 1313.

Then came the decisive moment for Scotland and, some believe, for Freemasonry. It happened early the following year at
Stirling, and came to be known as the Battle of Bannockburn.
Henry St. Clair and his son William fought there, alongside Robert
the Bruce.

> Before the close of the year 1313, all the towns and for-
> tresses of Scotland had yielded to the victorious Bruce
> with the exception of the Castle of Stirling, and the
> Governor of this stronghold had entered into an
> agreement with the Scots to surrender it into their
> hands if not relieved[152] before the feast of St. John the
> Baptist in the following year. Edward II and his bar-
> ons, who were now thoroughly aroused by the ex-
> treme urgency of the case, reconciled their differences,
> and, collecting the whole force of the realm of Eng-
> land, set forth to the relief of the garrison. Robert
> Bruce on his side was not idle. He ordered a general
> rendezvous of all the forces of Scotland at the Tor-
> wood Forest between Stirling and Falkirk, and not the
> last to arrive on that classic ground were Sir Henry St.

Clair, and his son, Sir William, with the men-at-arms and troops of Roslin. In the celebrated battle which ensued, both these knights greatly distinguished themselves, and for his good services at Bannockburn, and on other occasions, King Robert made Sir Henry a grant of the muir of Pentland and several other lands.[153]

One of the enduring legends of Bannockburn was that when the battle stood in danger of being lost, a force of Knights Templar showed up to aid Scotland and save the day. This would have been a remarkable accomplishment, since the Templar Order had already been disbanded by the pope prior to this time. Presumably these Templars had been in hiding for the intervening years, waiting for the right time to emerge. In return for their critical intervention, a grateful King Robert was said to have rewarded the Templar knights by creating Freemasonry. This would have allowed them to continue conducting their affairs with a new outward appearance. Various individuals and groups have supported this explanation since at least 1825.[154] In recent years Michael Baigent and Richard Leigh led the charge in championing this position.

> But what is most striking in the chronicles is the decisive intervention—when all the Scottish units were *already engaged* and the entire battle hung in the balance—of what the English regarded as a 'fresh force', which suddenly erupted with banners flying from the Scottish rear.
>
> According to some accounts, this fresh contingent consisted of yeomen, youngsters, camp followers and other non-combatant personnel.... It is a stirring, romantic story which does much credit to Scottish patriotism, but it does not ring true. If the intervention was indeed so spontaneous, so improvised and so unexpected, it would have caught the Scots as much by surprise as it did the English. That no confusion spread through the Scottish ranks suggests the inter-

vention was anticipated. Nor is it easy to imagine the heavily armoured English knights—even if they did improbably mistake a horde of peasants and camp-followers for professional soldiery—fleeing before an attack launched on foot. All the evidence suggests that the decisive intervention came from some reserve of mounted men. Who might these unknown horsemen have been?

Panic swept the English ranks. King Edward, together with 500 of his knights, abruptly fled the field....

Whoever the mysterious intruders were, they seem to have been instantly recognisable—which Templars would have been, by their beards, their white mantles and/or their black-and-white banner known as the 'Beauséant'. If they were indeed recognised as such, and if word of their identity spread through the English ranks, the result would have been panic of precisely the sort that occurred.[155]

Robert Cooper took the opposite view. He made a survey of writings from about the time of the battle, and showed many details of the fighting at Bannockburn were recorded, with no mention being made of participation by Knights Templar.[156] John Barbour was one such source, writing in 1375.

Then he [Robert the Bruce] sent all the small folk and camp-followers, and all the harness and victual that were in the Park, a great way from him, and made them leave the field of battle....[157]

At this moment, when the battle was in this fashion being fought, and either side was struggling right manfully, the yeomen, swains, and camp-followers who had been left in the Park to mind the victual, knowing for certain that their lords had joined battle and were in dire conflict with their foes, made one of themselves captain, and fastened broad sheets for banners upon long poles and spears, and said they would see the fight, and help their lords to their utmost. When all were agreed to this, and were come together in a body, they were fifteen thousand and more. Then they hastened forward all in a rout with their banners, like men strong and stout. They came with their whole host to a place where they could see the battle. Then all at once they gave a great shout, "Upon them! On them boldly!" and therewith they all came on.

But they were yet a long way off when the English, who were being driven back by force of battle as I have said, saw coming towards them with a shout a company which seemed full as great as the host they were fighting, and which they had not seen before....

When the King of England saw his men in sundry places flee, and saw the host of his foes become strong and bold, and the English array altogether defeated and without strength to withstand its enemies, he was so vastly dismayed that, with all his company, five hundred armed cap-a-pie, in utter disorder, he took to flight, and made for the castle.[158]

Those accounts given by people in the 1300s generally agreed that no Templars were seen, and that the number of people who suddenly appeared was quite large. About 20,000 Scots had been fighting the English to a standstill all day, and now 15,000 more Scots appeared. Seen from a distance, that could easily have been enough of a shock to unnerve the English soldiers and leaders.

Given the evidence presented by both sides, the overwhelming amount of it clearly points to the conclusion that the Knights Templar did not participate at the Battle of Bannockburn. And if they were not there, then they could not have given rise to Freemasonry after the battle. In other words, the events at Bannockburn have not produced a credible Templar-Freemason link.

However, the disproving of one possible link does not mean all possible links have been disproved. It only means that we now need to consider whether there were other, better links between the two. As it turns out, there were much better candidates for Templar-Freemason connections, as we see in due course.

Rejoining the St. Clairs after Bannockburn, Sir Henry's son William had been cited for bravery in that battle, and now showed bravery of a different sort. He boldly asked for the hand of Margaret Ramsay of Dalhousie, married her, and sired three sons. When Robert the Bruce died in 1329 after a long and momentous reign, it was his final wish that his heart be carried to the Holy Land. This romantic though quixotic mission fell to Lord James Douglas and William St. Clair, along with several other companions. When these men reached Spain, they decided to assist King Alonzo XI of Castile and Leon in his fight against the Moors. In a remarkable display of chivalry, both Douglas and St. Clair perished in a desperate battle at Theba just outside the fortress of Gibraltar.[159]

The heartbreak of that gallant death may have hastened the demise of the elder Henry St. Clair, who passed away within a year. That caused the mantle of the St. Clairs to fall to his grandson William, who became the 8th Baron of Roslin in 1331. This younger William was destined to add great fortune to the honors that his predecessors had amassed, because he married Isabel Forteith, who was heiress to the princely earldom of Strathearn and Orkney. Together they had three children, and built a splendid residence within the fortress that the St. Clairs had previously constructed. This converted the battlement known as Roslin Castle into an impressive and secure residence for their extended family.

His eldest son, Henry, succeeded to the title of 9th Baron of Roslin upon William's passing in 1358. To receive his due inheritance of the properties and title of Earl of Orkney, Henry had to endure the machinations of other claimants, but was finally confirmed in that right by the king of Norway in 1379. Though the rich Orkney Islands stood just north of the Scottish mainland, they had long since been conquered by the Norwegians, and it was to that king that homage needed to be given to receive those islands. This holding of lands from a foreign king was not unusual in those days, and even the king of England had given homage to French kings for the lands he held in that country.

Moving quickly to establish himself in the Orkneys, Henry built a navy of ships to protect his waterbound estates. Included in his legacy is the story of a possible trip to America at that early time, in the years before Columbus. This possibility was stimulated by what seemed to be carvings of American corn in Rosslyn Chapel, which was built by Henry's grandson. Since this has often been cited as a deep mystery involving the St. Clairs, it is worth taking a moment to shed some light upon it.

If Henry did somehow travel to America, he clearly would not have been the first to do so. In 982 AD, Erik the Red left Norway and sailed to Iceland, which had been discovered about 200 years earlier.[160] After killing several Icelanders and getting himself banished for three years, Erik put out to sea and was blown westward to a virgin land known as Greenland. There he founded two colonies that survived difficult conditions for the next 450 years, kept alive by trade via Iceland to Europe. During those years, a number of temporary settlements were started in America, most notably in Northeastern Canada. Henry St. Clair lived during a time when Norwegian trade routinely traveled westward to Orkney, Iceland and Greenland, with products from America and Greenland coming back in return. Could Henry have made that trip in his own ships or with the Zeno brothers from Venice as some suggest? Certainly he could have. Or might he have simply obtained ears of American corn from boats that stopped at Orkney? That could have happened also. Which of these he actually did is still being debated. But there was clearly nothing earth-shaking about doing either one. Columbus opened the southern route to the Americas in 1492, but the Norwegians had apparently opened the northern route many years earlier.

In 1400 AD, after a long and eventful life, St. Clair passed away and was succeeded by his son, also named Henry, who became the 2nd Earl of Orkney and 10th Baron of Roslin. The younger Henry expanded his family's estates further by marrying Egida Douglas, who was heiress to the earldom of Nithsdale. Together, he and Egida fathered one of the most remarkable members of this long and distinguished family, William St. Clair, who—among his other accomplishments—would be the builder of Rosslyn Chapel.

Rosslyn Chapel and Scotland's Grand Lodge

Upon the passing of Henry St. Clair in 1420, his son William took the reins of the family as 3rd Earl of Orkney and 11th Baron of Roslin. With an impressive castle as his family seat, and vast resources flowing to him that could be spent as he willed, William St Clair resolved to build a magnificent church unequaled for its beauty in Scotland. This would also be his thanks to the Almighty for his good fortune, and provide a final resting place for the bodies of his ancestors and heirs. To do this properly, he wanted to have four altars in the church, and set up a fund to pay for four clerics known as canons to pray one after another, twenty-four hours a day, for himself and his ancestors. This required the approval of Pope Eugene IV in Rome, with whom William had enough influence to request and receive the necessary grant of right for this special place that would become Rosslyn Chapel.[161]

He recruited the best masons he could find—whether local or foreign—and brought them to Roslin around 1441. As their first task, he instructed them to demolish his family's old stone manor house which had long stood on the site. At the same time he gave these masons parcels of land to the northwest of the worksite and allowed them to build homes for themselves using the old stones they salvaged from the demolition. Those old homes formed the town of Roslin, and several of these residences are still there, though the stones in their walls are chipped and much repaired.

> . . . .because he thought the massones, had not a convenient place to lodge . . . he made them to build the towne of Rosline, that now is extant [in existence] and gave every one of them a house and lands. . . .[162]

In the course of this work, St. Clair directed the masons to remove all of his family's ancient home except for the small chapel at the lowest part of the castle.[163] This modest chapel seemed to retain some special significance.

When formal approval was finally received from the pope in 1446 to begin building, the shift to construction proceeded quickly. A large foundation was prepared, a cornerstone was laid, and the building began. As the walls started to rise, an acknowledgement was carved on the exterior north side declaring that Rosslyn Chapel was dedicated in 1450. For decades the work continued under St. Clair's supervision, being only a short walk uphill from his castle. With loving attention to each detail, the vastly ornate stonework spread throughout the church.

Over the centuries that followed, Rosslyn Chapel took on an almost mystical quality. It became imbued with legends linking it to the Knights Templar, great treasures, grail quests, and the bloodline of Jesus Christ. Further legends linked it to Freemasonry, clandestine rituals, and complex symbology. Still more connected it to pagan practices, sexual orgies, and "green man" icons. Aspects of these legends sound too fantastic to be true, and perhaps they are. But it is possible that other aspects of those legends may have some validity. Consider what can actually be seen today.

Upon approaching Rosslyn Chapel, there is already a sense that this edifice is completely unique. No other church or building is similar to it on the face of the earth. For one thing, it is incomplete—hewn in two as if a mighty cleaver held by giant hand had come down and severed a cathedral in twain. A massive retaining wall was erected to close off that severed end. Walking closer, the flying buttresses overhead and intricate carvings in the stonework around each stained-glass window presage what is to come.

As you pass under the stone arch of the north doorway and enter the chapel, there is an immediate sense of being surrounded by such a wealth of visual images that the senses are overwhelmed. Your vision tends to race from delicate carvings close at hand to the soaring ceiling which arches over the rows of pews facing to the east. Turning in that direction and staying close to the wall, it is necessary to walk upon large floorstones worn smooth with use. No sign reveals that one of the stones underfoot was once the entryway to the burial crypt below.

For generation after generation, the Lord and Lady of the St. Clairs were laid to rest down there. Each time, the floorstone was lifted and the body was taken below by the few allowed to enter. The mortal remains were placed in the long, east-west underground chamber that reportedly traversed the length of the chapel, but ran southward only to the middle of the church and no farther. The crypt was lined with perfectly-cut ashlar stones, and if there once was a passageway to rooms under the other half of the Chapel, it has not been found. The legendary Holy Grail, Templar treasure, and proof of the bloodline of Jesus Christ have likewise never been found below, though not all are convinced that every possible storage place there has been explored.

The St. Clair men lived their lives so steeped in the honor and duties of knighthood that they refused coffins and other trappings of burial. Instead they insisted upon being placed beneath Rosslyn Chapel clad in full armor. To many, this recalled the exceptional devotion, even unto death, of the Knights Templar. The mystical lore inspired by the rites of the St. Clairs led people to say that the chapel seemed to be awash with flames whenever a St. Clair died. Sir Walter Scott preserved this enchantment in his poetic saga *Lay of the Last Minstrel*.

> O'er Roslin all that dreary night
>   A wondrous blaze was seen to gleam;
> 'Twas broader than the watch-fire's light,
>   And redder than the bright moonbeam.

Fig. 26 Rosslyn Chapel
The north doorway is on the left, with the floorstones over
the crypt being a few steps forward under these arches.

It glar'd on Roslin's castled rock,
    It ruddied all the copse-wood glen;
'Twas seen from Dryden's groves of oak
    And seen from cavern'd Hawthornden.
Seem'd all on fire that chapel proud,
    Where Roslin's chiefs uncoffin'd lie,
Each Baron, for a sable shroud,
    Sheath'd in his iron panoply.
Seem'd all on fire within, around,
    Deep sacristy and altar's pale;
Shone every pillar foliage bound,
    And glimmer'd all the dead men's mail.
Blaz'd battlement and pinnet high,
    Blaz'd every rose-carved buttress fair —
So still they blaze when fate is nigh
    The lordly line of high St. Clair.[164]

Returning upward into the passageway above the crypt, and standing on the large floorstones once more, it is possible to continue toward the front of the chapel by passing under a series of arches. These are separated from the body of the church by a row of pillars. Reaching the nave at the eastern end, the four Christian altars requested by William St. Clair are found, each having its own place along the wall. Oddly enough, they are set among detailed carvings that include prominent pagan "green men." In the years before Christianity came to Scotland, the early tribes included in their worship these icons of men's faces with vines and other greenery growing from their mouth. Also included in those pagan devotions were popular practices such as sexual orgies in the springtime. Rituals similar to those pagan rites were alleged to have taken place in the small fields near Roslin Castle at a later date, with the permission and possible participation of the St. Clairs.[165] This echoed the accusations against the Knights Templar of following non-Christian practices.

In the space before the four altars stand the famous three pillars that many people have associated with the three degrees of Freemasonry: Entered Apprentice, Fellow Craft, and Master. The column that receives the most attention is designated the Apprentice Pillar, and in fact it is the most visually striking. In essence it is a simple fluted column around which four vines seem to grow upward around the pillar from the intricately worked base to an ornate capital. The familiar legend associated with this particular column was that the master carver to whom the pillar was assigned went to Rome[166] before attempting the work so that he could see the original on which it was to be based. While he was gone, however, an apprentice executed the work brilliantly. When the master returned, he was so outraged at having been upstaged by the apprentice that he killed the young man with a blow from his mallet. A head carved elsewhere in the chapel once showed a mark on the figure's forehead, and it was believed that this was made for the apprentice. It is a beautiful legend. Yet some argue against it being true since there were only two Masonic degrees at the time Rosslyn Chapel was built, with the third degree being added only after Grand Lodges were formed several centuries later. However the head of each lodge was called the Master, which was a formally recognized position at that time even though it was not a "degree." It has also been said that the mark on the stone head was not on the original figure, but was added much later to resemble the story—though such an assertion would be difficult to prove one way or the other.

Moving to the south wall of the chapel and looking up, the "ears of corn" discussed earlier are clearly visible. They form an arch over the window, and are somewhat rectangular in design, but could easily be American corn. Many people have suggested that they had to be something else, because Columbus did not "discover" America until after Rosslyn Chapel was already built. Yet as we saw, in the early 1400s Norwegian settlers were already bringing back products from their temporary settlements in America.

Continuing toward the west along that same wall brings us to a doorway, where something else of interest waits just outside. Stepping through the doorway and then to the right, a stained glass window appears. On the lower left-hand side of the window frame rests a stone corbel carved with an intricate tableau. Of the two men pictured, the one in front has part of his clothing removed, and a rope known as a cable-tow is circled around his neck. This ritual is known to every Freemason, since each person participates in it before becoming a Mason. Considering the several details present in the image, the whole scene matches no currently known ritual or practice other than Freemasonry. The images have become worn with time, but observers in previous years recorded that the man standing in back had a large Templar cross on the front of his uniform. This would suggest that it was not a Masonic ritual being shown, but a Knights Templar ritual.

It might be possible that Freemasons were simply imitating the Templars in this regard, except for one thing. I have never met a Mason who knew that the ritual performed with a cable tow was once a Templar ritual. The Masonic ritual continues to be performed this way simply because it has always been done this way, without anyone knowing its origin. Certainly this single observation would not be enough to establish a Templar-Freemason connection. Yet it is worth keeping in mind as we see other elements emerge.

Going back inside the chapel, we then turn right and pass below the corn once again. In front of us, another remarkable sight appears: the Lower Chapel. Amid all the perfection of Rosslyn Chapel's design and crafting, the stairs to the Lower Chapel appear extraordinarily out of place. Located where they are, they required the fourth altar to be placed higher than the other three, since it sits atop the passageway through which the stairs descend. It also left almost no room in front of the altar for the canon to stand and say his prayers. If he stepped back too far from the altar, he fell down the stairwell. What compelling importance did the St. Clairs attach to the Lower Chapel, that they did not allow a single stone to be moved from it—even at the cost of forcing the design of their otherwise-magnificent Rosslyn Chapel to be made irregular at this point?

As we descend each of the twenty-five stone steps on the staircase and the several wooden steps at the bottom, we begin to see the ancient chapel. It is made entirely of stone and comprises only one-fifth the size of the grand edifice above. The amenities in this small space are basic, and it is very simply adorned. The St. Clair cross differed from the traditional cross in that it had many small, semi-circular "bites" taken out of its edges, creating a very distinctive image. The rounded roof of this Lower Chapel still bears the scalloped design drawn from that cross. At the far end of the room stands a simple altar. An impressive stained glass window rises above it, being about nine feet tall. The stone floor extends underfoot roughly 36 feet long and 14 feet wide, meeting the ashlar stone walls on all sides that rise to the curved ceiling above. The feeling of permanence and centuries permeates this solid structure. A modest fireplace rests nearby along the right-hand wall, and a doorway just beyond leads outside.[167] The left-hand wall likewise contains a doorway that once led outside, but was converted long ago to add a small storage or living area. The stonework of this addition is rough-hewn and made of odd-shaped rectangular stones rather than the carefully masoned stone blocks of the original construction and of Rosslyn Chapel above.

What was the importance of this rustic chapel below, and the intricately ornate Rosslyn Chapel above? Why were Christian, pagan, Templar and possibly Freemason images placed there? It now appears that Rosslyn Chapel may have been significant to the Templars and Freemasons, but perhaps not in the way we expected. To see those things in proper context, there is more we need to know about these unique places, events and people. It is there that we go now.

During the long life of William St. Clair, he did more than design and build Rosslyn Chapel. He held one of Scotland's highest offices, serving as Lord Chancellor from 1454 to 1456. Upon leaving that position he received the hereditary title of Lord Sinclair for his service to the crown.[168] Around that same time he resigned his title and lands as Earl of Nithsdale, which he had inherited through his mother, in exchange for receiving the title and lands of Earl of Caithness.[169] This new estate stood on the northernmost part of Scotland's mainland, facing the Orkney Islands.

That succession of good fortune was intruded upon by somber news. In July of 1469 King James III of Scotland married Margaret, the daughter of the Norwegian King.[170] Unfortunately the father of the bride found himself short of funds for the necessary dowry, so he put up the Orkney Islands as security for that wedding endowment. When it became apparent in 1470 that he still could not pay, the Norwegian king ceded the Orkneys to James III. Rather than renew the St. Clair rights to rule those islands in his name, James decided to keep them for himself. As token compensation to William St. Clair, the modest castle and lands of Ravenscraig near Kirkcaldy were given in exchange.

Being advanced in years by that time, William St. Clair decided in 1476 to break with custom and divide his estates among his three sons. By his first wife, Margaret Douglas, he had a son named William who was a wastrel and disappointment. That may have been the reason for this unusual dividing of the family's holdings. This son was invested with the title 2nd Lord Sinclair, but little else. By his second wife, Marjorie Sutherland, he had Oliver, who pleased his father well. Oliver received the title 12th Baron of Roslin and the largest share of all the family's estates. Marjorie had also given him a second son, who carried the traditional family name of William. This younger William received the title and lands of 2nd Earl of Caithness. Though Oliver had received the smallest title, the lands accorded to him were so extensive that it provoked jealousy and objection from his older half-brother. To keep the family peace, Oliver ceded to the older William the castle of Ravenscraig and some other lands to go along with that brother's honorary title of Lord Sinclair. When their venerable father finally passed away in 1484 the division of estates was complete.[171]

Since Sir Oliver, as he was known, had ended up with only a third of the estates of his father, it forced the family's desire to build Rosslyn into a vast and grand church to be met with a cold dose of reality. Rather than let his father's dream fall to ruin, however, Oliver had a large stone wall erected across the unfinished west side of the building. This marked the halfway point of what would have been the entire, magnificent church. The only part that had been built was the Lady Chapel and Choir, so it came to be known as Rosslyn Chapel.

To the extent that he could, Oliver kept some masons working to finish many of the adornments and details which had not yet been completed. At some point, unfortunately, the expense must have become prohibitive, for today one can still see sections that are remarkably free of decoration. He had a tiler roof the building with slate to make it habitable. Then he staffed the four altars with canons and set them to performing their daily prayers. His father's body was placed in the crypt below the Chapel, which satisfied the essential intentions and desires of his illustrious forebear.

Oliver's time came to an end in 1525, and he was succeeded by his son William as 13th Baron of Roslin. William married Alison Home, and produced an heir also named William. Other than that he managed to live a fairly quiet life.

In 1554 William's demise led to the younger William becoming the 14th Baron. With a measure of the earlier St. Clairs' energy and vision, the new master of Roslin set out to raise his family to prominence again. In time he even achieved the position of Lord Chief Justice of Scotland. His marriage to Elizabeth Kerr bore fruit in the form of a son whom they named Edward. Unfortunately, Edward died in 1582, but not before producing a grandson and heir.

It was in these latter years of William St. Clair's long tenure at Roslin that a man named William Schaw came to be Master of Works in Scotland. That in turn gave rise to a curious series of events that have been much debated in terms of their influence on Freemasonry.

The official duties of the Master of Works involved overseeing all construction and maintenance work on the king's castles, fortifications, and any other major project the king should desire. Schaw took these duties a step further, and began to involve himself more in the affairs of stonemasons than any of his predecessors had done. This new outreach included issuing his Statutes of 1598 and 1599, which receive more discussion later.

Then in late 1601 or early 1602, Schaw participated in the drafting of a most unusual letter to William St. Clair offering him the position of patron and judge for stonemasons in all their business matters. Since the king would have to approve such an arrangement, the signatories stated that if St. Clair wished to purchase from the king this hereditary honor, they would support it. Given St. Clair's position as Lord Chief Justice of Scotland, this seemed an excellent arrangement. Unfortunately, Sir William died at that time, so the letter and offer were presented to his grandson, who was also named William.

When young William became the 15th Baron of Roslin, he was somewhat of a dissolute character.[172] Nevertheless, the signatories of the letter clearly hoped he would mature with the responsibilities of the Barony, and be worthy of the stated offer. That was not to be. In addition to his arguments with local church ministers, the new Sir William was forced to confess to fornication with a local barmaid, and was unable to remember if all his bastard children had been baptized.[173] Given the other things on his mind, it was probably best for everyone that he did not take the trouble to petition the king for the honor and responsibility of being patron and judge for the stonemasons who had approached him.

One gets the impression that all of Scotland gave a collective sigh of relief when Sir William ran off to Ireland with his mistress in 1617, abdicating the Barony of Roslin. That felicitous act caused the title and family holdings to fall to his son, also named William in keeping with the family custom.[174] Installed as the 16th Baron, this newly-minted Sir William proved to be as honorable a man as his father was not. He worked to regain trust and honor for his family, and in 1622 was appointed sheriff for the shire of Edinburgh. Six years later, his reputation had apparently become well enough established that a second letter was offered to him by a number of stonemasons from across the center of Scotland, inviting him to become their patron and protector. Unlike his predecessor, William sought to obtain the king's approval of this right,. Unfortunately King Charles I replied on 27 February 1635 that the crown had never approved such rights for the St. Clairs in the past, and upon review was still not choosing to do so.[175]

It should be noted that those two letters from the stonemasons have sometimes been called the St. Clair Charters. That was an unfortunate name which has misled many people. A charter was an official document from the king, and it conferred specific rights to an individual or his heirs. Clearly these letters were not from the king. And King Charles even took the unusual step of confirming that no such rights had ever been granted. Any assertions that St. Clair acquired authority over stonemasons—or became Grand Master of Freemasons—due to these letters must unfortunately be found to have no merit. Eventually, of course, there was a relationship between the St. Clairs and Freemasonry, but it could not have been created or continued by these letters.

On a personal level, William St. Clair married Anna Spotswood, and they had three children together. When he died in 1650, his son John became the 17th Baron of Roslin. John was captured by the English and languished in prison for many years before returning home, where he died without issue in 1690. That event began a series of twists in the title to Roslin, and a landmark in the history of Freemasonry.

The title passed to Alexander—son of the late Baron's brother James—and this made him the 18th Baron.[176, 177] The main accomplishment in Alexander's relatively short reign was to produce a son and heir named William, who would become the first Grand Master of Freemasons in Scotland. When Alexander passed away in 1706, William became invested as the 19th Baron of Roslin.

Thirty years later Sir William had woven himself so deeply into the social fabric of his country that when Masons gathered at Edinburgh in 1736 to form a Grand Lodge for Scotland, he was the resounding choice to be Grand Master. In so doing, he formally declared that he was giving up any previous hereditary rights to the position of Grand Master which may have existed for his family. In return he accepted election to that same position in the newly formed Grand Lodge. William remained a Freemason thereafter, a time in which Masonry flourished in Scotland.

The "previous hereditary rights" he gave up were apparently those in the "St. Clair charters." As we have seen, however, these letters did not successfully confer any rights. The only offer the St. Clairs accepted and which resulted in investiture occurred in 1736 in the Grand Lodge of Scotland.

So we did not see a St. Clair become a Knight Templar, nor officially become a Freemason prior to 1736. Yet their close association with Templars, stonemasons and Freemasons has been amply demonstrated. To see the relationships that developed among these societies we now turn to the stonemasons. In their world a number of key events played out much differently than most people have assumed.

Fig. 27   William St. Clair, Grand Master of Scotland

Chapter 15

Master Masons to the Crown

Freemasonry is filled with references to stonemasons, using that craft in allegories or stories about how to live a better life. Yet Freemasonry is remarkably fuzzy about how working stonemasons would have developed a relationship with gentlemen and other members of society to allow a secretive society such as this to arise. Deciphering that relationship is clearly essential to determining how Freemasonry came to exist and what active role—good, bad or otherwise—it came to play. So it is into those formative years that we now go.

In 1481 John Mylne became Master Mason to the Crown of Scotland by the benefit of a hangman's noose.[178] His predecessor, Robert Cochrane, was accorded that public honor by dissatisfied nobles who resented the special favors bestowed upon this civil servant by King James III. Cochrane had actually held the title Master of Work, but was also a stonemason, one of the rare times that combination occurred. Traditionally, there was a Master Mason who actually built the king's projects, and above him was a favorite courtier of the monarch who held the title Master of Work and simply presided over those construction efforts. When Mylne became the king's Master Mason, the other title apparently fell dormant for a period of time. His family provided many Master

Masons to the Crown over the years, even while Freemasonry developed into its modern form.

Most stonemasons of that time earned their mason's wages in dust-filled workrooms far from the richly appointed chambers of kings and lords. Even so, their lot was far better than that of many others among the common people. Most commoners in that day were serfs tied to their farmlands by hereditary contracts from which they could never hope to escape. High above them, kings and lords lived in palaces and castles, while abbots and bishops ruled over rich abbeys and gilded cathedrals. Towns tended to be small, and contained the only free common people—the craftsmen and merchants who eked out a living in the narrow gap left between serfs and lords. To protect themselves, craftsmen in various towns began to band together, having at first the simple goal of preventing outsiders from coming into town to steal some of their modest livelihood. The only way an outsider could ply his trade in such a town was to present himself to the local craftsmen and be accepted as a member, pledging loyalty and obedience to their rules. By banding together they became the free and accepted members of the craftsmen's lodges.

Far to the south, London was already the largest city in Britain and had more craftsmen than other towns possessed. As a result it began to impose a degree of formality and structure that was uncommon elsewhere. One of those formalities was to grant craftsmen and merchants the "freedom of the city," after requiring them to go through an approval process and pay a fee. This gave a person the right to perform their trade or business in the city, with each trade group being authorized to decide which practitioners of their craft could receive that right.

> In 1376, the [City Hall] records show that the masons were now one of the forty-seven "sufficient misteries" of the City of London, when they were called upon to elect four men of the trade to serve on the Common Council, sworn to give counsel for the common weal, and "preserving for each mistery its reasonable customs."[179]

For whatever reason, the city chose to call these craft associations Livery Companies. There is, in fact, a Masons Livery Company still in existence today. Outside of London there was no rush to build a similar level of formality at that time. Almost all the towns and cities in England were quite small, and the voluntary arrangements of their local lodges seemed to work acceptably well, with little or no municipal support.

The second major city to formally recognize the craft was Edinburgh in Scotland, where the "Masons and Wrights" filed for incorporation together in 1475. Apparently neither group had enough members to justify filing separately. The "Seal of Cause" which granted their incorporation stated the city was giving its approval to the regulatory statutes that the two crafts had drawn up, and gave us a look into what they considered important affairs at that time.

> Four men to be chosen, "of the best and worthiest of the two crafts. That is to say two masons and two wrights...," sworn to "search and see" that all the craftsmen's work is lawfully and truly done.
>
> Complaints about any man or his work to be brought before the Deacon [the senior officer of the Incorporation] and the "four men," who shall cause the damage or wrong to be amended [repaired]. If unable to do so, the matter must go before the [town's] Provost and Baillies.
>
> New craftsmen coming to town to seek employment, or to take work on their own account, to be examined by the "four men" as to their competency, and if admitted, to pay 13/4 stg.[180] to the maintenance of the Altar.
>
> Apprentices to be taken for a minimum of seven years, and they pay an entry fee of 6/8 to the Altar.
>
> Runaway apprentices or other bound "servants" are not to be employed; a scale of penalties for the masters who give them work.
>
> An apprentice at the end of his term to be examined by the "four men," to ensure that he is qualified

to become "fellow of the craft." If found worthy, he pays 6/8 to the Altar and may enjoy the privileges of the craft. If not, he must continue in employment until he is fit to be made freeman and fellow....

The crafts to be each responsible for the decent burial of the Brethren of their crafts.[181]

It was apparently traditional in Edinburgh at that time for newly incorporated crafts to build a small chapel onto some part of St. Giles' Church, to house their altar and meeting place. The beautiful "north porch" constructed by the stonemasons remains one of the most visible and striking parts of that church today. St. Giles—now designated a cathedral—stands near Edinburgh Castle, with the famous High Street passing directly beside the north face of the cathedral. That means the north porch built by the masons is prominently in view on the High Street. The two chapels they constructed within the porch—one for masons and one for wrights—are visible through stained glass windows. Between those chapels a pair of massive doors is sometimes used to provide entrance, with an even larger stained glass window above them. The east chapel still reflects the use given to it by those masons. Dedicated to the two Saints John,[182] its stained glass windows show Solomon building his Temple, then Zerubbabel rebuilding the Temple in later years.

That incorporation of masons and wrights in 1475 gave rise to the Lodge of Edinburgh (Mary's Chapel). The lodge acquired this name when it was relocated to the church known as Mary's Chapel, about 440 yards east of St Giles, on a street called Niddry's Wynd. Through some miracle, the records of this lodge, from 1599 forward, have been preserved and tell us in remarkable detail about the membership and activities of the lodge during that time.

It was six years after this incorporation that John Mylne became Master Mason to the Crown. By so doing he established a family that would be intimately involved with many of the major events believed to be important in the evolution of Freemasonry. Mylne was responsible for the work on numerous royal palaces and fortifications, but became particularly well known for his

Fig. 28   Stonemasons' chapel in St. Giles Cathedral, Edinburgh

work at Stirling Castle. His two children, Alexander and Robert, likewise became well trained in this craft prior to his passing, which occurred sometime before 1513.

His son Alexander was educated at St. Andrews before becoming Abbot of Cambuskenneth near Stirling.[183] Yet he also followed in his father's footsteps by supervising the building of a local bridge among other projects. Those successes attracted the attention of the king, who appointed Alexander Mylne as Master Mason to the Crown about 1517. In addition to serving the king he also served in Parliament from 1532 to 1542, and remained active in Scottish life until 1548.

Alexander's brother, Robert Mylne, apparently earned his living as a supplier of building materials such a stone and oak, but it was not known if he worked as a mason like his father and brother.[184] Robert's son Thomas, on the other hand, definitely carried on the family tradition.[185] He served as Master Mason to the Crown from 1561 to 1579. He also received the honor of being named a burgess at Dundee in 1593.[186] Thomas took care to educate his son John in the craft, and prepared him for the tumultuous times that would be written large in the lore of Freemasonry.

John Mylne first worked with his father as a stonemason, then succeeded his mentor as the royal Master Mason after 1579, being appointed by King James VI.[187] In this capacity he built the landmark Drum House during 1584-1585 and performed numerous projects in Dundee, where he was made a burgess in 1587. While Mylne was engaged in these projects, a man named William Schaw was made Master of Works and began to build his own career. It should be recalled that the Master Mason performed the actual construction activities, while the Master of Works was generally a well-born courtier appointed by the king to oversee the Master Mason's efforts. The actions taken by Schaw would have a tremendous impact on the legends of Freemasonry, as well as on the Mylne Master Masons and the St. Clairs of Roslin.

William Schaw was born into the influential Schaw family of Sauchie, although in a lesser branch.[188] Even so, family connections were apparently strong enough to gain him a start in life as page to Mary of Guise, the grandmother of King James. Many years later, in 1583, James rewarded his courtier with the title

Master of Works. Yet the services for which Schaw was primarily being retained were illustrated immediately after his appointment. The king sent him on a diplomatic mission with Lord George Seaton to renew Scotland's friendship treaty with France.[189] Since he was not a mason, this trip was also a chance for Schaw to learn something of French architecture, which he did on excursions with the Lord's son, Alexander. Upon their return from this diplomatic mission, Lord Seaton asked Schaw to oversee work on an addition to his palace, giving him a chance to see how construction work actually took place. Upon the elderly Lord's passing soon thereafter, the work continued at the request of his son, the new Lord Alexander Seaton.

Schaw was one of the courtiers who went with James VI to Norway in 1589, where the king married Anne of Denmark. When Schaw returned, he took responsibility for having the palaces at Holyrood and Dunfermline repaired and readied for the new queen. Well pleased, Queen Anne made Schaw her Chamberlain in addition to his other duties. Thus involved in court, Schaw's involvement with building continued to be relatively modest.

It should be noted that the Master of Works position had only a limited area of responsibility—to manage the construction and repair of buildings and fortifications belonging to the king or queen. Quite apart from this, the largest number of projects in those days were performed for the religious leaders of Scotland, and consisted of cathedrals, churches and monasteries, well funded by their rich coffers. The nobility also raised and repaired their great homes and collegiate churches, such as the St. Clair Castle and Rosslyn Chapel, which they handled outside the purview of the king's builders. The towns had their bridges, buildings and civic halls as well. Thus the Master of Works and Master Mason to the Crown tended to have only a small number of projects under their control. These were often lavish and worthy projects—given the king's means—but few in number. Stonemasons and their lodges served all of these religious, noble, royal and civic clients. That enabled the lodges to maintain a large degree of independence and self-determination for themselves.

Then in 1598, Schaw set out to make a serious change in this balance. During the last years of his life, Schaw developed an interest in bringing all the stonemasons' lodges in Scotland under his direct supervision. On the 28th of December in that year he issued what became known as the Schaw Statutes which set out regulations under which all of Scotland's stonemasons and their lodges were directed to begin operating. This was an extraordinary step which none of his predecessors had seen fit to take. And it had the potential of dramatic consequences for the stonemasons' lodges.

Recognizing that what he proposed was new and unusual, Schaw made a point of writing in the statute that his right to impose these rules came from his relationship with the Scottish king. He also gave himself the title of Warden General, and declared that all of this was done with the consent of the governed.

> The statute ordinances to be observed by all the master masons within this realm, set down by William Schaw, Master of Work to his majesty, and general Warden of the said craft, with the consent of the masters hereafter specified.
>
> And for fulfilling and observing of their ordinances, set down as said, is the whole of the masters convened the foresaid day, binding and obliging them hereto faithfully. And therefore have requested their said Warden General [Schaw] to subscribe their presence with his own hand, to the effect that an authentic copy hereof may be sent to every particular lodge within this realm.[190]

This ordinance largely repeated items covered in the incorporation given to masons and wrights in Edinburgh a hundred years earlier, with several additional details regarding items such as payments. In addition, it declared that anything not covered in the statute was to be done as in days of old. Therefore the articles of the statute were not particularly radical or new. The unusual and new aspect of the ordinance was Schaw's attempt to impose one particular set of regulations on all Scottish towns and lodges, without the participation of most of those towns and lodges in this process.

Over the years, the general assumption by most people has been that this was a good thing, that everyone must have accepted it, and that Schaw's Statutes contributed greatly to the formation of Freemasonry. In 1988, David Stevenson went so far as to declare that Schaw was the founder of the Masonic movement.[191] Other authors then took up the Schaw flag and ran forward with it, calling Schaw "the father of Freemasonry and the first modern Freemason,"[192] and also "the architect of the Craft."[193] Those are serious claims. Let us look a little deeper into these assumptions and statements.

In his statute, Schaw stated that these things were done with the consent of the governed. Yet only some masons from lodges near Edinburgh attended the meeting and, apparently, authorized him to write their names at the bottom of the document.

Even if they had reservations during this meeting, it would have been difficult for individual craftsmen to contradict the royal Master of Works, who said he spoke with the voice of the king. Whether they wished to be part of it or not, they would no doubt have been relieved to discover Schaw was willing to have the regulations comply with what they were basically already doing, provided the lodges be placed under his control. If there were any problems with having Schaw as Warden General, those could be dealt with in the future. For the moment the craftsmen suffered no direct loss, so they seem to have agreed to add their names.

Of all the lodges in Scotland, only Kilwinning was bold enough to assert its objection. In doing so, this lodge forced Schaw to issue a second statute the following year, in which a modicum of authority was won for Kilwinning with respect to Western Scotland. Once again, Schaw was willing to yield minor points, as long as he would hold the ultimate control.

It was not clear what the lodges stood to gain from these ordinances. They received no new powers or revenues that would benefit their lodges. On the other hand, it was amply clear what they stood to lose—their independence. These lodges had come into existence voluntarily in the many towns they occupied across Scotland. Traditionally they wrote their own rules, which the town councils generally supported. Edinburgh was the largest city in Scotland, but its lodge did not rule the others. Independence was as Scottish as tartan and bagpipes.

Up to that time, the religious leaders, nobles and civic leaders had all governed their own projects and kept them separate from those of the king. The Master of Works had no say in their affairs, unless they should request support for some reason. Schaw proposed to change that way of life with a single stroke, bringing all stonemasons, their lodges and their work under his control. The reaction from town councils, abbots, lords and gentry of Scotland was nowhere recorded, but the encroachment on their right to decide their own affairs would not normally have been met with much enthusiasm.

One of the most serious clues that something might be amiss with these statutes was the absence of the king's Master Mason from this process. John Mylne was a mason in every sense of the word. He made his living in that craft, and served as Master of the lodge at Scone. He also came from a family of Master Masons to the Crown. If anyone at that time served as a bridge between stonemasons, the king, and other gentlemen, it was the king's Master Mason. He lived with one foot in the lodge and one foot in the royal court. In any rational approach to uniting the lodges under a representative of royal rule, he would have been involved in some way. We find instead that he was left out of the process. Schaw did not mention him or his office in the statutes, did not give him a role in the new arrangement, nor obtain Mylne's signature upon the document.

If the purpose of these regulations was to benefit the public and not Schaw himself, there was a straightforward way to do it. Schaw could have simply gone to Mylne and asked him to be the Warden General. In that way Schaw would still have held control, as Mylne's superior officer, yet Mylne would get the honor of the position. And the masons could have been governed by one of their own. When Shaw set Mylne aside from the entire process, he showed what was actually happening.

John Mylne's comments about this state of affairs were not recorded, but his actions were definitely noted. Mylne went over Schaw's head and invited King James VI to become a mason. In

1601, the king was admitted into the Lodge of Scone by the Master of the lodge, John Mylne.

> In the reigne of his Majesty King James the sixt, of blessed Memorie, who, by the said John Mylne was by the king's own desire entered Freeman, Meason and Fellow-Craft. During his lifetime he mantayned the same as ane member of the Lodge of Scoon, so that this lodge is the most famous lodge within the kingdom.[194]

Normal courtesy for a significant event such as this would have been for the Master Mason to the Crown to have involved his superior officer. This could easily have been done by admitting William Schaw into the Lodge of Scone beforehand, then allowing him to participate. If one were truly generous, he could have arranged for Schaw to become acting Master of the lodge for the purpose of admitting the king. No record has ever been found of Schaw being made a mason at Scone or any other lodge.

That same year there was another thrust and parry in this exchange. That involved the letter sent from several stonemasons' lodges to the head of the St. Clair family, asking him to be their patron and protector. This in itself was a strange occurrence. Schaw had placed himself over all the lodges, and his statutes seem to show he was acting with the authority of the king. So if the lodges were happy being ruled by him, what greater access to king and power could they have wanted for their protection? Yet for some reason the lodges felt a need to approach St. Clair and ask him to be their protector.

After Mylne had made King James a mason, this action by the lodges would have left Schaw out in the cold in terms of exercising authority over the lodges. Under the circumstances he seemed to have done what any good politician would do—he put a brave face on it and added his name to the letter. By so doing, he might have hoped to retain the position of Warden General and some modest authority, even if St. Clair accepted the offer and became the protector of the lodges and the conduit for grievances. Half a loaf was better than none. In any event, there was a poison-pill placed in the letter—possibly at Schaw's instruction—that could render useless this offer to the St. Clairs. The requirement was that this offer would not be complete upon acceptance by St. Clair, but required the king's approval as well.

How motivated—or desperate—were the masons in the lodges? They wanted to present this letter to the aged but highly respected William St. Clair, the Lord Chief Justice of Scotland. By the time they were able to deliver the letter, however, Sir William had died and left his grandson, also named William, at the head of the family. This was the William who was described as "a lewd man who was forced to run away to Ireland although...this was more to do with trouble with the Presbyterian Church than his adulterous affair with a miller's daughter."[195] Even so, the Masters of the lodges chose this dissolute and dishonorable younger St. Clair rather than William Schaw, and went ahead with the letter anyway.

When Schaw died shortly thereafter, all parties involved seemed relieved to drop the question of presiding over stonemasons' lodges in Scotland. The next Master of Works, David Cunninghame, showed no interest. William St. Clair dallied amid his own difficulties until 1617, when he abdicated and left his son to deal with matters involving the St. Clairs. As we have seen, that son who was also named William, was an honorable and forthright man in the best St. Clair family tradition. However the offer from the stonemasons' lodges had lain fallow for fifteen years, and he did not pick it up.

During that period, Queen Elizabeth I died and left the crowns of England and Ireland to King James of Scotland. This was a turbulent time, for Elizabeth had been the daughter of King Henry VIII, the man who split from the popes in Rome and created the Church of England during the Protestant Reformation. King James was still a Roman Catholic when he raised his scepter over England, and that inherent conflict came to dominate much of his life. Feeling the larger kingdom to the south required his personal attention, James moved to London with his court. By so doing, he became a more distant ruler of his native land. However the competition for control of the stonemasons' lodges in Scotland was not over.

Chapter 16

Stonemasons and Gentlemen

$\mathcal{T}$he Schaw storm of thunderclouds rose again in 1625 when King James, who had worn the triple crown for twenty-two years, passed away and caused his son to become Charles I, king of England, Scotland and Ireland. The young monarch made it one of his first acts to confirm many royal officers in their existing positions, including James Murray as Master of Works in Scotland. Perhaps motivated by that confirmation, Murray then attempted to re-assert control over the stonemasons' lodges.

If there had been any question before about whether the lodges wanted to be ruled by the Master of Works, the situation was made sufficiently clear now. The lodges issued a new letter in 1628 to the honorable William St. Clair, who had now been eleven years at the head of his family. Displaying a markedly different feeling toward this issue than did his predecessor, St. Clair picked up the standard and carried it into battle. He actively pursued the king's confirmation of his role as patron and protector of stone-masons and their lodges in Scotland. In this he was energetically opposed by Murray, the Master of Works.

In 1629, while the struggle over this issue continued, King Charles appointed Anthony Alexander as co-Master of Works alongside James Murray. Alexander was the son of the Secretary of State for Scotland, a powerful position in Charles' administration. This proved to be a boon for Murray, who otherwise lacked the social status and influence in Scotland to compete with Sir William St. Clair. Even so, Charles attempted to extricate himself from this dispute by writing to the Scottish Privy Council on the 4th of March in 1631 that he would approve St. Clair's request to be patron and protector of the stonemasons and lodges in the land, unless any valid objection should be raised.[196] Unmollified by the passage of time, Murray again objected, this time joined by Alexander, which cast the proposal into limbo again.

At that point the Mylne family re-entered the fray. John Mylne, the Master Mason of the previous king, had sired a son who was also named John and taught him the craft. When the elder Mylne died in 1621, an unrelated builder was given the honor of being Master Mason. Now, ten years later, the younger John Mylne was appointed Master Mason to the Crown.[197] Mylne brought with him significant credentials. He completed several noted projects in Perth, north of Edinburgh, and others in Scone, Edinburgh, and Aberdeen. He was no less active at home, marrying Isobel Wilson and producing two sons, John and Alexander, who followed him in the trade. Mylne also took time to serve as Master of the Lodge of Scone from 1621 to 1627. Called to Edinburgh for work at Holyrood Palace, he there received his commission as the king's Master Mason. Having taken up residence in the city, he joined the Lodge of Edinburgh (Mary's Chapel) on 9 October 1633.[198] It was at this juncture that he and his lodge brothers found themselves caught in a precarious position between St. Clair and Murray. The workingmen had expressed a desire to have the Baron of Roslin be their champion, yet the Master of Works held some degree of authority over them due to Schaw's earlier actions.

It should be noted that up to this point, stonemasons' lodges seemed to consist completely of craftsmen. The lodge members were workers who shaped stones, raised buildings, built bridge spans and the like. They signed apprentices to seven-year terms and occasionally fined fellow stonemasons who broke the rules. For those who postulated that Freemasonry rose exclusively from the stonemasons' lodges, the subsequent experiences at Lodge of

Fig. 29 John Mylne the Younger, Master Mason to the Crown

Edinburgh (Mary's Chapel) have often been cited as a clear example of how this transition to Masonry came about. For that reason they bear closer examination.

By some miracle, the records of this lodge have been preserved from 1599 onward, providing a remarkable look into what actually transpired. The first entries in the minutes of the lodge indicate this was an ongoing organization, with previously-elected officers. Their focus was entirely on stonemasons' issues. Due to the general illiteracy of this time, the person who kept these minutes simply guessed at the spelling of words, which means they now require some translation. With that done, we see this early entry reflecting their ongoing activities.

> 31 July 1599
> On this day George Patoun, mason, granted and confessed that he had offended against the deacon and masters (of the lodge) for placing of a cowan (non-member) to work at a chimney head for two and a half days....[199]

By 1634, however, William St. Clair's attempts to keep the Master of Works from controlling the stonemasons' affairs began to spill over into the lodge's activities. Anthony Alexander requested that he be made a member of the Lodge of Edinburgh (Mary's Chapel), and asked John Mylne to sponsor him. Mylne would have been in no position to refuse the co-Master of Works, who was his superior officer. In a related action which seemed of no particular significance at the time, but which would have a clearer meaning later, two other gentlemen were admitted along with Alexander. One of them was Lord Alexander, the eldest son of the 1st Earl of Stirling, who was Anthony Alexander's older brother. The other man was Sir Alexander Strachan, Baronet of Thornton in Kincardineshire, who held an important position as a collector of the king's revenues in Scotland.[200]

Other than the admitting of King James VI to the Lodge of Scone, which was indirectly documented, this admitting of three gentlemen who were not stonemasons was the first time such an event was directly documented in a lodge's records. A separate "minute" was recorded for each new member.[201]

> The 3 day of July 1634
> On which day the Right Honorable My Lord Alexander is admitted fellow of the craft by Hugh Forest, deacon, and Alexander Nesbet, warden, and the whole rest of the master masons of Edinburgh and thereto every master has subscribed with their hand or set their marks.
>
> > (Beneath this minute were the marks of Hugh Forest and Alexander Nesbet, and the written names of J^n Watt, Thomas Patersone, Alexander, A. Strachan, Johne Mylln, Thomas Ainslie, Robert Gray)
>
> The 3 day of July 1634
> On which day Antonie Alexander, Right Honorable Master of Work to his majesty by admission of Hugh Forest....(goes on similar to above)
>
> At Edinburgh the 3 day of July 1634
> On which day Sr Alexander Strachan of Thorn(ton) is admitted fellow craft by Hugh Forest....   (goes on similar to above)

The normal process of a seven year apprenticeship was waived for these gentlemen. They were accepted and passed to the position of Fellow Craft on the same evening.

Only a few months after the admitting of these men to the lodge, James Murray died on the 29th of November, vacating the senior Master of Works position. Alexander lost no time in petitioning King Charles for appointment as the sole Master of Works for Scotland. His request was granted on the 15th of December by the king in London, needing only the formality of being stamped by the State seal held at the Exchequer in Scotland. At this juncture the amount of prestige and influence exercised by the St.

Clairs in Scotland came into full view. Sir William raised his objection to Alexander's appointment, and—in direct contradiction to the king—caused the Exchequer to withhold the seals. Incensed by this act, Charles I wrote to the commissions of the Exchequer on the 27th of February in 1635, stating his displeasure at St. Clair's "pretending ane heritable charge of the Maissones of our said kingdome, though we have never given a warrant for strengthening of aney heritable right."[202] He also asked for any proof that such a warrant had ever been issued to St. Clair's father, believing there to be none. In fact, no such warrant seems to have been issued, and certainly no such document has ever been found.

In a show of support for Alexander, Charles granted him the dignity of a knighthood. Thus reassured of royal favor toward his efforts, the newly-minted Sir Anthony followed his elevation by performing an alarming act. He compiled a list of masons whom he renounced, and sent it to London, to be considered in resolving the issue of his control over the lodges.[203] As fortune would have it, the issue became mired in the government and no action was reported as being taken against the masons named. But the fact that he took this step spoke volumes.

After joining the lodge in 1634, Sir Anthony rarely ever attended a meeting, nor did the two men admitted with him. They came as a group in 1635 when John Mylne's son Alexander was made a mason in the lodge. This appears to have been a courteous act. The three men came again in 1637 when David Ramsay, a favorite of the king, came to Edinburgh and asked to join the lodge. That Ramsay was said to have been an avid student of Rosicrucianism, which could be identified with Freemasonry,[204] suggested that he came due to his own interests. It is unfortunate that Sir Anthony and his two associates by-passed the regular lodge meetings and only came for this pair of events.

Before Sir Anthony could press his case further, the king became distracted by troubles with the Scottish Covenanters whose rebellion consumed his time and thoughts. As a result nothing came of Anthony's pleas to the king, the matter was dropped, and the Scottish lodges—for all intents and purposes—remained independent. If either William Schaw or Sir Anthony Alexander had succeeded in establishing the Master of Works as de facto Grand

Master over all the lodges, it would have been as a government-appointed position—and one not necessarily filled by a mason. Instead that question hung in abeyance for a hundred years until 1736. In that year Scottish Masons met and chose their own Grand Master, from amongst themselves.

Being caught in the middle of that tug-of-war for control of the lodges seemed to take its toll on John Mylne, causing him to resign his position of Master Mason to the Crown in 1636. Yet he insured the office stayed in good hands by yielding it in favor of his eldest son, John. The senior Mylne continued to ply his craft for some years thereafter, but in the gentler climes of Kirkcaldy and Dundee to the north.

His son, who became known as John the Younger, had already proved his worth by assisting on the work at Holyrood palace. He was a member of the lodge in Edinburgh, and became honored as a burgess of Edinburgh in 1633. John the Younger would hold this position of king's Master Mason for thirty-one years, during which time he managed to serve the lodges and the king without detriment to either.[205]

If there was a smooth transition from stonemasons' lodges to Freemasonry, as many have suggested, the Schaw Statutes and St. Clair letters did not reveal it. Did it come in the years which followed, when a number of extraordinary events took place?

On 20 May 1641, John Mylne the Younger and another representative from the Lodge of Edinburgh (Mary's Chapel) went to Newcastle in England where they admitted two gentlemen, Robert Moray and Alexander Hamilton, into the lodge.[206] Moray and Hamilton were Scottish officers, and this extraordinary lodge meeting took place beside a battlefield between the Scottish and English armies.

Among the stonemasons' lodges whose records have survived, it was rare to find a person who was made a mason outside of the lodge room, although it could be done. The Moray and Hamilton ceremony was not just performed outside of the lodge, it was performed outside of the country. In fact, this is the first officially recorded time a gentleman was made a mason in England, by any lodge. This action was accepted by the lodge in Edinburgh and became official. Robert Moray would later be raised to knighthood and become instrumental in the Invisible College and Royal Society in London.

His admission to this Scottish lodge was followed five years later by a similar honor bestowed on an Englishman. This event seemed to be the first time an English lodge admitted a gentleman who was not a working mason. At that occasion on 16 October 1646, Elias Ashmole reported he was made a mason in a ceremony conducted at the home of his father-in-law, in the presence of other gentlemen. The odd thing about Ashmole's admission into masonry was that none of the people present appear to have been stonemasons. This stood in marked contrast to what was happening in Scotland. Was England following a different path? The search for an answer takes us southward to London.

The Masons Livery Company in London, which originally was strictly a working lodge, was going through its own changes. It had been a group of craftsmen in 1481 when King Edward IV granted to the Company the coveted right to wear a distinctive Livery and march in the city's formal ceremonies. In the group's internal records, which were preserved from 1620 onwards, there was a clearly seen preoccupation with trade affairs and membership. Fees were collected at all four levels of membership: becoming an entered apprentice, "coming on the yeomandry," being made a Master Mason, then coming on the Livery, which was the highest class of membership.

However in 1621 a new class of fee was recorded. For some reason, men who were already masons within the Company, and even some who held the high position of Liverymen, were charged a new fee to be made Masons. Later, even the Warden, the second-highest officer in the Company was charged a fee for his "acception." Two entries in 1650 seem to show individuals, possibly gentlemen, joining the Company at a high level and paying fees for "coming on the Liverie & admission uppon Acceptance of Masonry." Harry Carr sought to explain those strange events this way.

> Up to this time (1650) the majority of men who had
> joined the Acception were masons by trade who had

gone through the usual stages of apprenticeship, the "yeomandry," and occasionally the livery. In a few instances where records are incomplete their precise status in the trade and in the Company is doubtful, but the historian of the London Masons' Company (E. Conder, *The Hole Crafte and Fellowship of Masons*) concludes from his analysis of the records that several men were being admitted to the Acception who had no connexion at all with the trade or the Company.[207]

These activities in London seemed to show stonemasons bringing people from outside the craft into masonry. Did this then lead to Freemasonry as we know it today? Many have been sure that it did.

Regretfully, no documentation connects the Masons Livery Company with any of the lodges that formed the Grand Lodge in 1717. The Masons Livery Company, which still exists today as a charitable organization, took this matter a step further with its own clarification. It acknowledged past rumors, but asserted that it had no direct link to Freemasonry.[208] This has made the matter more of a mystery.

The question of connections between working stonemason lodges and Freemasonry was further complicated by the fact that virtually no records exist from English lodges prior to 1670. Of the four lodges that formed the Grand Lodge, none seem to have records that go back before 1695. Working lodges of stonemasons certainly existed outside of London, since great structures such as York Minster had to be built in these places. Yet none of their records have been preserved for us other than an occasional sheet of paper. They give us no record of English lodges transitioning from working stonemasons to Freemasons.

In Scotland, however, it was a different story. There we can definitely find records of transitions that occurred in some of the lodges. When changes came, however, they seemed to have had more to do with sharp drops in membership and natural disasters.

These disasters were a chain of raging fires that destroyed much of Edinburgh in the years before 1674, racing through the wooden buildings that filled the city up to that time.[209] To prevent this from happening again, the Town Council ordered that all damaged buildings be replaced with ones made of stone. This incredible bonanza of work for stonemasons would give the impression that it was ushering in a golden age of prosperity for the Edinburgh lodge. In fact, the opposite took place. The city of Edinburgh immediately became flooded with people from other towns and countries willing to do masonry work. Local contractors gladly threw these new workers onto job sites to meet the incredible demand for construction. As a result, the lodge in Edinburgh began to have trouble getting apprentices to pass to Fellow Craft, since that required payment of fees as well as additional obligations. Apprentices who had finished their term of service could find more work than they could handle, so there was no incentive for them to go up to a higher level within the craft.

The increase in work also led to a new lodge being started at Canongate, in the eastern part of the city. That encroached on the monopoly once held by the Lodge of Edinburgh (Mary's Chapel). This tearing of the fabric continued when another lodge was formed in 1688 by members seceding from Mary's Chapel. In fact, many incoming stonemasons seemed to find work in Scotland without having to join any lodge at all. Having lost control of masonry work, membership in the Lodge of Edinburgh (Mary's Chapel) dwindled. It became pre-occupied with finances rather than masonry work. Even its own journeymen took the lodge into the Law Courts in 1715 to get more oversight of the funds being managed. The death knell for this honored working lodge came in 1726 and the following year. This was nine years after Freemasons in London had already formed their Grand Lodge.

> In December 1726 one of the members, James Mack, reported that a number of "creditable tradesmen" in the city were anxious to join the Lodge, and were each of them willing to give "a guinea in gold for the use of the poor." The proposed candidates were all men from other trades, and although the golden guineas were very tempting, the diehard operatives in the Lodge rejected the proposal.

A month later Mack returned to the attack, at a meeting which he had apparently called without permission of the Master of the Lodge. The question of the proposed admissions was reopened, and there was a thundering row. The Master and Warden "walked out," and the remaining five proceeded to elect new officers, choosing Mack as "preses" or Master. Three "entered-apprentices" from other lodges, *all non-operative*, were admitted and passed F.C.;[210] and seven burgesses, *none of them masons*, were received "entered apprentices and fellow crafts." In February 1727 another eight non-operatives were admitted, and the operative character of the Lodge was completely lost. The extent of the change may be judged from the fact that in 1736, when the Lodge compiled its first complete code of By-laws, not a single regulation was made which concerned the mason trade. The transition was virtually complete![211]

In other words, this was not the gradual, evolutionary change evoked by the word "transition." It was more consistent with the term *coup d'état*, in which new people abruptly took over the prior organization and put it to new use.

With the Lodge of Edinburgh being an ancient "flagship" of stonemasonry in Scotland, the other stonemason lodges eventually followed its course, without the need for an explosive meeting. They either brought in many members from outside masonry, or closed their doors and went out of existence.

So the easy route of assuming that stonemasons' lodges made a gradual transition to Freemasons' lodges has not turned out to match the actual events. It was seen earlier that William Schaw was far from being the father of Freemasonry. Other difficulties followed, such as the major stonemason lodge in London—the Masons Livery Company—having had no visible or claimed role in the 1717 emergence of Freemasonry in that city. Then came the abrupt takeover of Edinburgh (Mary's Chapel). All the easy explanations of Freemasonry being created by stonemasons' lodges seem to be in somewhat of a shambles.

Clearly we need to know more before we can say what actually happened at that time. Freemasonry came from somewhere, and had some relationship to stonemasons' lodges. But what happened during those secretive early years? Was the relationship of gentlemen's lodges to the stonemasons' lodges only symbolic, or was it something more?

And what of the other early paths that have been suggested for Freemasonry, such as some relationship to the Knights Templar? Alternatively, was Freemasonry just an eating and drinking fraternity and nothing more? To explore these different paths we need to look deeper into the deeds of Freemasons and other gentlemen from the time of the Templars up to the emergence of Freemasonry into public view.

The Brotherhood

The knights among the Templars had come from the noble families of Europe. For the most part they were the younger sons in those households, where only the eldest could inherit the title and lands of the family. As we saw earlier, sending younger sons to be monks was a time-honored way to remove them from contention for the family title. When the Templars were arrested in 1307 and some of those sons were subjected to torture, while all the rest were declared heretic, the anger of those noble families must have been difficult to contain. Yet contain it they did, for the king had ordered it, and the pope affirmed it. Those were powers that could not be challenged.

But these families, indirectly attacked in this way, could still care for their sons. When the trials ended and their slain brothers were mourned, the surviving knights needed to look forward and emerge from the covert houses in which they had taken refuge. Their families could not welcome them openly and risk the wrath of king and Church, but they could help quietly—restoring their sons to some semblance of their former life. Given a reasonable estate, with a manor house and fields to support it, the fugitive knight could assume whatever name he chose, register his property, and eventually return to a significant role in society. Freed from the restrictions of celibacy, he could sire his own children, and teach them the lessons he learned during a difficult life. One of the strongest lessons would have been about the brotherhood that ultimately saved his life. A return to the lodging house where he lived during the most difficult years would have been natural, along with feeling a strong need to respond to brothers in distress—even as he had once been in need himself, and received that relief.

The clerical brothers among the Templars had likewise folded their green robes for the last time, laid them down, and gone to live in that underground world. They took with them a high degree of literacy and whatever level of skill in finance, commerce and legal matters they had been able to hone while in the Order. Upon the cessation of their brothers' trials and tribulations, these men would have had to move on, just as their knightly brothers had done. Yet a different world awaited them. There were no rich family members to embrace them, nor were fertile estates given to them. Yet they were not without strengths of their own. The monetary, legal and organizational skills that enabled them to build and operate one of the greatest financial systems in the world were still with them. Using a covert piece of former Templar property as collateral, or imposing upon a noble brother for such a lien, they would soon be back in business again, serving as a trader, builder, financial provider or practitioner of the law.

These former clerics no longer needed to send the earnings of their labor to battlefields in the East to be consumed in the fire of warfare. So any profits could now stay and multiply in their own well-trained hands. Mindful of the dark days when they needed shelter, and received the assistance of Templar brothers, they would likewise be unable to refuse requests for help. Employing their former servingmen or clerical brothers when asked, or providing professional assistance to noble brothers when needed, their life went on. The clandestine lodging places they once occupied would not likely have been forgotten. Returning to spend an occasional evening with former brothers would have sufficed to keep the memory alive. Like their knightly brethren, they could also give themselves children to carry on their name and their small but growing fortunes. How much they would tell their children about the life they had lived would depend on each man. But the lessons they learned—the brotherhood, the wariness of unlimited church or state power, and the blessings of literacy—these they could pass on to their children with an urgency their children might not understand. Those lessons would stand them in good stead in a difficult world.

When the Templars' large preceptory in London was seized by the king after 1307, it was recorded that a number of clerical practitioners of the law were in residence there, and that they claimed to hold leases. Though the preceptory property passed through several hands thereafter, it was always leased to these barristers. In due course the property was deeded to the barristers' legal associations and became two of the Inns of Court—known as Inner Temple and Middle Temple. These barristers still occupy the Templar grounds and buildings today. It is not known if those original clerical practitioners once wore green robes.

The servingmen of the Templar Order did not have the bountiful opportunities accorded to the knights and clerics. They had lived the life of tradesmen and assistants, earning their room and board with the skill of their hands and the sweat of their brow. But they had also learned discipline and the same high standards as the knights and clerks who considered themselves among the best in the world at what they did. That was a thing of value. And they had experienced something that was both wonderful and terrible: though they may have come from mean circumstances, they had been treated like brothers by men of noble blood and high education. It would be difficult for them to go back to being a piece of chattel on a rich man's property, a condition that afflicted most of their peers in those days.

When they no longer had to live in hiding and could go out into society as their own man, it would be understandable if they did so with some trepidation and concern. A few might not have ventured out at all, preferring to stay on as innkeepers in the old lodgings. There they would be hosts for the private gatherings of their brothers—the men who had once been Templars. Those stepping out into the world would of course have made their first request for employment to the former knights and clerics of their order, who could not have refused them. The former servingmen had skills at maintaining estates, assisting gentlemen, and performing trades such as masonry and carpentry. These were all valuable services that could help their more fortunate brothers sustain their properties and holdings. When they had their feet under them, these working brothers might then move on to a higher position, or go into their own trade as a master.

For almost two hundred years the Knights Templar were renowned for their unquestioned devotion to God, courage, secrecy, financial prowess, discipline and unity. It was intended to be a good preparation for battle. It may also have been a good preparation for life.

It is not known if Thomas Gresham was a Freemason, but his actions influenced and advanced Freemasonry to such an extent that the question is a reasonable one. He was born into a family of gentlemen who identified themselves as being from the noble line resident at Gresham manor in Norfolk. Yet he could trace his own heritage back only to John Gresham in 1340 at the nearby town of Aylmerton. This situation would be typical for a younger son or grandson being given a small property but excluded from the primary family title. The father of that John Gresham had his identity obscured for some reason during those post-Templar years.

By the time Thomas Gresham was born around 1519, his father and uncle were well established merchants in London. They prospered in the importing and exporting of goods between England and various countries in Europe, and both men had served as Lord Mayor of London for a period of time. Each of them had also been knighted by King Henry VIII for service to the crown. Using this favorable heritage as a springboard, Thomas Gresham went on to exceed both his forbears in the art of trade and financial management, amassing a great fortune in the process. One of the landmarks in his career came in 1565 when he offered to build a central exchange for the City of London, to be used by merchants dealing in foreign trade. All the City had to do was donate the land. The City astutely accepted this offer, and the Royal Exchange was born. Gresham's return for this was a princely £700 per year in rents that he collected from the merchants who opened offices in the Exchange. This widely-celebrated establishment was officially opened by Queen Elizabeth I, who granted use of the royal title.

Beyond all the national acclaim, however, there was a more private side to Thomas Gresham. It compelled him to write into his will that the two crown jewels of his estate, the Exchange and his nearby manor on Bishopsgate, should be used to create a college for higher education—the first to be built in London. As incredible as it may seem, there were only two universities in England at that time, and they were located in the cities of Oxford and Cambridge. London was unrepresented. Upon his passing, there was a delay in launching the college due to his wife being allowed to live in the manor for the remainder of her life. After seventeen years, however, Gresham College was opened to great acclaim in 1597.

This college grew into more than a commitment to higher education, for it had several other unique attributes. It was free of charge to all the citizens of London, an exceptional aspect in itself. This was made possible by the land and buildings being donated free and clear, with rents from Thomas Gresham's Exchange covering all of the operating costs. Next, the choice of subjects to be taught was quite unusual. He funded chairs for professors in geometry, astronomy, physic,[212] law, divinity, rhetoric and music. The last five were the traditional subjects taught in colleges at that time. However neither Cambridge nor Oxford had chairs in geometry and astronomy. It should be noted that geometry was a central part of Freemasonry, as evidenced not only by internal Masonic teachings but through the immediately recognized square-and-compass symbol by which it is known around the world.

The choice of astronomy as an endowed chair was a little more subtle. Up to this time, higher education was almost exclusively the domain of the Church. As noted earlier, religious clerics were the literate individuals in Europe, with nobles having a smattering of that art and commons receiving almost none at all. The original purpose of the universities was to educate and graduate clerics, with positions as university instructors being almost completely limited to clerics as well. When Henry VIII replaced the Catholic Church with the Church of England in 1534, the new Protestant

Fig. 30 Thomas Gresham founded Gresham College,
the first home of the Royal Society.

practitioners simply stepped into the shoes of their Catholic predecessors. As late as the 1700s, graduates of Oxford became ordained ministers before they could teach. The new religious leaders simply extended the long-standing role the Catholic Church had played in determining what was proper education and what was heresy. In 1543 Nicolaus Copernicus published his controversial finding that the earth revolved around the sun. The Catholic Church denied this as heresy. By 1579 Gresham made his own position clear by establishing a professorship to teach astronomy at his college, regardless of the feelings of the Church. To put this in perspective, Galileo Galilei publicly declared his support for the findings of Copernicus in 1610 and was put on trial for heresy. He was found guilty, and died under house arrest in Italy.

Control by Church and state blanketed all aspects of life at that time, not just education. Those who wore the crown or the mitre could—after serious deliberation or on a whim—make decisions to their liking and enforce them by casting people into prison or taking their life. The Knights Templar were not the only ones to whom this happened, but they were a clear example. Gresham College made no requirement that professors have a predetermined religious background. There also was no funding from the state, and therefore no control by the state over class content. Moreover, the lecture classes were not limited to clergy or nobles. All could come and meet on the same level, and receive an education. This college would also be one of the catalysts for Freemasonry's emergence into public view in the years which followed.

In Scotland we saw the Mylne family produce many generations of prominent stonemasons, and it began when the first John Mylne was chosen Master Mason to the Crown. This was not a position one achieved simply by hewing stones. The king had to know the craftsman personally, or the craftsman needed connections with prominent families who could influence the king to make such an appointment. As there was no indication that Mylne knew the king personally, he reasonably needed to rely on the latter route. Personal connections such as this generally worked for one man, but rarely for his son, as illustrated by the many different Masters of Work and similar positions in Britain that were constantly awarded to new men from different families. The odd thing about John Mylne was that different members of his family were appointed to be the king's Master Mason from 1481 to 1710. Each time a new king's whim might point toward appointing someone from outside the family, influence was brought to bear and a new Mylne was granted the next appointment. There is no way for us to know how this family of simple stonemasons came to be on intimate terms with so many influential nobles or merchants, or how that close relationship was passed down from generation to generation. All we know is that it seemed to have happened.

Several Mylnes were Master of the Lodge of Scone[213] and Perth, as well as being members of the Lodge of Edinburgh (Mary's Chapel). In 1641, when a later John Mylne was Master Mason to the Crown, he also led the Edinburgh lodge during the historic entering of Sir Robert Moray and another gentleman.

Moray was the son of Mungo Moray of Craigie, a town on the outskirts of Scone.[214]   Robert's grandfather was the 8th Lord of Abercairney, and could trace an unbroken line back to Sir William Moray in 1289. It is interesting that Robert Moray's family and Mylne's family lived side by side near Scone for many generations. There also seemed to be sufficient connection between them that Mylne would travel to England for the purpose of entering Moray into masonry. There is no way to know if the Morays were among the connections that enabled the Mylnes to be Master Mason to the Crown for most of the years during a 229-year span of time, nor how these stonemasons and nobles originally found common ground. But these are the facts as they occurred.

The young man who would become Sir Robert Moray, Freemason and confidant of several kings, left home at the age of twenty-four to join the Scots Guards. Being from a noble family but without a grand inheritance, this was his best chance for adventure, fame and fortune, especially since the Guards were employed by Louis XIII of France on the continent. Those duties gave Moray the unexpected reward of working closely with Cardinal Richelieu—the French cleric and prime minister whose power rivaled that of the king. In 1638 Robert returned to serve in the Scottish army at Edinburgh, a group that came to be known as the Covenanters. Displaying commendable leadership and experience, he was named General of Ordnance in the Scottish Army that invaded England and captured Newcastle-upon-Tyne. It was there that he was initiated into masonry on 20 May 1641 by a small delegation from Lodge of Edinburgh (Mary's Chapel). Moray adopted the five-pointed star as part of his mason's mark, and employed it often in signing letters from that time forward.

When Cardinal Richelieu died on 4 December 1642, it was Robert Moray who carried this news to Charles I, the king who reigned over England, Scotland and Ireland. Those two men's lives became closely entwined thereafter. Only nine years older than Moray, Charles was the son of King James VI of Scotland. Like his father, Charles was burdened with the difficult task of balancing competing demands from his Scottish, Irish and English dominions. Charles' relations with his subjects was further strained by his belief in the divine right of kings, which caused considerable conflict with the fairly weak Parliament. When he declared war on Spain, Parliament audaciously attempted to limit his access to funds to prosecute that war. So Charles summarily dismissed the Parliament and began to assess additional taxes without the consent of the governed. He allowed Parliament to remain disbanded for eleven years.

His relationships in Scotland were not much better. Charles attempted to impose the Church of England's practice of ecumenicalism (where bishops provided leadership) in place of Scottish presbyterianism (where elected members of congregations provided the leadership). That drove away many religious leaders. Among Scottish nobility, many were offended that Charles lived in London and favored English nobility for prestigious positions. The incursion by Moray and the Scottish army into Northern England, which resulted in the capture of Newcastle, was a bid to force Charles to finally come to terms with Scotland's demands. The plan succeeded, and Charles was forced to summon a new Parliament to approve the Treaty of London, yielding to Scots their self-determination in religious matters and removing numerous supporters of the Anglican Church of England from Scottish government positions.

When Parliament continued to press for redress of perceived abuses of power by Charles, he angrily burst into the House of Commons on 4 January 1642 to arrest some of its members and confront Oliver Cromwell. This forced a rupture between king and Parliament that quickly moved to the battlefield. Charles transferred his court to Oxford, raised an army, and rallied the northern and western counties of England behind him. Parliament stayed in London, assembled an army of its own, and rallied the southern and eastern counties behind its angry rebellion. The debilitating English Civil War ensued.

Many Scots felt reassured by the king's previous concessions, and saw in England's troubles a chance to win additional grants from their distant monarch. Others were decidedly less forgiving and felt a common cause with the Parliamentarians. It was during these tumultuous days that Robert Moray had come to Charles with the news concerning Cardinal Richelieu. Charles seemed to quickly see the value of this Scot who knew his way around the French court, and asked for Robert's help in mitigating his current difficulties. Accordingly, the king conferred knighthood upon Moray on the 10th of January in 1643, and sent him to France as the crown's emissary. All of these things would be important in Moray's later Masonic activities.

Unfortunately, King Louis XIII died four months later, and Sir Robert Moray found himself without traction in the new French court. Still only thirty-four years of age, Robert was resilient enough to begin building rapport again by accepting a commission as Colonel of the Scots Guard in the service of the French king. On campaign in Germany later that year, he was captured and held in Bavaria for ransom. Seventeen months later, the prime minister of France, Cardinal Mazarin, finally paid the £16,500 demanded by the Germans and obtained Moray's release on 28 April 1645.

Just over a month later, while Robert was still recovering from his ordeal, he learned that the army of Charles I had been destroyed at the town of Naseby about sixty miles northwest of London. This was a pivotal victory by the military forces of Parliament under Sir Thomas Fairfax and Oliver Cromwell, but Robert knew the fighting was not over. As in any swordfight, a series of parries and thrusts were made by both sides. Everything boiled down to the Siege of Oxford in April of 1646. The king managed to escape, only to find himself out of options. Rather than surrender to English Parliament forces, Charles gave himself up to the Scottish army at Newark, about fourteen miles northeast of Nottingham. He then relied upon the Scots' previously-established willingness to negotiate, and Moray rushed back from France to participate. There, beside the woods made famous by a man named Robin Hood, Moray counseled the king to escape. Upon hearing that the plan called for him to dress like a woman, Charles indignantly declined and remained in captivity. Sir Robert stayed at the king's side as negotiations opened between the Scottish and English forces on how to resolve the crisis without renewed fighting.

Robert Moray's loyalty to his king would come to pay tremendous dividends for Freemasons and Britain.

Chapter 18

Invisible College
and Royal Society

While Sir Robert Moray and King Charles were encamped in the North, a completely different meeting took place in Central England that was of considerable significance to Freemasons. This was the private ceremony in which Elias Ashmole was made a Freemason. He was far from being the first gentleman to be so raised, for he was brought in by other gentlemen. However he was the first Englishman for whom written records clearly showed admission into Freemasonry. And his contributions would go beyond his lodge membership.

Ashmole's family had been rich in name but poor in purse when he was born in 1617 at Lichfield near Birmingham. Those family connections were useful to him as a young solicitor in London, where he labored as a lawyer on civil affairs. There he married a woman in similar circumstances, Eleanor Mainwaring, whose poor but aristocratic family helped establish him among the society of the day. Being a supporter of Charles I, Elias was soon appointed King's Commissioner of Excise—that is to say tax collector—at Lichfield in 1644. This was followed by a more influential posting as ordnance officer at Oxford during the time this city served as Charles' headquarters in his war with Parliament.

For whatever reason, Oxford became a touchstone for a number of illustrious men who found their way into Freemasonry during this time. Ashmole lived in one of the university halls, where he undertook the study of mathematics and physics. Those subjects then drew him into astronomy, astrology, and magic. When the war turned against Charles late in 1645, Elias prudently moved to Worcester to accept the position of Commissioner of Excise. With this came a nominal appointment as an artillery captain in Lord Astley's Regiment of Foot, though he was not known to have seen actual combat duty. In any event, Worcester fell to the army of Parliament in July of 1646, and Elias retired to the home of his father-in-law, Peter Mainwaring.

It was at this time that Ashmole recorded in his diary the following entry for 16 October 1646:

> 4^H.30 P.M. I was made a Free-Mason at Warrington in Lancashire, wth Coll: Henry Mainwaring of Karincham in Cheshire. The Names of those that were then of the Lodge, Mr Rich Penkett Warden. Mr James Collier, Mr Rich Sanchey, Henry Littler, John Ellam, Rich Ellam, & Hugh Brewer.[215]

Though Elias was now connected through the invisible links of a secret society with Sir Robert Moray, the two men would not meet for several years. In the meantime, Elias's wife passed away, casting him back into the social pool. There the Englishman found a new mate and proceeded in 1649 to wed Mary, Lady Mainwaring, a distant member of his first wife's family. This brought him rich estates around Bradfield in Berkshire, about forty miles west of London. Being independently wealthy, he was then able to pursue his many interests which included—in addition to Freemasonry—translating several Latin texts on alchemy, compiling a catalogue on botany with John Tradescant, developing his own catalogue on the Roman coin collection of the Bodleian Library, and compiling several lavish editions on coats of arms. In 1660 the king appointed him Commissioner, then Comptroller, for the Excise in London. This was followed by the position of Accountant General of the Excise, which made him responsible for much of the king's revenue. With it came considerable income for himself as well as patronage power.

Ashmole then received a doctorate in medicine from the University of Oxford in 1669, and eight years later made a significant gift to the university. It would bring him a measure of lasting fame, for his donation was the Ashmolean Museum. This donation included the fabulous botanical collection assembled from around the world that his friend John Tradescant had deeded to him, and to which he had added considerable materials of his own. The collections came to Oxford with the proviso that the university erect a suitable building to house the materials, and that the museum be open to the public. Similar to the endowment of Thomas Gresham, this gift broke new ground by creating one of the first museums in Europe not held for private use, but for public use and benefit. Oxford followed through, and the Ashmolean Museum has become one of the premier collections of manmade artifacts and natural specimens around the world.[216, 217]

In this same vein, the scientific world and Freemasonry were about to join in a major undertaking, as we will soon see.

The exploits of his fellow Freemason, Sir Robert Moray, were also intricately woven into the events of this time. After Robert's attempts to help Charles I escape proved fruitless, that monarch was turned over by the Scots to the English Parliamentary forces in exchange for enough money to pay the Scottish soldiers' wages. Yet even that resolution did not bring peace. By early 1648, Charles promised sufficient concessions to Scottish leaders that they rallied to his cause and the Civil War began again. With this, the patience of Oliver Cromwell and the other Parliamentary leaders ran out. Charles was put on trial at Westminster for high treason and publicly executed on January 30, 1649.

Not content to let the matter rest, Robert Moray hurried to France where the late king's son, also named Charles, lived in exile. Sir Robert and other Scots then managed to persuade the young Prince of Wales to return to Scone, the ancestral home of Scottish kings located north of Edinburgh. In that auspicious place

Fig. 31   Elias Ashmole, raised as a Freemason in 1646

the royal heir was crowned King Charles II of Scotland on the 1st of January 1651. To gain the English crown as well, Charles set off at the head of a military force, made up chiefly of Scots, to confront the Parliamentary army. This confrontation occurred at Worcester in Western England during September of 1651, but did not turn out well for the young monarch. He was compelled to retreat from the field, and had to take up residence in France once again.

Sir Robert stayed in Scotland this time and was elevated to the position of Lord Justice Clerk, one of the highest judicial positions in the land. He was also named a Privy Councillor, or personal advisor to the king. After participating in an unsuccessful Scottish uprising in 1653, Moray judiciously spent several years in continental Europe where he rejoined Charles II.

The death of Oliver Cromwell five years later left the Parliamentarians in England divided and unable to rule their country. As a last resort, they agreed to the return of Charles, and to his being crowned King of England and Ireland. The young Scottish monarch returned to England and began his reign there on the 29th of May in 1660. His formal coronation followed later at Westminster Abbey, not far from where his father had been executed eleven years earlier.

A few months after he helped Charles take his place as king of England, Sir Robert Moray found himself at an historic meeting in Gresham College. The men gathered at Gresham on the 28th of November in 1660 were involved in a conspiracy to overthrow the control held by church and state over what could be understood, believed and taught in the realm. Thomas Gresham had planted the seeds for this conspiracy when he founded his college. It was now sixty-three years later and the people attracted to his cause—including Moray and other members of the secret society that has come to be known as the Invisible College—were preparing to storm the barricades of power.

The cautionary tale of Galileo Galilei was still fresh in the minds of those nervous men, since he had died under house arrest only eighteen years earlier for the heresy of declaring that the earth revolved around the sun. Moray's associates had been making numerous scientific discoveries about the world, and were doing so without the permission of the church. That meant they risked denunciation—and the punishment Galileo received—each time they dared put some part of their findings forward to the public. Their animated discussion that night in 1660 turned to the need for the king's stamp of approval on their inquiries—an official imprimatur—so that they could publish without fear of arrest or charges of heresy. If that could be achieved, they hoped for a revolution which could improve the life of every person, high and low.

In this regard Sir Robert Moray was a critical player at the table. He came to them fresh from having helped install the new king of England, and had unparalleled access to the crown. That night at Gresham he agreed to carry forward their proposal, and the Royal Society came into being.

Over the years the Royal Society would produce ground-breaking work on steam engines, electricity, biology, medicine and many other areas of endeavor. Gifted people such as Isaac Newton would take turns leading this radical group, and others including Benjamin Franklin would be elected to its membership. But these were still the early days, and Moray actively joined in plotting the society's course.

One of the other catalysts around whom these men gathered was Christopher Wren, the professor of astronomy at Gresham College. It was after his lecture at the college that the historic meeting was held to launch this society. Both Wren and Moray were Freemasons, and in some unknown way Sir Robert's sympathies to the cause of Wren and these co-conspirators had become known.

It seems clear, however, that this event at Gresham was not a wholly Masonic meeting. Although a number of practices from Freemasonry were clearly incorporated into their proceedings, the group did not meet with full Masonic ceremony and observances. This suggests that some of the participants were not Freemasons but simply shared the same values as those who were members.

They did not seem like typical revolutionaries who worked by candlelight in musty cellars while writing emotional manifestos. Instead they were twelve gentlemen[218] who met in well-appointed rooms and brought results of their experiments and explorations in chemistry, architecture, mathematics, astronomy, languages and other diverse interests. For at least fifteen years they met in secret, due to the risks involved in what they were doing. As a result this group became known as the Invisible College, as described here by one of its members, Robert Boyle, in 1646.

> The best on't is, that the corner-stones of the *Invisible* (or, as they term themselves, the Philosophical) *College*, do now and then honour me with their company, which makes me as sorry for those pressing occasions that urge my departure....[219]

John Wallis, an active member of the group, described their proceedings this way.

> About the year 1645, while I lived in London (at a time, when, by our Civil Wars, Academical Studies were much interrupted in both our Universities)...I had the opportunity of being acquainted with divers worthy Persons, inquisitive into Natural Philosophy, and other parts of Humane Learning; and particularly of what hath been called the New Philosophy, or Experimental Philosophy.
>
> We did by agreement, divers of us, meet weekly in London on a certain day, to treat and discourse of such affairs. Of which number Dr. John Wilkins (afterward Bishop of Chester) Dr. Jonathan Goddard, Dr. George Ent, Dr. Glisson, Dr. Merret, (Drs. In Physick) Mr. Samuel Foster then Professor of Astronomy at Gresham College, Mr. Theodore Hank ...and many others.
>
> Our business was (precluding matters of Theology and State Affairs) to discourse and consider of Philosophical Enquiries, and such as related there-unto; as Physick, Anatomy, Geometry, Astronomy, Navigation, Staticks, Magneticks, Chymicks, Mechanicks, and Natural Experiments....

About the year 1648/1649, some of our company being removed to Oxford (first Dr. Wilkins, then I, and soon after Dr. Goddard) our company divided. Those in London continued to meet there as before (and we with them, when we had occasion to be there) and those of us at Oxford with Dr. Ward (since Bishop of Salisbury) Dr. Ralph Bathurst (now President of Trinity College in Oxford) Dr. Petty (since Sir William Petty) Dr. Willis (then an eminent Physician in Oxford) and divers others, continued such meetings in Oxford; and brought those Studies into fashion there....[220]

Several similarities between their unusual practices and those of Freemasonry are readily apparent. Meeting in secret was one of those similar elements, but one that a group of people could decide to do for many reasons. And clearly their secrecy was weakly enforced, for one of the participants wrote about their activities and sent it to someone who was not there.

As we will soon see, Freemasonry was still in the stage where its brothers met and acted in complete secrecy. Their meetings were not advertised, the places where they met were not identified, and their members were not known other than the handful we have been able to discover. It was truly a secret society in every sense. After Freemasons emerged into the light of day in 1717 all of that changed. Freemasons could then truthfully say they belonged to a "society with secrets" from that day forward. However that day had not yet come.

Returning to the meetings of the Invisible College, John Wallis noted another interesting practice in these gatherings. They precluded "matters of Theology and State Affairs." In other words, religion and politics were off limits.

As every Freemason knows, there is a firm prohibition against the discussion of religion or politics in any Masonic meeting. This suggests early Freemasons experienced harsh lessons with those topics and learned to keep them out of their meetings. That does not mean religious values were not important in Masonry. Quite the opposite. No one could become a Mason unless they believed in God. It was one of the unshakable requirements.[221] But there was no requirement on how a brother was to believe in God. His religion was his own affair, and in no way was it allowed to interfere with his being a brother to another man.

If the Invisible College sprang from the university system, as the appearance of such highly educated people might suggest, how could they not have allowed the discussion of religion at their meetings? Divinity was one of the main subjects taught and discussed at every university of that day. In addition, the Catholic Church was the first sponsor of the university, then that role was taken over by the Anglican Church. To teach there, one had to be ordained and become a deacon. Moreover, the whole purpose of this conspiratorial group was to limit the Church's ability to control what was known and taught. Clearly this was not a university institution.

Were these rules drawn from some society other than Freemasonry? It has not been unusual for groups to informally have a preference that religion and politics not disturb the peace of their gatherings. They might even suggest such discussions were impolite. However there was almost never been a written or absolute requirement that those subjects not be discussed in meetings. That was a rare prohibition.

This rule shared by the Invisible College and Freemasonry produced surprising results. Consider one of the college's members, John Wilkins, who graduated from Oxford and received ordination as a minister. In 1641 he anonymously published the first book in English on cryptography titled *Mercury, or the Secret and Swift Messenger*. Anonymous publication was one way to get around the risk of publishing new material that might offend someone in the church or government and draw an accusation of heresy or treason. His work in this book eventually led to the invention of the telegraph. Seven years later, when he was already a member of the Invisible College, Wilkins was named warden of Wadham College in Oxford University. In 1656 he married the sister of Oliver Cromwell, who at that time was Lord Protector of England. His powerful relative arranged for Wilkins to be named Master of the prestigious Trinity College at Cambridge University. In other words, he was deeply involved on the Parliamentarian side in the English Civil War.

Sir Robert Moray, on the other hand had been a personal advisor to Charles I and then held an even closer advisory role to his son, Charles II. Few could have been identified as more committed to the royal side in this civil war. So how could John Wilkins, brother-in-law to Oliver Cromwell, be involved in the Invisible College with Sir Robert Moray? It should be remembered that Cromwell presided over the execution of young Charles' father. Charles II returned the favor by having Cromwell's body dug up and decapitated posthumously. If the subject of politics had ever come up, Wilkins and Moray would surely have been at each other's throat. But the Freemason rule was applied, and neither man spoke of religion or politics in those meetings. In the absence of that divisive discussion, they were able to develop a deep respect for each other's abilities and contributions. At the meeting in 1660 when the Royal Society was created, Sir Robert Moray was chosen as president of the group, and John Wilkins was named its secretary.

It is also notable that Elias Ashmole was at Oxford in 1645, and a year later was made a Freemason. For some reason this was considered the most suitable place for members of the Invisible College to live and work outside of London. Among the other unexplored questions involving Oxford and the secretive societies of interest to us was the matter of the Knights Templar presence in that city. When first Grand Master Hugh de Payens visited England in 1128 along with a group of his Templar brothers, Oxford was the only university in Britain.[222] It undoubtedly would have drawn the attention of the literate brothers among them. Years later, when the Sandford estate near Oxford was donated to the Templars, it was quickly elevated to serve as an important Templar center.[223] Although a map of this estate has not been recovered, it apparently was the large property bounded by Temple Road, Marsh Road, and Oxford Road. It thus stood only one-and-a-half miles from Magdalen College on the Oxford University campus, a distance that could be walked in thirty minutes. Being a prominent estate, this Oxford land could not be concealed when disaster struck in 1307, so the displaced Templars were forced to abandon it and find other accommodations in the area.[224] More investigation is needed before it can be determined what happened at Oxford during all these occurrences, but when combined with the Invisible College and other activities we will see at Oxford, it is somewhat intriguing.

The Royal Society became officially sanctioned when Sir Robert Moray followed through on his commitment to speak with Charles II and obtained for his compatriots the formality of a Charter of Incorporation on the 15th of July, 1662.[225] At this event William Vicount Brouncker was named president of the Society. A second Charter was requested and issued the following year, listing Charles II as Founder, and expanding its official name to The Royal Society of London for Promoting Natural Knowledge.

Membership in the Royal Society subsequently became a veritable Who's Who of famous individuals. Nor was it just a social club. These men soon produced a stream of discoveries that extensively expanded the level of knowledge in the arts and sciences, from which we still benefit today. In addition to Sir Isaac Newton's contributions on gravity and physics, Christopher Wren made a lasting impression on architecture in England. Edmond Halley produced work in astronomy that earned him a comet named in his honor. Robert Hooke created the term "cell" to describe the basic unit of life. Freemason Elias Ashmole, also among the first people invited to be a fellow of the Royal Society, became recognized for his work in botany and chemistry.

Of these men, Christopher Wren was particularly intriguing. This was not only due to his being part of the Invisible College, but because he continued to be involved in Freemasonry through the time the first Grand Lodge was formed in 1717.

Chapter 19

A Bill of Rights
a Breath of Fresh Air

Who was this Christopher Wren, that men both influential and royal felt drawn to be near him? Born a minister's son, his father was Dean of Windsor, the town that embraced one of the king's palaces. He was two years younger than Charles II, though it is not clear the two lads knew each other at Windsor. Christopher started at Wadham College in Oxford University when he was eighteen, studying Greek and Roman classics, and it was there that he met John Wilkins who was the warden at Wadham. Wilkins was believed to have expanded Wren's interest in drawing and mathematics into the broader range of arts and sciences. When he received his master's degree in 1653, Christopher stayed on at Oxford to perform research experiments, and was believed to have become involved in the Invisible College with Wilkins and others at that time.

Four years later Wren accepted an appointment as Professor of Astronomy at Gresham College and moved to London to begin teaching. There he continued the pattern of Gresham professors being intimately involved in the Invisible College. From 1637 to 1660 these professors included Samuel Foster (1637, 1641-52), Mungo Moray (1637-41), Sir William Petty (1651-61), Lawrence

Rooke (1652-62), Jonathan Goddard (1655-75), and Sir Christopher Wren (1657-61).

The Invisible College began to meet each week after Christopher Wren's lectures at Gresham, and it was at one such post-lecture meeting on 28 November 1660 that they founded the Royal Society. Thereafter the Royal Society continued to meet at Gresham College for the next fifty years. During much of that time Robert Hooke was curator of the Royal Society's collections, and also served as the Gresham Professor of Geometry (1665-1704). Only in 1710, when Sir Isaac Newton was its president, did the Society finally seek its own facility and move to a pair of houses in Crane Court, near the New Temple grounds. Years later, Gresham College also moved, taking over historic Barnard's Inn, just off High Holborn in London. While tracing the life of Sir Thomas Gresham, I came to his College one day and arrived just in time to attend a lecture on the East India Trading Company that was absolutely fascinating. As a result I can attest that the lectures do in fact continue, are still free and open to the public, and are a piece of living history worth experiencing.

In 1661 Christopher Wren received an appointment as Professor of Astronomy at Oxford, which was too great an honor to pass up even though it meant he had to commute to London to participate in Royal Society meetings. As fortune would have it, however, he was not at Oxford long. A fiery holocaust consumed the city of London on 2 September 1666, and changed the course of his life. The conflagration broke out on Pudding Lane near the center of the market district and ran uncontrolled for four days, incinerating two-thirds of the city before it burned out. This Great Fire of London destroyed 13,200 homes and 88 churches—including the cathedral of St. Paul—as well as most of the prominent buildings of the day. Only Westminster and the outlying areas were spared. Virtually the entire population of the Old City within the Roman walls was rendered homeless.

Searching for a magician to restore London, the king chose Christopher Wren whom he knew from the Royal Society. The monarch was also familiar with Wren's design of the Oxford Sheldonian Theatre and numerous other buildings. The incumbent as King's Surveyor of Works, Sir John Denham, should

Fig. 32 Sir Christopher Wren

have had this honor, but was a political appointee with no knowledge of architecture or building. Upon Denham's death on 10 March 1669, Wren received the formal title of King's Surveyor to go with the duties he was already performing. He would serve in this influential capacity for almost fifty years, giving London its new physical shape and appearance. Dubbed a knight in 1673, Sir Christopher oversaw the raising of literally thousands of buildings in London, many of which have survived to this day. His masterpiece was St. Paul's Cathedral, for which he is most famously remembered. Wren also designed the massive column known as The Monument near London Bridge which commemorated the Great Fire. It can still be ascended via an internal staircase of 311 steps to a viewing platform above, from which some parts of Christopher Wren's London can be seen.

As noted earlier, this rebuilding work brought vast numbers of stonemasons and carpenters to London. Ironically, this demand for construction became so great that the stonemasons' guild, known as the Masons Company, was stripped of its protections from competition. Anyone could be a stonemason without having to join the guild. As a result, the Masons Company withered and became a social charity organization. Sir Christopher had no known association with the Masons Company, but instead belonged to a different group that would soon emerge into public view, and this was Freemasonry.

At that time Sir Robert Moray was in the last years of his life, but remained active in the Royal Society. He guided into being the Society's prestigious publication *Philosophical Transactions of the Royal Society*. This was how he described it in his letter to noted Dutch mathematician Christiaan Huygens.

> ...we shall print what passes among ourselves, at least everything which may be published. Then you shall have copies among the first, and if there is something withheld from publication, it will be much easier for me to communicate it to you than to have to send word of everything by letter.[226]

This publication continues to be issued from the row of town-houses that serve as the current home of the Royal Society. These occupy No. 6 through No. 9 of Carlton House Terrace in London, situated between Buckingham Palace and Trafalgar Square.

The king retained Sir Robert as a member of the royal Privy Council out of gratitude for his many years of service, and granted him an apartment at the Palace of Whitehall. There Moray was able to pursue his interest in chemistry, and had space to conduct his experiments. When he died on 4 July 1673, Sir Robert was buried in Westminster Abbey by order of the king. His name is etched on a memorial plaque set in the floor, just in front of the tomb of Geoffrey Chaucer.

King Charles II passed away twelve years later, and in doing so he unwittingly set off a series of events that paved the way for Free-masonry to emerge into public view. Charles died without producing a legitimate heir, and the twelve illegitimate children he brought into the world were regrettably unable to inherit. So his crown passed to his brother James. That caused his brother to become James II of England and Ireland, and James VII of Scotland. Normally this would not have been a problem, but James had converted to the Roman Catholic faith. And he now wore the crown of a kingdom which King Henry VIII had split away from the Catholic Church in 1534 to create the powerful Church of England. That Anglican Church was the one to which most of his subjects now belonged.

Undaunted, James began laboring to roll back the Protestant tide by appointing Catholics to senior positions—a direction that did not prove to be terribly popular. These stark religious differences were aggravated by James' belief in the absolute power of kings. This was the same belief that had gotten his father, Charles I, beheaded in public. It therefore came as no surprise to his contemporaries when James had to weather two rebellions against the crown during the first year of his reign. These he quickly put down, but outspoken opposition by Parliament continued until he felt compelled to peremptorily disband that body. It did not meet again during his reign.

Miraculously, in spite of these difficulties it seemed that James might yet weather the crises that beset him. This was due to both of his daughters being Protestants. One of them, Mary, was also married to the Protestant William of Orange, who ruled the Dutch Republic. Although manifestly unhappy, the not-so-loyal opposition seemed resigned to tolerating James' reign and waiting for the day one of his children would ascend the throne. Then in 1688 James had a son by his Catholic wife, and that changed everything. The existence of a Catholic heir caused rebellions to break out across the land with greater force than ever before. This groundswell became known as the *Glorious Revolution.* Initial protests grew into military campaigns when James' daughter Mary and her husband William of Orange brought an army to England from the Netherlands. Upon arrival that army was joined by many Protestant English leaders and troops, allowing the Glorious Revolution to press forward strongly.

In less than gallant manner, James decided not to fight and instead threw the Great Seal of the Realm into the Thames River before he fled to France. A Parliament was quickly assembled to deal with the situation, and it promptly decided that James' actions amounted to abdication. As a result, the crown was offered to his daughter Mary and her husband William, to rule jointly — but only under specific written conditions.

It was quite rare for members of the public to confront a monarch with conditions before granting a crown. It reflected the deep pressures building up in Britain to severely limit those excesses of power that had been exercised in the past by king and church. One of the clearest examples of this excess had been the harsh treatment accorded to the Knights Templar. That had left a striking and vivid picture in people's minds of king and church wrongfully taking people's life, liberty and property — with no recourse but what the king or church might give. Inquisitions, executions and the recent civil war had kept those fears fresh.

Those concerns were made clear to William and Mary, along with the necessary provisions that would henceforth limit the monarchy. The new royal couple approved those conditions. Parliament then formally ratified this English Bill of Rights. While this bill had some provisions particular to the English situation, such as rules governing the succession of monarchs, many of its other provisions would be echoed later in the United States Bill of Rights.

Prior to these bills being written, we saw in the formation of Gresham College and the Royal Society a strong desire to escape the arbitrary rule of church and state. The charter of the Royal Society did this for scientific inquiry and removed from it the repressive charges of heresy that had been used by the church. The English Bill of Rights now did the same for all the people of the kingdom and removed the repressive force of arbitrary power by church and state. And that was not the only similarity with the Royal Society charter.

The newly-adopted certificate of rights was a strange creation. It represented neither a sole victory for the Parliamentary forces, nor a sole victory for Royalist partisans. The recent civil war had led to direct confrontations over whether to continue the powerful monarchy or disband it altogether. Now, for some reason, another force emerged during the decision-making process. It reached people on both sides of this divisive issue, and brought them together to meet in the middle. There they agreed on the compromise that was artfully penned. It protected people from exercise of arbitrary power, rather than simply yielding to an absolute monarch or abandoning the monarchy altogether.

Similar to the situation that occurred in the Invisible College and Royal Society, it would be wrong to think a remarkable outcome like this was driven only by an invisible secret society such as Freemasonry. Clearly there were other large and powerful forces at work. The nose-to-nose confrontation of Catholics and Protestants could not be denied. Nor could the Parliamentarian versus Royalist confrontations be underestimated, after having so recently ripped the country apart. Yet despite those volatile forces, no pitched battles erupted this time. No public executions were held at Whitehall. No riots filled the streets to leave nobles and commoners injured and fearful.

This time the course of events leaned closer to the process that formed the Royal Society. There, in what could have been a tense situation, the brother-in-law of Lord Protector Oliver Cromwell faced the Privy Councillor to the King—and took each other by the hand instead of by the throat. What John Wilkins and Sir Robert Moray had done in private, now lords and commons did in public. The force of this public agreement was such that a king and queen were required to accept these clear limits on their power. It was a new moment, and a new day.

Freemasonry quietly existed underground at this time, surfacing only in the person of Moray, Ashmole and the others who have been named here. Private meetings were held and men came to the aid of their brothers. They waited and worked patiently for the day when arbitrary power by church and state might be sufficiently overcome. But had it finally happened? Was this Bill of Rights enough of a restraint on the king's power, and on his ability to champion a monolithic church? If it was, then would this restraint last, or would it soon be overthrown in a return to the bloody excesses of the past? Those living in the shadows had to wait a little longer to see what would happen. The declaration of rights had to pass the test of time. And the test of successive coronations.

As fortune would have it, the next several reigns passed quickly.

Queen Mary died five years after she was crowned, leaving William to rule alone. He passed away in 1702, and conferred the throne upon Mary's sister, Anne. Even though Queen Anne was the second daughter of James II, she did not go back to his policies. The Bill of Rights remained in effect. After a reign of twelve years, she left the crown to distant relative George I in 1714. Having passed through the reigns of all these men and women, it seemed clear that the protections were going to last. There was no more need for secrecy.

Freemasons continued to meet in private, but for the first time began to take their meals in public places. Members of several lodges discussed the possibility of coming fully into public view. If this was to be done, it would be a major step that could not be undone later—so the decision was not taken lightly. By all indications some brothers and lodges waited and watched the actions of their more outspoken brethren. When the day finally came, only four lodges were bold enough to come forward.

The men of those four lodges met at the Apple-Tree Tavern in London and agreed to hold the first Grand Lodge banquet on 24 June 1717. When that day arrived, they celebrated in the manner of those long confined to back rooms who were now set free.

Accordingly

On St. *John Baptist's* Day, in the 3d Year of King George I. *A.D.* 1717. the ASSEMBLY and *Feast* of the *Free and accepted Masons* was held at the foresaid *Goose and Gridiron* Ale-house....[227]

Among the Freemasons choosing to emerge during this watershed event was John Desaguliers, of the lodge that met at the Rummer and Grapes Tavern in Channel Row, Westminster. Being also a member of the Royal Society, he and others formed a bridge between the old and the new. Desaguliers also served as the third Grand Master, and remained active in Freemasonry all his days.

Other brothers such as Christopher Wren were of an older generation. Sir Christopher was eighty-four when the Grand Lodge was formed. He chose not to give up the secret practices of a lifetime.

His situation was similar to that of most men who became Freemasons prior to 1717, in that no records have survived which show the actual date he became a Freemason. The most likely time would have been upon his joining the Invisible College when he worked with John Wilkins at Oxford. Many years later, written information indicated he belonged to the Lodge of Antiquity in London, and was its master in 1680.[228] Lodge records from the days before Freemasonry's emergence are scarce, but we are fortunate to have notes preserving information about the internal affairs of the Lodge of Antiquity and the man who was perhaps its most well-known member.

The Lodge once possessed minute books going back to 1721 but the first two, covering the years 1721 to 1733, are missing, and the years 1734 and 1735 are absent

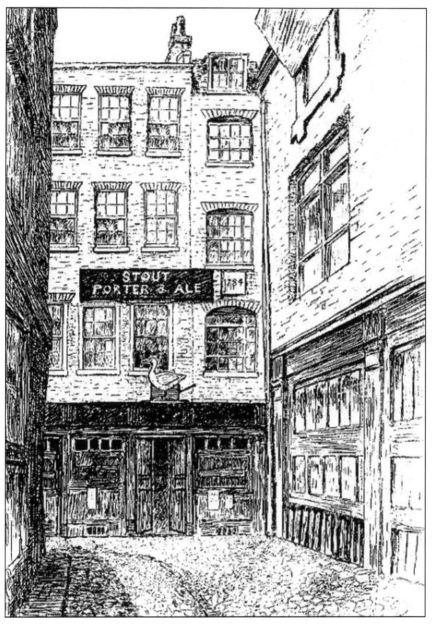

Fig. 33   Goose and Gridiron Ale-house.

from the third. From then onwards there are minutes....

There is a legend, strong in the Lodge from the earliest years, that Sir Christopher Wren was once Master. He lived from 1632 to 1723 and his son, also Christopher...was a member of the Lodge and Master in 1729.... A note supposed to be copied from the Lodge minutes of 1723 refers to "The three mahagony Candlesticks presented to the Lodge by its Worthy old Master Sir Christopher Wren ordered to be carefully deposited in a Woodn Case lin'd with Cloth to be Immediately purchased for that purpose." The Lodge still has them.... If these notes be accurate (and there is no obvious reason to doubt them) then they date back to Sir Christopher's own lifetime and the legend was certainly current in his son's, when it could easily have been refuted."[229]

Christopher Wren declined the honor of serving as the first Grand Master,[230] but remained active until his death at ninety-one years of age.[231] He was buried in the southeastern cove of the crypt under St. Paul's Cathedral, beneath a stone slab marked with a Latin inscription[232] which is translated as follows.

> Below lies the builder
> of this church and city,
> Christopher Wren;
> who lived beyond ninety years,
> not for himself, but for the public good.
> Reader, if you seek his monument,
> look around you.
> He died on the 25th of February, 1723, aged 91.

Wren had lived to see the public emergence of Freemasonry, whose lodges were now starting to come out of the shadows in rapid-fire fashion. By making this drastic change, Freemasonry was no longer a secret society. Yet it was still a society with secrets.

Chapter 20

Lodges Young and Grand

After the uncovering of those first four lodges in London, other Masonic lodges began to emerge in many widely scattered cities. They also appeared in the open countryside. It soon became apparent that for some time Freemasonry had been quietly going about its affairs all across Great Britain. This was amply illustrated by a remarkable occurrence that took place thirty-one years *before* the emergence of the lodges in London. Robert Plot recorded an intriguing look at Freemasonry during the days when it was still a secret society. This was contained in his 1686 book *Natural History of Staffordshire*, a county in the English Midlands north of Birmingham.

> ...the *Customs* relating to the *County*, whereof they have one, of admitting Men into the *Society of Freemasons*, that in the *moorelands* of this *County* seems to be of greater request, than any where else, though I find the *Custom* spread more or less all over the *Nation*; for here I found persons of the most eminent quality, that did not disdain to be of this *Fellowship*.

Into which *Society* when any are admitted, they call a *meeting* (or *Lodg* as they term it in some places) which must consist at lest of 5 or 6 of the *Ancients* of the *Order*, whom the *candidates* present with *gloves*, and so likewise to their *wives*, and entertain with a *collation* according to the Custom of the place. This ended, they proceed to the *admission* of them, which chiefly consists in the communication of certain *secret signes*, whereby they are known to one another all over the *Nation*, by which means they have maintenance whither ever they travel: for if any man appear though altogether unknown that can shew any of these *signes* to a *Fellow* of the *Society*, whom they otherwise call an *accepted mason*, he is obliged presently to come to him, from what company or place soever he be in, nay tho' from the top of a *Steeple*, (what hazard or inconvenience soever he run) to know his pleasure, and assist him: *viz.* if he want *work* he is bound to find him some; or if he cannot do that, to give him *mony*, or otherwise support him till *work* can be had.[233]

Any Freemason will recognize the above customs as still being very much alive in Masonic rites and practices today.

Before Robert Plot penned the above observations, he took his degrees at Oxford University, then became a fellow of the Royal Society in 1677. Plot was subsequently recruited by Elias Ashmole to be the first Keeper of the new Ashmolean Museum when it opened its doors at Oxford in 1683. With Elias Ashmole being a Freemason and Robert Plot choosing to write about this society with some familiarity, it is not difficult to conclude how the Keeper came to possess this information. It also seems to continue the involvement of men at Oxford with Freemasonry.

In Yorkshire and Northern England, other early lodges were also in evidence during those years before 1717. One of the early documents of Freemasonry known as the Scarborough manuscript had this note written on it.

M[emoran]dum Thatt att A private Lodge held at Scarborough in the County of York the tenth day of July 1705 before William Thompson Esqr P^{r}sident of the said Lodge & severall others brethren ffree Masons the severall psons whose names are herevnto Subscribed were then admitted into the Said ffraternity....

Meanwhile records from the Old Lodge at York show that the position of President or Master of that Lodge was held by a series of gentlemen in the years between 1705 and 1713, including Sir George Tempest who was a Baronet, Lord Bingley who was Lord Mayor of York, and several other gentlemen of distinction. The minutes of that Lodge were preserved from 19 March 1712 to 1730, and included the following.

December the 18: 1713
At a private Lodge held then at the house of Mr. James Borehams Scittuate in Stonegate in the City of york Mr. Tho: Hardwick, Mr. Godferey Giles and Mr. Tho: Challener was admitted and Sworne into the Honoble Society and Company of ffree Masons before the Worshipfull

        Sr Walter Hawxworth Kn^t and Barr^t President
        Tho: Hardwick
        Godfrey Giles
        Thomas (his T marke) Challoner

These lodges, scattered across the central and northern reaches of England, must have been aware of the emergence of four London lodges into public view, and the formation on 24 June 1717 of the Grand Lodge. Yet at first the watchful waiting continued. This was reflected in the fact that eleven years after that formation there were only 57 lodges recorded on the Manuscript List of the Grand Lodge. One year later, the number stood at 61. However rate of growth began to pick up after that, and ten years later the number of member lodges had tripled.

Even so, that still did not represent all the hidden Masonic lodges across Great Britain that had existed before 1717. Though the Old Lodge of York showed a continuous record of minutes from 1712 to 1730, and was clearly a lodge of gentlemen having significant rank, it still had not joined the Grand Lodge. Eventually, however, it did take that step, becoming the 236th lodge certified by the Grand Lodge, and still bearing that number today. The assumption that individual lodges came into existence on the day they were acknowledged by the Grand Lodge has proven to be far from the truth. Some lodges were new, of course. But for many lodges in the early 1700s their long history of private, secretive existence was kept that way, and their actual day of formation was never disclosed. Only by discovering copies of lodge minutes such as those at York have we gotten a glimpse into that dim past that is still concealed and never revealed.

Ireland had active lodges as well and—just as several lodges in London had gotten together to spontaneously create a Grand Lodge—the same took place in Dublin eight years later. The Grand Lodge of Ireland's earliest known record was this account in the *Dublin Weekly Journal* dated 25 June 1725.

> Thursday last, being St. John's Day, Patron of the Most Antient, and Rt. Worshipful Society of Freemasons; they met about Eleven o' the Clock, at the Yellow Lion in Warbroughs-street, where there appear'd above a 100 Gentlemen. After some time spent, in putting on their Aprons, White Gloves, and other parts of the *Distinguishing* Dress of that Worshipful Order, they proceeded over Essex-Bridge to the Strand, and from thence to the King's Inns....

The following year, Freemasons in the Irish city of Cork met in similar manner to form the Grand Lodge of Munster—that being the ancient name for southwestern Ireland. After seven years of operating alongside their brothers in Dublin, the men of Munster agreed to be absorbed into the Grand Lodge of Ireland. This seemed to be a time of ebb and flow in Freemasonry, with brothers seeking a reasonable balance of control and freedom in which to practice their craft.

Similar changes took place back in England, where the Old Lodge of York formed its own "Grand Lodge of All England at York" in 1725. Naturally that declaration came as something of a surprise to the Grand Lodge in London. This proclamation was followed shortly thereafter by three lodges in Chester forming their own Grand Lodge. To head off this growing wave of Northern defections, the Grand Lodge in London dispatched its much-honored past Grand Master, John Desaguliers—who was then serving as Deputy Grand Master—as a goodwill ambassador to the brothers in Chester. Desaguliers, who had already done much to shape Freemasonry after its 1717 emergence, apparently charmed the brothers at Chester into accepting the title of a Provincial Grand Lodge and operating under the aegis of London. The new Provincial Grand Master confirmed this in a letter to the Grand Master at London in 1727.

> ...[Thank you] for the great honour done us by your Worship's most affectionate L're and the kind visitation of our Lodges by your most acceptable Deputy.... [And we offer] most Chearfull obedience and extensive gratitude to our Superiors in London and Westminster.

This curious arrangement of establishing a "Provincial" Grand Lodge was then repeated in several other northern counties that included Lancashire, Northumberland, and County Durham. Similar relationships were established with the two western regions identified as North and South Wales.

Provincial Grand Lodges also began to crop up in the colonies of North America. Freemasons had met in ad-hoc American lodges ever since they first arrived in wooden sailing boats and started to hew farms, towns and cities out of the wilderness. The Grand Lodge of England acknowledged their growing status by granting a patent to Daniel Coxe in 1730 to serve as Provincial Grand Master for New York, New Jersey and Pennsylvania. This was to be a two-year term, with election of a new Provincial Grand Master to follow every two years thereafter. Coxe, however, was still in England in 1731, and there was no indication that he ever exercised this authority. In 1732 William Allen was apparently elected by local lodges to serve as Provincial Grand Master of Pennsylvania, since he presided over a meeting held at that time. He was followed in this capacity by Humphrey Murray in 1733. The position took a step up in prestige when Benjamin Franklin was chosen to serve as Provincial Grand Master of Pennsylvania in 1734.

Born in Boston on 17 January 1706, Ben Franklin was only twelve years of age when he started down the path that brought him to Masonry by becoming apprenticed as a printer to one of his older brothers. Having a great deal of self-confidence, he set sail for London six years later to make his own way in the world. There he took work as typesetter for a printing house located in the decommissioned church of St. Bartholomew the Great, more popularly known as St. Bart's. The rag-tag commercial rooms built onto the side of the church can still be seen today. St. Bart's stood only a few blocks north of St. Paul's Cathedral, in whose courtyard resided one of the four Masonic lodges that had brought Freemasonry out into the open only seven years earlier. Franklin lived in the epicenter of Freemasonry at that time and it may well have influenced his later decision to join this society.

When he returned to America and settled in Philadelphia, Franklin became a printer in his own right and was soon publishing a leading newspaper known as the *Pennsylvania Gazette*. Socially active in the city, he took a significant step in 1731 at age twenty-five when he was initiated into St. John's Lodge and became a Freemason. Three years later the energetic and popular Benjamin Franklin was Grand Master of Pennsylvania. That same year he began to publish Masonic writings to share Freemasonry with the other men he was coming to know in the American colonies. Since these colonies would not issue the Declaration of Independence— on their way to becoming the United States of America—until forty-two years after Franklin went to press, it would be fair to say that he helped Freemasonry become firmly rooted in the New World.

Fig. 34   Benjamin Franklin, Grand Master of Pennsylvania

Yet all was not a bed of roses. A measure of confusion occurred in the colonies when Henry Price received an appointment from the Grand Lodge of England to serve as Provincial Grand Master for New England in 1733. Price was a resident of Boston, Massachusetts, but apparently insisted that his rights extended to include New York, New Jersey and Pennsylvania as well. This did not seem to faze the brothers in Pennsylvania, who carried on as before. Price certainly established his Provincial Grand Lodge in Massachusetts, but it is not clear how much farther his influence extended.

Far to the south on the rugged coastline of the New World, James Edward Oglethorpe established the colony of Georgia in 1732. Oglethorpe was a Freemason born in Surrey just outside London to parents who were well-connected in society and of reasonable means. Entering Corpus Christi College at Oxford in 1714, he soon discovered his interests were elsewhere and dropped out to join the army of the Prince of Savoy. Upon his return to England he was promptly elected to Parliament. Oglethorpe used that public position to strongly advocate the traditional Freemason position of opposing debtors' prisons, and seeking instead to secure work for those in need. To accomplish this he proposed to re-settle debtors to a new colony to be named Georgia, where each would receive land to work and support themselves. His proposal struck a positive chord, and in 1732 he set out for the wilderness at the head of the first colonists, creating a settlement near the current location of Savannah, Georgia.

Oglethorpe created the first Masonic lodge in Georgia on 21 February 1734 and it became known as Solomon's Lodge No. 1. He also served as that group's first Worshipful Master. In 1735 the Grand Lodge of England appointed one of the members of that lodge, Roger Hugh Lacey, to serve as Provincial Grand Master for Georgia.

The colony of New York then followed suit when Captain Richard Riggs was appointed Provincial Grand Master in 1737, although he did not arrive in that colony until the following year. Very little seems to have occurred in New York during the fourteen years of his tenure. In 1751 Francis Goelet was named as successor to Riggs, and seems to have continued in that same manner.

An event of some importance to Freemasonry happened the following year in Virginia when a twenty-year-old youth named George Washington was accepted into the Fredericksburg Lodge on the 4th of November in 1752. The young Mason then began to make his way in the world as an officer in joint British and American military campaigns against the French and their Indian allies. The widespread popularity of Masonic lodges among military units, where a sense of camaraderie helped to make up for often-dismal living conditions, may have contributed to Washington's ability to get along well with officers from the British camp. When alliances shifted at the beginning of the Revolutionary War—with the French coming to the aid of the Americans against the British—Washington was just as comfortable working with Freemason officers among the French, such as the Marquis de Lafayette.

When the American colonies finally declared their independence from England, the "Provincial" status of their Grand Lodges disappeared. A full-bodied Grand Lodge was then declared in every U. S. state, and that tradition has continued to the present day.

In 1736 Scotland also took the plunge and created its own Grand Lodge. There was a longstanding tradition of Freemasonry in Scotland. But there was an even longer tradition of proud independence. When those two forces finally reached a good balance, the Masonic lodges yielded their independence and came together to form the Grand Lodge of Scotland. The assembled brethren chose William St. Clair as their first Grand Master, and thereby began a new tradition rooted in the old.

Only two years after Scottish Masons took that step, this fraternal society was acknowledged in a completely different way. That unfortunate recognition came about as the unintended result of a Scot's efforts in France.

Chapter 21

Vestiges of Knighthood, Vatican Vitriol

Chevalier Andrew Michael Ramsay did not seem like the kind of person who could trigger opposing waves of euphoria and dread over possible connections between the Knights Templar and Freemasonry. The son of a common baker in Ayr, Scotland, thirty miles southwest of Glasgow, he was good enough with books to gain admission to the University of Edinburgh in the year 1700 at the tender age of fourteen. After three years on campus he put his youth and education to good use by becoming the tutor for a succession of prominent men's sons. This innovative occupation brought him to France in 1710 where he promptly became involved with highly-placed members of the royal court.

Among those French leaders was the Archbishop of Cambrai, François Fénelon, who converted Andrew to Roman Catholicism. This was a remarkable accomplishment, since Andrew was—and continued to be—a practitioner of the *Quietism* cult that had been condemned by several popes.[234] His circle of friends in Paris grew to include Philippe d'Orleans who, as Regent, ruled France on behalf of five-year-old Louis XV. It was from the Regent's hands that Andrew received the Order of St. Lazarus, which conferred upon him the title of *Chevalier*, or French knight. As Chevalier

Ramsay, he wrote several books that won scholarly and social acclaim, followed by the distinction of being awarded an honorary doctorate at Oxford. Around that same time, on 16 March 1730, he was initiated as a Freemason at the Horn Lodge of London, along with a number of other distinguished gentlemen.

Andrew's involvement with Freemasonry deepened upon his return to France, and by 1737 he was serving as the Grand Orator in Paris. In that capacity he produced the work that cast him into the pages of history. From his pen flowed the "Discourse pronounced at the reception of Freemasons." This subsequently gained both fame and notoriety as *Chevalier Ramsay's Oration*. In this work he traced the roots of Freemasonry not to stonemasons as others had done, but to the knights of the Crusades.

> At the time of the Crusades in Palestine many princes, lords, and citizens associated themselves, and vowed to restore the Temple of the Christians in the Holy Land, to employ themselves in bringing back their architecture to its first institution. They agreed upon several ancient signs and symbolic words drawn from the well of religion in order to recognize themselves amongst the heathen and Saracens. These signs and words were only communicated to those who promised solemnly, and even sometimes at the foot of the altar, never to reveal them.... Sometime afterwards our Order formed an intimate union with the Knights of St. John of Jerusalem.[235]

Although he did not directly name the Templars in his oration, the Knights of St. John—otherwise known as the Hospitallers— were united with only one other order, and that was the Knights Templar.[236] Word of Ramsay's findings generated a surge of interest in this new, knightly view of Freemasonry. Ripples of excitement crossed the borders of France into neighboring lands, and spread across the Channel into Great Britain.

Yet before that positive wave swept north, a bitterly negative wave swept south. This resulted from Ramsay's assumption that his oration's air of knighthood and French pride would be appreciated in the court of Louis XV. Accordingly he sent a copy of his speech to Cardinal Fleury, the king's prime minister, on 20 March 1737. The immediate and sharp rejection of Ramsay's oration by Cardinal Fleury indicated that the connection of crusading knights with secretive Freemasons had touched a raw nerve.

The Templars had been brutally tortured and burned at the stake by representatives of the Vatican. Consequently the possibility that brothers-in-arms or family members of the fallen might take revenge against the Church seemed to have been more than a passing discussion after those public executions. Secret societies would reasonably have been high on the Vatican's watch list during the years and centuries that followed. Whether or not the Church had its own information of a connection between those mistreated knights and the Freemasons who later emerged from hiding, we cannot know.

When Ramsay issued his oration, however, it was like a match thrown onto fuel-soaked kindling. There was an immediate eruption. Within eleven days, Cardinal Fleury issued an interdict banning all Freemason meetings in France. He and other members of the College of Cardinals then involved the pope and pressed for action.

Pope Clement XII cooperated by publishing his papal bull *In eminenti* condemning Freemasonry on 28 April 1738. This official letter denounced Masonry using the Latin and French names for the group, *Liberi Muratori* and *Francs Massons*.

Clearly the Catholic Church or any other group was entitled to defend itself when attacked. Over the centuries there was no question that kings such as Philip IV of France and leaders of other religions had attacked the Church. Responding to those actions in the form of an official papal bull was quite reasonable.

What made *In eminenti* so unusual was that the now-public organization identified as Freemasonry was not known to have done anything to attack or harm the Catholic Church during the twenty-one years since it came into public view in 1717. Nor did the written document give any specific cause for the pope's action. He attributed his motivation only to having heard "common gossip" and "rumors" about Freemasonry. That was deemed enough to publish a public condemnation. If this sounds too ridiculous to be believed, feel free to visit the Vatican website and read the full text.[237]

Having no overt action by Freemasons to which objection could be made, Clement used the following logic to justify the harsh punishment of excommunication used against them. First, *In eminenti* stated that Freemasons took an oath of silence about what they did in secret. Second, it was asserted that crime generally showed itself by the things criminals say. Third, since Freemasons observed secrecy, the Church must have the "greatest suspicion" that they were doing something wrong, and that they must be "depraved and perverted." He succinctly summed up the charges this way, "For if they were not doing evil they would not have so great a hatred of the light." In other words, if he did not know what they were doing, they must be doing evil.

What was the appropriate punishment for keeping secrets? Freemasons were "condemned and prohibited," and anyone involved with them or helping them in any way was to suffer the "pain of excommunication."

Perhaps even more curious than that attempt to justify harsh punishment was why the Vatican took any action at all. By the time this papal order was written, the highest imaginable number of visible Masonic lodges worldwide would have been on the order of 600. That would have meant a total membership of 15,000 to 30,000 at the most. This was about the same population as one good-sized town. In a world of roughly 750 million people at that time, how could such a small number of individuals possibly be worth the pope's attention, let alone a formal letter attempting to charge them with a vague offence?

This over-reaction to the appearance of Freemasonry was almost as if the Vatican recognized a feared old foe re-emerging on the battlefield.

In eminenti even borrowed some of the language used against the Knights Templar by King Philip of France and the earlier pope, who was also named Clement.[238] Anyone who gave assistance was to suffer the penalty of excommunication, the same sentence levied against those who helped the Templars. Clement XII ordered not only "bishops and prelates" to deal with Freemasons, but promised to send "inquisitors for heresy" into the fray against them as well. This echoed the earlier pope's action, jumping to the equivalent of Code Red. Without waiting for inquisitors to take to the field and find any wrong-doing, the pope proceeded directly to punishment, instructing his inquisitors that they "are to pursue and punish them with condign penalties as being most suspect of heresy."

In eminenti was an unusual step for the Church to take against these newly-emerged Freemasons. But it would not be the last. The Vatican continued to issue letters, culminating in a major denunciation in 1884 by Leo XIII titled *Humanum genus*. This time the papal bull accused Freemasons of actual charges. Freemasons were condemned for advocating the separation of Church and State. They were further condemned for supporting the election of government leaders by the people. And Masons were condemned for allowing the education of children by teachers who were not members of the Church.

> Therefore, in the education and instruction of children they allow no share, either of teaching or of discipline, to the ministers of the Church; and in many places they have procured that the education of youth shall be exclusively in the hands of laymen, and that nothing which treats of the most important and most holy duties of men to God shall be introduced into the instructions on morals.
>
> Then come their doctrines of politics, in which the naturalists lay down that all men have the same right, and are in every respect of equal and like condition; that each one is naturally free; that no one has the right to command another; that it is an act of violence to require men to obey any authority other than that which is obtained from themselves. According to this, therefore, all things belong to the free people; power is held by the command or permission of the people, so that, when the popular will changes, rulers may lawfully be deposed and the source of all rights and civil duties is either in the multitude or in the governing authority when this is constituted according to the lat-

est doctrines. It is held also that the State should be without God; that in the various forms of religion there is no reason why one should have precedence of another; and that they are all to occupy the same place.

That these doctrines are equally acceptable to the Freemasons, and that they would wish to constitute States according to this example and model, is too well known to require proof. For some time past they have openly endeavoured to bring this about with all their strength and resources.

This was the nature of the terrible crimes of which Freemasons stood accused. It can be freely acknowledged that Freemasons were guilty of these things. Did that make them depraved and perverted? Probably not.

A document from the Vatican Secret Archives sheds considerable light on the issue of lingering guilt and embarrassment in the Vatican due to its violent treatment of the Knights Templar. This is the *Chinon Parchment* written in France during 1308. It has been suggested that this ancient manuscript—which the Vatican "rediscovered" in 2001—somehow exonerated the Church for its actions against the Templars.[239] It has also been said that Chinon cleared the record of that knightly order by showing they were innocent of the charges of heresy against them. But those claims may not be true.

After arresting many Templars in France on 13 October 1307, King Philip worked tirelessly to obtain whatever confessions he could muster from the imprisoned men of the Order. With persistence, he was rewarded with enough bits and pieces of induced confession to justify his confiscation of their possessions. Pope Clement V meanwhile asserted the Vatican's longstanding position that the members of its various orders could not be tried by secular courts outside the Church. He followed that by jumping into the fray to hold his own trials of the Templars. For this purpose he ordered three cardinals to proceed to the city of Chinon

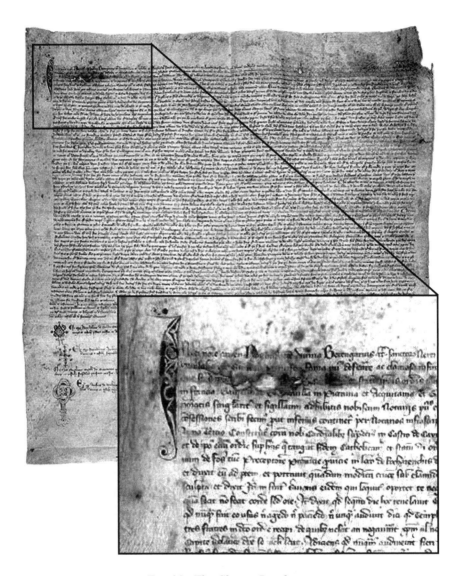

Fig. 35 The Chinon Parchment

in Western France for the first great trial of Jacques de Molay and the other leaders of the Knights Templar.[240]

That trial took place from the 17th to the 20th of August in 1308, and its proceedings were duly recorded by scribes on what has become known as the *Chinon Parchment*. De Molay and the other men were brought from prison for that purpose, and during the trial they repeated their earlier confessions of acts which could be considered heresy, and they repented. In return they were absolved and reconciled with the Church. This amounted to a "plea bargain" in which they pled guilty to less than all of the charges against them. Other Templars had already signed similar confessions and gained their freedom, so the leaders of the Templars no doubt expected the same. Yet their freedom did not come.

It is possible that this trial and the parchment at Chinon may have been valiant attempts by the pope to save his people and, if that was true, be a highly commendable act. Yet his actions from that moment forward lend themselves to no such gentle interpretation.

In September of 1309, before any of the Templars in Great Britain had been called as witnesses to support or rebut any accusation against them, the Catholic Archbishop of Canterbury posted in all churches of the land a bull from the pope:

> ...wherein the Pope declares himself perfectly convinced of the guilt of the order, and solemnly denounces the penalty of excommunication against all persons, of whatever rank, station, or condition in life, whether clergy or laity, who should knowingly afford, either publicly or privately, assistance, counsel, or kindness to the Templars, or should dare to shelter them, or give them countenance or protection, and also laying under interdict all cities, castles, lands, and places, which should harbour any of the members of the proscribed order.[241]

This was a declaration of the Templars' guilt prior to their trial. That unequivocal act did not show the pope as impartial, let alone reconciled with the Templar Order by the actions at Chinon. But there was more to come. During the following year the Templars in English prisons were questioned many times without obtaining proof of their guilt, so sterner measures were ordered.

> At first, king Edward the Second, to his honour, forbade the infliction of torture upon the illustrious members of the Temple in his dominions—men who had fought and bled for Christendom, and of whose piety and morals he had a short time before given such ample testimony to the principal sovereigns of Europe. But the virtuous resolution of the weak king was speedily overcome by the all-powerful influence of the Roman pontiff, who wrote to him in the month of June, upbraiding him for preventing the inquisitors from submitting the Templars to the discipline of the rack. Influenced by the admonitions of the pope, and the solicitations of the clergy, king Edward, on the 26th of August, sent orders to John de Crumbewell, constable of the Tower, to deliver up all the Templars in his custody, at the request of the inquisitors....[242]

In France, also during 1310, a number of Templars who had previously confessed under duress now fully asserted their innocence. As we have seen, King Philip had fifty-four of these men brought before the archbishop at Sens, a city to the southeast of Paris, who passed judgment on those Templars on behalf of the Church.

> "...you have fallen into the sin of *heresy*. By your confession and repentance you had merited absolution, and had once more become reconciled to the church. As you have revoked your confession, the church no longer regards you as reconciled, but as having fallen back to your first errors. You are, therefore, *relapsed heretics* and as such, we condemn you to the fire."[243]

They were burned at the stake the following day. This showed how fleeting the reconciliation with the Church was for those

Templars. At Chinon, we saw Jacques de Molay and the other Templar leaders were not found innocent as some have suggested. They were required instead to falsely declare they were guilty of some form of heresy. The Church then pardoned them for their guilt, and pronounced them to have been reconciled. Even so, the pope then left de Molay and the other officers to languish in prison for six more years. On 18 March 1314, after a quick trial in front of three cardinals appointed by the Vatican, all were condemned to spend the rest of their life in prison. Having finally had more than he could bear—of giving "confessions" in hope of winning freedom for himself and his men, but never gaining that reward— Jacques de Molay stepped forward at the trial and loudly declared his innocence, and the innocence of his Order. One of the other Templar officers joined him in that affirmation. This declaration of their innocence made them "relapsed heretics."

> The same day at dusk they were led out of their dungeons, and were burned to death in a slow and lingering manner upon small fires of charcoal which were kindled on the little island in the Seine, between the king's garden and the convent of St. Augustine, close to the spot where now stands the equestrian statue of Henry IV.[244]

The confessions obtained from these men at Chinon worked against them when they later pled their innocence. In what sense can it be construed that the *Chinon Parchment* ever established the innocence of the Templars? How could it be said that *Chinon* relieved the Church of any guilt or embarrassment over the treatment of the Knights Templar? None of those things seem to have occurred.

The raw nerve touched in the College of Cardinals by Chevalier Ramsay's declaration that Freemasons were linked to the Knights Templar was an indication that all had not healed between the Templars and the Vatican. If Ramsay's assertion was without merit, it could easily have been ignored. The excessive response to these newly-emerged Freemasons—a response elevated all the way to a papal bull and excommunication—showed the members of the Vatican took Chevalier Ramsay's claim very seriously.

While the Vatican moved in the direction of suppression, other people in the North moved in the opposite direction. A wave of revival and emulation of these Templars began, showing they still stirred admiration and fascination hundreds of years after their disappearance.

Chapter 22

Knights Arise,
Peasants Revolt

After *Ramsay's Oration* the desire among many Freemasons to re-create the Templar experience spread quickly across France, England, Scotland and Ireland. It took root in that fertile soil and gave rise to Knights Templar groups known as encampments. Is it possible that those revivals contain useful clues regarding what happened to the original Knights Templar?

The proposal by Ramsay was somewhat vague, but served as a good starting place for these revivals because it had several bits and pieces of history in it. A number of Crusader groups became well-established in Europe, including the Knights Templar, Hospitallers, and the German Order of Teutonic Knights. However Ramsay presented few if any facts to support his statements, causing Masonic scholar Albert Mackey to dismiss his findings, a path that many have followed.

Other investigators stepped in to fill the gap by proposing the original Templar encampments lay in hiding and came riding forward in later years, leading to the rise of the Masonic Knights Templar. This included the Battle of Bannockburn where Templars were said to have come to the rescue and helped win independence for Scotland. Yet as we have seen, the actual facts of history do not support any appearance by the Templars at that battle.

The rise of Masonic Knights Templar in Ireland was also pointed to as a possible connection back to the original knights via Kilwinning.

> In October 1779, Archibald, Earl of Eglinton, who was at that time the Grand Master of Lodge Mother Kilwinning, issued a charter for a new lodge to be formed in Dublin to be called the "High Knight Templars of Ireland Lodge". This lodge became the Early Grand Encampment of Ireland, and when Scottish Grand Lodge issued a directive in October 1800 "prohibiting and discharging its daughters to hold any meetings above the degree of Master Mason, under penalty of forfeiture of their Charter," many Scottish masons applied to the Early Grand Encampment of Ireland for charters, to work the Knight Templar degrees in Scotland.[245]

The difficulty with this possible connecting path was that the Templar heritage of Lodge Mother Kilwinning was traced back to the Battle of Bannockburn, where Robert the Bruce was said to have shown his gratitude to the Knights Templar by endowing Lodge Mother Kilwinning with privileges that enabled the Templars to go underground and continue as Freemasons. If the Knights Templar were not at Bannockburn, which now appears to be the case, then there were no Templar services for the king to reward. Hence this possible path of connection via Ireland fails to work.

York presented another possible link. Rites leading to the Knights Templar degree were practiced there in Northern England, though it was an addition to the craft degrees rather than a separate preceptory or encampment.

> On June 2, 1780, the Grand Chapter resolved that "the Masonic Government, anciently established by the Royal Edwin and now existing at York under the title

of The Grand Lodge of All England, comprehending in its nature all the different Orders or Degrees of Masonry, very justly claims the subordination of all other Lodges or Chapters of Free and Accepted Masons in this Realm." The Degrees were five in number, viz. the first three, the Royal Arch and that of Knight Templar. The Grand Lodge, on June 20, 1780, assumed their protection and its Minute-book was utilized in part for the preservation of the records of the Royal Arch and Knight Templar Degrees...the draft of a certificate preserved at York for the five Degrees of January 26, 1779, to November 29, 1779, is the earliest official document known in Great Britain and Ireland relating to Knights Templar in connection with Freemasonry.[246]

At that same time there was evidence of a Templar preceptory in the southern part of England at Bristol that seemed to have earlier roots, as A.G. Mackey noted in 1870.

There is at Bristol in England a famous Preceptory of Knights Templar, called the Baldwyn, which claims to have existed from time immemorial.... The earliest record preserved by this Preceptory is an authentic and important document dated December 20, 1780.[247]

The Templars at Bristol and York were also investigated by J.S.M. Ward who wrote in 1921.

In England we find that Bristol, Bath and York all have old Masonic Templar Preceptories, and were the sites of medieval Templar Preceptories.

All three are remote from the central Government in London, and therefore members of the Order were less likely to be thoroughly dispersed.[248]

This observation suggested that in 1307 the Templars at preceptories in the fairly remote cities of Bristol, Bath and York were not completely dispersed. If that was true, perhaps they only had to wait quietly before re-emerging as Masonic Templars in 1780.

Unfortunately each of these forays into possible links between the original Templars and the Masonic Templars who came later has been disproved over the years by recourse to historical facts and records, as we saw in detail at Bannockburn. Or else they lacked any meaningful supporting evidence during the centuries that elapsed between the old and new Templars.

In addition, notice that during the twenty years from 1717 to *Ramsay's Oration* there were no Masonic Templar degrees or encampments seen to exist in any country. As a result, we have to reluctantly conclude that the original Knights Templar did not lead directly to the Masonic knights. But what about the possibility of following some other path that was not direct? John Robinson had some interesting insights in this direction.

John J. Robinson was an American historian in Carroll County, Kentucky who immersed himself in Medieval studies. This came after a long life in which he had been a business executive and member of the U.S. Marines. That meant he followed the tradition of Thomas Gresham, John Desaguliers, Benjamin Franklin and others who earned enough when young that they were freed to make significant contributions in later years. Robinson's specialty became the Middle Ages and especially the Crusades, which led to some intriguing discoveries about the Knights Templar and Freemasonry.

While investigating an often-overlooked affair in England referred to as the Peasants' Revolt of 1381, he stumbled upon a shadowy society. It was an integral part of this revolt in which more than a hundred thousand people stormed across the countryside into London, burning down palatial manors on the way. Many years later the event made a significant impact on Winston Churchill, who was moved to remark in *The Birth of Britain*:

> Throughout the summer of 1381 there was a general ferment. Beneath it all lay organization. Agents moved round the villages of central England, in touch with a "Great Society" which was said to meet in London.

This possibility of there being a "Great Society" operating in secret across the length of England made the Peasants' Revolt especially intriguing. That was joined by another puzzle: the rebels seemed to have an especially strong antipathy against the Knights Hospitaller, as Robinson noted:

> All of the religious orders owned properties in London, but only the Hospitaller property was deliberately sought out for destruction, and not just the major establishments at St John's Clerkenwell, and the "Temple" area between Fleet Street and the Thames. The chroniclers state that the rebels sought out every Hospitaller house and rental property to smash or burn it. For that purpose native Londoners had to have been involved, not just to identify such property, but to lead the rebels to it; at that time London streets were not marked by sign posts, and not until hundreds of years later would London have a system of numbered buildings....
>
> In all of the destruction in London, why did the rebels not burn the records stored in the Hospitaller church off Fleet Street right where they found them? Why go to all the trouble of carrying boxes and bundles out of the church to the high road, away from the building, unless it was to avoid the risk of damage to the structure? How was this church different from any other property? Only in that it had been the principal church in Britain of the Knights Templar, consecrated almost three hundred years earlier,[249] in 1185, by Heraclius, the patriarch of Jerusalem. The manner of its consecration alone didn't set it apart, however, because the patriarch had also consecrated the Hospitaller church at Clerkenwell in 1185, during the same month that he had dedicated the Templar church; yet no consideration was given by the rebels to protecting the church at Clerkenwell.[250]

The violent treatment of Hospitaller property and respectful treatment of Templar property suggested something about the Knights Templar might be behind this revolution. As we have seen, the Hospitallers were strong rivals of the Templars during the years both existed, and the black knights were one of the principal beneficiaries from the disbanding of the Templars in 1312. Pope Clement V had ordered all the property of the Templars be handed over to the Hospitallers, a fact that could well have embittered many of the outlawed Templars.

This desire to strike back at Hospitallers was seen by Robinson as a major impetus behind the Peasants' Revolt, and that may well have been true. But a different motivation may also have existed.

The Templar property turned over to the Hospitallers would have included the records of estates and personnel, to the extent that those records escaped destruction on the days the Templars fled. Those documents would have hung like a sword over the heads of the escaped Templars and their heirs. The pope's charges of heresy and orders of excommunication against them had never been revoked. Penalties or social stain could still fall upon the families of former Templars if those records were ever released. When the archives were taken out of Temple Church and burned, that threat was permanently erased.

Either way, the Peasants' Revolt gave indications that the Templars who went underground and disappeared from public view seemed to remain in touch with each other, and were able to act together to represent their interests. And that they were doing so in secret.

Of course there were other causes for the Peasants' Revolt beyond the motivations of this Great Society. Those who tilled the land and worked their crafts struggled under difficult burdens of oppressive laws at that time. Anger and passions were primed and ready to break lose in wanton rioting, looting and destruction. What made this revolt surprisingly different than the riotous behavior that normally accompanied such outbursts was how much it remained under control. The leadership kept order, targeted some individuals and specific places while sparing others. And left evidence of highly coordinated activities in different cities.

These things were reflected in the testimony of people who participated in the revolt, as Robinson noted.

> ....Messengers came into Cambridgeshire from London and from John Wrawe in Suffolk, both reporting high levels of success and urging the locals to rise. On June 14 the first rebel attack in Cambridgeshire singled out a manor of the Knights Hospitaller at Chippenham. The next day the revolt exploded at a dozen different places throughout the county. Men rode through the county announcing that serfdom had ended. One man, Adam Clymme, ordered that no man, whether bound or free, should obey any lord or perform any services for him, upon pain of beheading, unless otherwise ordered by the Great Society....[251]

Robinson raised the possibility that this Great Society might have been the remnants of the Knights Templar who were driven underground in 1307. He also noted the other "secret society" that might have existed in England at that time was Freemasonry. If Masonry did indeed exist then, was there any known connection between it and this revolt, or with the Knights Templar? A deeper look into both societies yielded some interesting discoveries.

Many words, symbols and practices used by Freemasons in lodge rituals have no real meaning in English. Yet it was certainly possible that they had some meaning hundreds of years ago in Freemasonry's early days. From his background in Medieval studies, Robinson was aware that Hugh de Payens and a large number of Knights Templar were from France. French was also the official language still used in English courts until 1362, a holdover from the Norman Conquest of England led by William the Conqueror. So might the explanation for some words in Freemasonry be found in Medieval French?

One of the mysteries he addressed was the name of the central figure in the Masonic Third Degree initiation ritual, Hiram Abiff. This man was described in the Bible as the master builder of Solomon's Temple, and was known simply as Hiram with no last name. Yet in Masonic lore he was always called Hiram Abiff and was identified by the initials H.A. or H.A.B. This path did not look promising to Robinson when there turned out to be no Medieval French word corresponding to "abiff." But the reference in some sources to H.A.B. was intriguing. It would only be written that way if the name had originally been in three parts, as in Hiram A. Biff. In French the word "biffer" meant "to strike out or eliminate." In Masonic tradition, Hiram is struck upon the head with a mallet and killed. So "Hiram à biffe" or "Hiram who was struck and eliminated" apparently became his identifying name. Over the hundreds of years that this name was passed down in oral tradition, the original meaning had been lost and Masons simply repeated and wrote what they heard, which was Hiram Abiff.

If that had been the only puzzling Masonic expression which made sense in Medieval French, it would simply have been interesting and "maybe" true. But this was only the first of many cases where a Medieval French key opened the lock.

Masonic lodges have always been guarded by an officer at the door who only allowed Masons to pass, and at all other times kept the lodge doors closed during these secret meetings. In the Knights Templar this same practice was observed, and the officer at the door carried a drawn sword to enforce the security of the Templar meetings. Today the Masonic officer at the door wears a jewel or insignia that depicts a drawn sword as his mark of office. As we have seen, stonemasons' lodges had no such tradition of an officer at the door, nor of anyone with a drawn sword to enforce security.

This could have simply meant Masons decided much later to copy the Templar practice for fun—if it were not for the peculiar name of this officer. Masons call him the Tyler. If all Freemasons had once been stonemasons, it would be reasonable to assume he was named after the "tiler" who set tiles. That kind of tiler, however, had nothing to do with guarding doors, or even making doors. On the other hand if we look to Medieval French, we see that the word *tailleur* meant "the one who cuts." The cloth-cutter has come down to us with the name *tailor*. In similar fashion, the man at the door who cuts with his sword appears to have come down to us as *tyler*. The French word fits the insignia and function of this officer in Freemasonry.

To pick another Masonic usage that has no real meaning in English, the identifying sign given when a Mason enters the lodge is called the *due guard*. When looking back into Medieval French, it is found that the expression once had a clear meaning. The traditional term for a knight or soldier's protective gesture was "gest du garde." This became shortened in usage to "du garde." English-speaking people heard these words, repeated them, then began to write them as "due guard" in Masonic usage.

This French connection not only sheds some light on current Masonic practices, it gives us two other gifts. The first is a connection between present-day Masonry and the 1300s, when French was still the language of gentlemen and the courts in England. The other is the observation that Masonry still contains many usages which were simply repeated verbatim by its members without really knowing what those things originally meant. Masonry became like a time machine into which various things from long ago were placed and preserved for us to see today.

One of those long-standing usages we still see is the presenting of a white lambskin apron to each brother as he completes the Third Degree ritual and becomes a Master Mason. This apron has long been considered one of the clearest links to stonemasons of old. The reality, however, is somewhat different. No records have been found showing a stonemason wearing an apron of expensive white lambskin. Such work apparel would have been destroyed during the first day on the job by dirt and gashes from rough pieces of stone. Stonemasons wore clothing of sterner stuff. Who, then, wore white lambskin aprons?

The written Rule of the Knights Templar set a requirement of chastity within the Order. To help brothers keep this vow it required them to wear a girding garment of white lambskin around their loins at all times. This was not taken off for any reason, even for bathing. For that reason it became a distinguishing mark of the Templars by which they identified their fellow brothers. This was a custom not generally seen by or known to the public. For that reason there was no public catch-phrase or emulation of "wearing lambskin like a Templar." Much like the words in French repeated by people after the original meaning was lost, the wearing of white lambskin "aprons" was done by Masons for one reason only: because it had always been done. So the tradition continued.

A related tradition existed in Freemasonry, and that was the wearing of gloves during meetings and official events. This is still the practice in many lodges. We saw the printed report that Masons put on white gloves before the Irish Grand Lodge meeting in 1725, so this custom was present when Masonic lodges first emerged into public view. But was this a new tradition adopted by these "public" Masons for fashionable or other reasons? In 1686, when Freemasonry was still a secret society, we saw Robert Plot describe a ceremony in which Freemasons were presented with gloves by the new brothers coming into Masonry. Clearly then, this has been a longstanding custom.

Going back a step further, it was seen that the clerics of the Knights Templar, in addition to their green robes with the red Templar cross, also wore gloves in the performance of their duties.

> Their Rule required that the Templar priests wear gloves at all times to keep their hands clean "for when they touch God" in serving Holy Communion.[252]

While this obligatory practice of hand covering applied to all priests among the Knights Templar, in most other religious groups the wearing of gloves was extremely rare. It was generally limited to bishops and higher prelates. It was a distinction and honor that would have been cherished by the Templar clergy. These clerical brothers would have been well represented among the surviving Templars since they were responsible for the safe houses in which the Templars took refuge. If they brought with them any small, inconspicuous thing as a reminder of brighter Templar days, it would reasonably have been their gloves.

The white lambskin aprons and gloves were among the first clear connections that linked Masons to the Knights Templar. Yet they were certainly not the last. Consider the square and compass, by which Freemasonry is still recognized all over the world.

Robinson noted that, like most people on the run from authorities, the fugitive Templars would have met in isolated forests and temporary rooms where they could bring all that they needed for their ceremonies, then go away as quietly as they came. In case they were stopped by the authorities—which was apparently a frequent occurrence in those days of runaway serfs, highwaymen and other fugitives from the law—the covert Templars could not be carrying obvious symbols of a secret society. That would have led to immediate arrest and whatever punishment local authorities chose to dole out. So the things these "conspirators" used in their ceremonies had to be items of innocent appearance—until they were properly brought together during the secret rites.

Today, Masonic oaths are taken on a Bible, with a compass and square resting on top of it.[253] This is different than the Templar oaths, which were taken on a Bible by itself. Those Templar Bibles were written by hand and were in Latin, as were all the other Bibles of that day. Printed Bibles in local languages did not yet exist in the 1300s. And those hand-copied Latin Bibles were primarily kept in churches. If the early secret society in Britain during the Peasants Revolt was related to the suppressed Templars in some way, then in place of a Bible it would reasonably have needed to use some other symbol during the oath-taking. Robinson searched through all the religious symbols available, and finally came up with one that was surprisingly good. The Poor Fellow-Soldiers of Christ and the Temple of Solomon were of course familiar with the Seal of Solomon, the symbol used by one of their principal benefactors. This seal resembled the six-pointed Star of David, except that it was made of two triangles, one white and one black. It would have been instantly recognizable to all of their brothers, just as it was on this old medallion.

> The "Mémoires de la Société Royale des Antiquaires de France"…contains a most curious and interesting account of the church of Brelevennez, in the department des Cotes-du-Nord, supposed to have formerly belonged to the order of the Temple, written by the Chevalier du Fremanville. Amongst various curious devices, crosses, and symbols found upon the windows and the tombs of the church, is a copper medallion, which appears to have been suspended from the neck by a chain. This decoration consists of a small

*Fig. 36   Masonic square and compass upon
the six-pointed Seal of Solomon*

circle, within which are inscribed two equilateral triangles placed one upon the other, so as to form a six-
pointed star. In the midst of the star is a second circle,
containing within it the lamb of the order of the Temple holding the banner in its fore-paw....[254]

Yet carrying symbols that resembled the Jewish Star of David
in staunchly Catholic Europe at that time would have been a severe problem. It could have easily led to that undesired arrest by
the authorities of church and state. However, if one simply
dropped the two horizontal lines from the Seal of Solomon, an
immediately recognizable design was formed—that of a square
and compass.

Men could then go to their meetings carrying a square and
compass without arousing any suspicion. If stopped by authorities
of the king or Church, they could simply say, "I am a mason," and
go on. In addition, stonemasons were not like the serfs or local
craftsmen who were confined to the estate on which they were
born. As masons, the brothers could travel in their own country
and in foreign lands. The compass and square they carried were
their passport, requiring only a local mason as a character witness.

This custom of traveling masons became so well established in
Europe that even as late as the 1600s Freemason Sir Robert Moray
used it to gain the right to be in the Netherlands. Moray went to
live in that country for a period of time, and in the local archives[255]
the following entry was recorded by the authorities.

On the 10th of March, 1659, appeared Sir Robert
Moray, Knight, born in Scotland, Privy Councillor of
the King of Great Britain in Scotland, and Colonel of
the Scottish Guards in the service of His Majesty, the
King of France, aged fifty years, presented by Everard,
master of the Craft of masons. He took under this craft
the necessary oath, and the right of citizenship was
granted him, according to custom. [256]

So we see evidence linking Freemasonry closer to the Knights
Templar in the square and compass symbol, aprons, gloves and

numerous ancient words still in use. Yet as persuasive as this evidence seemed to be in 1989 when Robinson introduced many of these points, the debate over a connection between the Knights Templar and Freemasonry continued. Fortunately more evidence has now become available to help fill in some missing pieces of this large jigsaw puzzle and make the final picture easier to see.

Our earlier exploration of the Knights Templar has already filled in the importance of that society's three sub-orders: white-robed brothers from noble families; green-robed brothers imbued with secrecy, literacy and clerical skills; and black/brown-robed brothers bearing the tools of their crafts.

They all contributed to the skills and resources used by the Templars when they came under attack in 1307. Especially significant were the long overlooked contributions of their green-clad clerical brothers, and the financial network that allowed their funds to flow secretly and securely. The conversion of that network and secrecy during the several months of warning in England, Scotland and Ireland afforded the Templars a form of underground railroad into which they were able to step and disappear from view.

Now the filling in of missing pieces continues as we unroll some actual manuscripts from Medieval and later times that have been preserved in remarkably good condition. With all the things we have discovered up to this point, we can now read them with clearer vision and understanding, seeing further evidence that went unnoticed before.

Old Charges and Cooke's Tour

After Freemasonry emerged from secrecy into public view during 1717 a treasure trove of ancient Masonic manuscripts was discovered. These parchment manuscripts became known as the Old Charges, to distinguish them from newer documents produced after the founding of the Grand Lodge in England. These documents described how a person would be "charged" in Masonry to follow good rules in life. Each was couched in the language of stonemasons, but was good advice for anyone.

James Anderson was one of the Masons involved in the founding of that Grand Lodge and he was granted access to all those manuscripts. From them he drew much of the material used in his influential *Constitutions of the Free-Masons*, published in 1723. [257]

This *Constitutions* document was particularly useful, since very few Masons were ever given access to the original manuscripts to learn what they contained. Yet Anderson's cleansing and summarizing process also washed away many of the rich details that could convey to us valuable descriptions of Freemasonry in its early days as a secret society. Those details and rich descriptions are recovered here.

Unrolling these parchment manuscripts and examining them carefully we are able to fill in many gaps in the picture of Freemasonry's relationships with stonemasons and the Knights Templar—whether those relationships be near or far. The overall picture, as we have seen, was reasonably clear up to the time most of the Templars escaped into protective secrecy in 1307. It also was quite clear after Freemasons emerged from secrecy in 1717. In between those two events we have managed to fill in some pieces with the help of Sir Robert Moray, Thomas Gresham, John Mylne, the St. Clairs and many others. To these accounts we now add actual manuscripts written by people who lived during those days and saw the events transpire.

These Old Charges manuscripts not only contained guidelines for living as a good member of society but also provided curious references to stonemasonry mixed with things completely outside the experience of stonemasons. The documents have been reliably dated, and cover the period from 1390 through the 1700's. Each one was copied by hand from an earlier manuscript.[258] Usually written on parchment and rolled into long scrolls, there were a few preserved as separate pages of parchment sewn together. These Old Charges ranged in appearance from almost illegible scrawls hastily done, to beautiful calligraphy illuminated with intricate drawings. Altogether, about 120 of these documents were found in different collections. I was allowed to examine many of these original, fragile documents preserved at the United Grand Lodge of England, as well as faithful reproductions of those held in other hands. They were remarkably revealing.

Rather than speak in generalities, however, let us consider the actual content of one of the earliest Old Charges documents: the Cooke Manuscript. This was written around the year 1450, and appeared to be copied from an even older document. The content of this manuscript was first translated from Old English into modern English by Matthew Cooke,[259] in whose honor the original document was named.[260]

One of the first significant details of the Cooke Manuscript was not only that it opened with a prayer, but the particular form this prayer took.

> Thanked be God, our glorious Father, the founder and
> creator of heaven and earth, and of all things that
> therein are, for that he has vouchsafed, of his glorious
> Godhead, to make so many things of manifold virtue
> for the use of mankind....

In those times, religious expression was a prominent part of
English society, so it was not entirely unusual for a prayer to be
included in the document. The slightly more traditional beginning
would have been to acknowledge a temporal authority such as a
king or lord,[261] but that was not a requirement. Beginning with a
prayer does, however, suggest that the group by which this was
written had some religious orientation or stronger than normal
religious commitment. The strangest aspect of this was that the
Catholic Church was still the dominant religion in Europe at that
time, yet after acknowledging God, neither the Church nor the
pope was mentioned anywhere in the document.

That curious combination is reminiscent of an unusual requirement made of each person seeking to enter Freemasonry. The
candidate had to believe in God. However he was not required to
believe in a particular religion. This was a highly unusual combination, to say the least. Most organizations have avoided this difficult subject by making no requirement that a person believe in
God. Those that did have such a requirement normally went a
step further and required a belief in Christianity, or some other
specific doctrine. Freemasonry did not. So while the Cooke Manuscript prayer would be odd for most other groups, it was a perfect
fit with the practices of Freemasons.

However it was not a good fit for stonemasons. Great Britain in
the 1400's was almost 100 percent Christian, with a small number
of Jews and people of other faiths. To be Christian in those days
before the Protestant Reformation meant that one was Catholic. In
addition, stonemasons earned a large part of their living by building churches and cathedrals, so their employers were devout
Catholics. There was no benefit for stonemasons to be anything
other than staunchly Catholic at that time. In fact, any lack of enthusiasm in that regard could be punishable by inquisition and
death, as many in Europe had already discovered. A document of

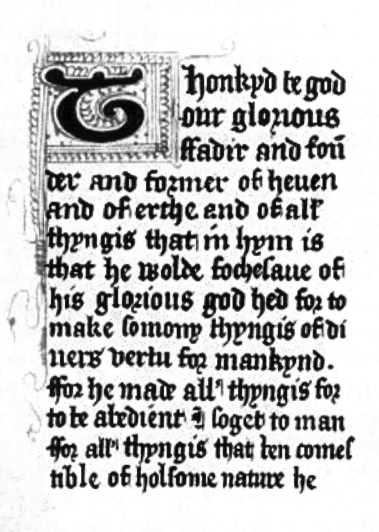

Fig. 37   Cooke Manuscript, the second oldest of the Old Charges
of Freemasonry, begins this way in Old English.

guidelines for stonemasons could easily have avoided mention of religion at all—just as the charters granted by towns to stonemasons often did. Alternatively, such a manuscript could bless God and the pope, as was common for documents mentioning religion. It was unnecessary for stonemasons to put their neck on the chopping block by invoking God but not the Church or the pope. This by itself would not be sufficient proof that the manuscripts were not created by stonemasons, but it raises reasonable questions.

The Knights Templar, on the other hand, had lived their life deeply connected not only to the service of God, but tied to the pope in every way. The Grand Master of their Order reported directly to the pope, and only to him. So from this standpoint, they also would seem ill-suited to be associated with the Old Charges manuscripts. Of course we now know that was not their whole story. In 1307 the pope abandoned them, giving them up to be arrested, tortured, and then burned alive. Understandably, that lessened their attachment to the pope. This left the surviving Templars deeply conflicted. They had dedicated their lives to God's service, and the trial testimony of captured Templars showed that these men still felt strongly compelled in that direction. Yet the brothers seemed understandably split on how to view the religion to which they belonged. That they would create a legacy of love for God—yet omit any reference to the Church or the pope from their writings—would be consistent with what we know about them.

The next part of Cooke—and usually in other Old Charges as well—was a clear appreciation of the seven arts and sciences, along with a brief description of them. In this group, geometry was given special mention, as shown here.

> These seven sciences are as follows:
> The first, which is called the foundation of all science, is grammar, which teacheth to write and speak correctly.
> The second is rhetoric, which teaches us to speak elegantly.

The third is dialectic, which teaches us to discern the true from the false, and it is usually called art or sophistry (logic).

The fourth is arithmetic, which instructs us in the science of numbers, to reckon, and to make accounts.

The fifth is Geometry, which teaches us all about mensuration, measures and weights, of all kinds of handicrafts.

The sixth is music, and that teaches the art of singing by notation for the voice, on the organ, trumpet, and harp, and of all things pertaining thereto.

The seventh is astronomy, which teaches us the course of the sun and of the moon and of the other stars and planets of heaven.

Our intent is to treat chiefly of the first foundation of Geometry and who were the founders thereof.

It should be pointed out that in those days normal university education was built around the arts and sciences, but with a particular purpose in mind. That purpose, as we saw earlier, was to train new priests and other clergy, with a smaller number of the nobility receiving some part of that education. It was common for kings and lords to require clergy be present at official events to record whatever was necessary, since most of the highly-born people could not write themselves.

Recall for a moment the typical stonemasons' lodge. Standing around blocks of stone upon which they worked, these were rough-handed, unschooled, and largely or completely illiterate men. Now try to imagine them sitting down and attempting to write a document that went into something they never had, and never would have: a university education. And try to imagine these working men putting themselves through all that just to introduce the subject of geometry.

If they hired a scribe to write down their words, and spoke from their own experience, it would have produced a far different discussion. That would reasonably have produced an interesting document based on the precise squaring of stones, the careful matching of uniquely-shaped columns and arches, and the art of carving which causes faces and flowers to emerge from previously shapeless blocks of stone. In England I was able to talk with a number of stonemasons who were still plying this ancient trade. They shared with me some of the love they felt for their work, and I learned that they have their own expressions and view of the world. None of that springs from the pages of these manuscripts. An entirely different hand and mind seems to have created them.

On the other hand Freemasons had a clear relationship with the arts and sciences. We saw some of them dedicated much of their life to gaining the right to pursue the arts and sciences, and helped to form the Royal Society. Other Freemasons continued that tradition at the Royal Society, including John Desaguliers and Benjamin Franklin.

Even today the arts and sciences have significant roles in the traditions and rituals of Freemasonry. This is perhaps clearest in the rite of the Second Degree that involves the Winding Staircase. Each of the seven arts and sciences is an essential step in the staircase. The connection between Freemasonry and the invoking of the seven arts and sciences in the Old Charges seems to be quite clear.

Among the Knights Templar, the only group that had a close connection with the arts and sciences would have been the green-robed clerics.[262] These men were well-educated, just like the other clergy of their day. Their experience made them highly skilled in languages of the East and the West, and they were sufficiently capable with numbers to create and maintain the financial consortium that spread from Europe to the Middle East.

After 1307, the Templars who survived had access to funds and property gleaned from the former Order and could afford good education. Like many other men no longer living under vows, they were able to start their own families and make decisions about how to raise their children. Among well-to-do families, home schooling was a popular decision. It allowed their children to achieve a bare minimum of literacy and numbers, with some learning only enough to sign their name. Given the important role education played in building their financial empire, the Templar survivors would reasonably have given more attention to home-schooling and university education than the average family that inherited its power and position. In any event the experiences of Templar survivors, and especially the clerics among them, would have been consistent with the discussion in the Old Charges manuscripts of the seven arts and sciences.

The Cooke Manuscript then recited a "traditional" history of Masonry that was more of a fanciful construction than real record. That is why these accounts are called "traditions" in Masonry. This is some of the imaginative content found in this part of the manuscript.

> Before Noah's Flood by direct male descent from Adam in the seventh generation, there lived a man called Lamech who had two wives, called Adah and Zillah. By the first wife, Adah, he begat two sons, Jabal and Jubal. The elder son Jabal was the first man that ever discovered geometry and masonry, and he made houses, and is called in the Bible the father of all men who dwell in tents or dwelling houses. And he was Cain's master mason and governor of the works when he built the city of Enoch, which was the first city ever made and was built by Cain, Adam's son, who gave it to his own son Enoch, and give the city the name of his son and called it Enoch, and now it is known as Ephraim. And at that place was the Science of Geometry and Masonry first prosecuted and contrived as a science and as a handicraft. And so we may well say that it is the first cause and foundation of all crafts and sciences. And also this man Jabel was called the father of shepherds. The Master of History says, and Beda De Imagine Mundi and the Policronicon and many others more say, that he was the first that made partition of lands, in order that every man might know his own land and labour thereon for himself. And also he divided flocks of sheep, that every man might know his own sheep, and so we may say that he was the inventor of that science.

So here was a man named Jabal, in the eighth generation after Adam, described as the master mason for Adam's son Cain—even though the two men would have been separated in time by about 200 years.[263] Somehow the author of the tract also professed to know Jabal was a master mason, and governor of works. All of this appeared to be imaginatively expanded from the Bible, which told us only this.[264]

> And Lamech took unto him two wives: the name of the one was Adah, and the name of the other Zillah. And Adah bare Jabal: he was the father of such as dwell in tents, and of such as have cattle. And his brother's name was Jubal: he was the father of all such as handle the harp and organ.
>
> *Genesis 4:19-21*

After that, the rest of the tradition wended its way through the work of Euclid in Egypt, Solomon's Temple, Medieval France, and finally England. Its fanciful creations seemed to have the purpose of sketching a mythological tradition, far removed from reality, that might capture one's imagination the way Greek mythology had once been wont to do.

One discernible reason to create such a mythology would be to fill a blank spot for people who had no idea of their actual history. A second reason could be to help people conceal a history they did not want to come to light. Stonemasons might have fit into the first explanation, since they were not well-educated in history and the like. Freemasons might fit either the first or second explanation. Templar survivors would clearly fall into the second explanation, being fugitives from the law. All things considered, this does not seem to be one of the "tipping points" that help us resolve the remaining parts of this puzzle.

The actual "charges" in the Old Charges were guides to good moral conduct. They were the things each person was "charged" to do in living a good life. These were presented as if said to a stonemason, yet were good allegories for anyone on how to live an honorable life. Freemasons have continued to use this same process for many centuries. The first two articles in Cooke illustrate how this worked.

> The first article is this. That every master of this art should be wise, and true to the lord who employs him, expending his goods carefully as he would his own were expended; and not give more pay to any mason than he knows him to have earned, according to the dearth [or scarcity and therefore price] of corn and victuals in the country and this without favouritism, for every man is to be rewarded according to his work.
>
> The Second article is this. That every master of the art shall be warned beforehand to come to his congregation in order that he may duly come, unless he may [be] excused for some cause or other. But if he be found [i.e., accused of being] rebellious at such congregation, or at fault in any way to his employer's harm or the reproach of this art, he shall not be excused unless he be in peril of death. And though he be in peril of death, yet must he give notice of his illness to the master who is the president of the gathering.

The stonemasons of that day could have lived according to such rules, and may in fact have done so. There were nine articles and nine points in these charges, and they could have easily been passed down verbally from masters to apprentices at that time. They were short enough to be easily memorized and followed, so stonemasons had no need to write them down—even if they had known how to write. In any event, memorization would have been the best way to keep these charges on stonemasons' minds every day in the workplace.

For Freemasons, these charges are reflected in rites still being used today. In the Entered Apprentice degree, when a new Mason is charged to properly use a twenty-four inch gauge or ruler, he is actually being urged to divide his twenty-four hour day properly to meet all his obligations.

This was much like the popular sayings in Benjamin Franklin's *Poor Richard's Almanack*, where good advice was dressed in other clothes. The *Almanack's* expression "a stitch in time saves nine" clearly had meaning beyond sewing—it offered practical advice for life. Freemasons used the charges, the tools, the arts, and the lodges of stonemasons as a way to look inside life, and find a better way to live in society. The Old Charges manuscripts appear to have served that same role.

A guide to good behavior in society would have been as attractive to survivors of the Knights Templar as it would have been to any other conscientious member of society. Yet for them, the applicability of the Cooke Manuscript went a step farther than that. Just before the "charges" were listed, a story was told that these guidelines were needed because of unidentified defects among stonemasons around 930 AD. The story may or may not be true, but the choice of words was quite interesting.

> ...in the time of king Athelstan, sometime king of England, by common assent of his Council and other great lords of the land on account of great defects found amongst masons, a certain rule was ordained for them.

Monastic orders were governed in those days by a Rule. That was the primary use of the term when expressed in this manner. The word "ordained" could mean "ordered" but was most closely associated with religious usage, as in "the novice was ordained into the clergy."[265] Stonemasons were not a religious order. As such, they were not ordained, and did not receive a Rule from the Church. It is possible that this was simply a colorful reference, but it would be a highly unusual reference for a stonemason to make about his own occupation. On the other hand, it would be a term familiar to the descendants of a religious brother such as a Knight Templar, whose family had been deeply marked by that experience.

Earlier we saw the possibility of Freemasonry evolving from Medieval stonemason lodges had serious problems, which made that avenue less likely than it may have seemed before. The Cooke

Manuscript has shown us other difficulties with this possibility. That poses a dilemma, because for some reason the tools and practices of stonemasons were chosen to be used in the allegories and symbols of Freemasonry. Examining many collections of those Masonic symbols for clues, I discovered something interesting.

The symbols of Freemasonry contain numerous references to ancient works. The Great Pyramid is portrayed, often with the all-seeing eye. Solomon's Temple appears often, including its details such as the winding staircase and the twin pillars *Jachin* and *Boaz*. Arches were used in Mesopotamian times and became highly popular among the ancient Romans. The tools of compass, square, plumb and level were also known and used in antiquity. Yet oddly enough, ***there are no significant symbols in Masonry relating to Medieval buildings such as cathedrals***. This is true even though those were the main product and hallmark of Medieval stonemasons. There is no depiction of Notre Dame Cathedral, Westminster Abbey, or other prominent church. There are no church towers in general, nor naves or flying buttresses.

The Masonic symbols that constitute the core of Freemasonry suggest that the connection with stonemasons did not take place during the Medieval period. Instead they point to stonemasonry as it existed in ancient times. Following that thread causes us to look again at the green-robed clerics among the Knights Templar. The Lebanese Christians in this group clung strongly to their Phoenician roots, as many Lebanese people still do today. Their Phoenician forebears had been present at the building of the Great Pyramid, and provided Hiram Abiff along with other masons for the raising of Solomon's Temple. That gave the Knights Templar their strongest link back to the temple for which they were named. It is a link that would have been cherished and remembered.

When the time came for fugitive Templars to choose a new name for themselves, a common name so that they could pass without being arrested, they chose to be Masons. And they chose as their symbols those things that would remind them of their past.

At the end of the Cooke Manuscript came the words, "Amen, so mote it be." This was done as if one were closing a prayer. Even

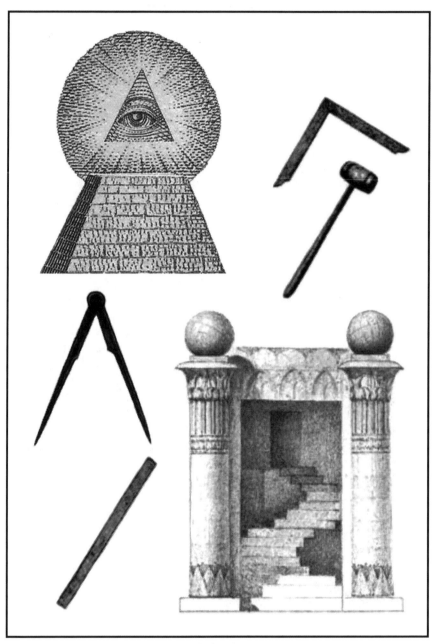

Fig. 38 Symbols of Freemasonry

today, Freemasons end each prayer with the word "Amen"—to which the brothers respond, "So mote it be."

The Cooke Manuscript has given us an interesting look into the lives and practices of an unusual group of people in Britain around the year 1450. To discover more about the early days of this society, let us step back further in time, to see what happened in the 1300s when the Knights Templar were being disbanded.

Regius, Templars and Freemasonry in the 1300s

Our search for Freemasonry's early connections to other societies and the driving force behind its growth brings us at last to a manuscript older than Cooke. It has exceptional value because of its distinctive content. This is the Regius Manuscript,[266] the first of the Old Charges. It was written about 1390, and seemed to make reference to a related document written earlier in the 1300s.[267] Regius was the only Old Charge written as a poem, and it described events such as one might find in a gentleman's household. Due to its age and unique content, Regius provides a remarkable window into the years following the disappearance of the Knights Templar.

As the first of the Old Charges, it also reveals some things about the early days of Freemasonry. The manuscript opens in this manner.

> Here begin the constitutions of the art
> of Geometry according to Euclid.
>
> Whoever will both well read and look
> He may find written in old book

> Of great lords and also ladies,
> That had many children together, certainly;
> And had no income to keep them with,
> Neither in town nor field nor enclosed wood;
> A council together they could them take,
> To ordain for these children's sake,
> How they might best lead their life
> Without great dis-ease, care and strife;
> And most for the multitude that was coming
> Of their children after great clerks,
> To teach them then good works;

The first sentence was written in Latin, showing that the author was a highly educated person, and not a lightly trained noble or non-literate stoneworker. The rest appeared in Old English and was composed into rhyming meter extending 794 lines, which also indicated a high degree of literacy. The intended audience for the work seemed to include lords and ladies, with an eye toward providing guidance for their families.

Curiously, Regius focused on a specific concern for those families: they often had many children, but only one of those children could inherit the noble title and lands of the family. What was to be done with the other children who would receive no income property? The daughters were not a concern, since they would normally be married off to good families. However the younger sons posed a serious difficulty. In exploring the lives of the Knights Templar earlier, we saw their Order was part of the solution to this problem. Younger sons traditionally were prodded into taking vows in religious orders. There they became well educated, but lived a dull life—unless they took their vows with the Knights Templar. Then they lived a chivalrous life in a profusely well-endowed order.

With the fall of the Knights Templar, that option no longer existed for them.[268] This poem suggested Masonry could be appropriate for younger sons who might previously have been urged to be clergy or Templars.

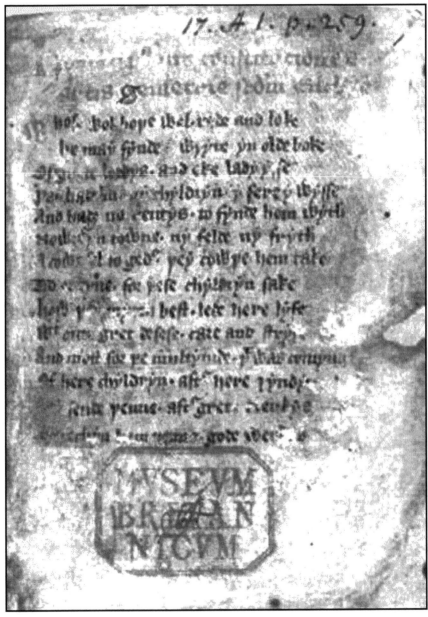

Fig. 39 Regius Manuscript, the earliest of the Old Charges of Freemasonry, begins this way in Latin and Old English.

And pray we them, for our Lord's sake.
To our children some work to make,
That they might get their living thereby,
Both well and honestly full securely.
In that time, through good geometry,
This honest craft of good masonry
Was ordained and made in this manner,
Counterfeited of these clerks together;
At these lord's prayers they counterfeited
geometry,
And gave it the name of masonry,
For the most honest craft of all.

Note the observation in Regius that geometry was worked by clerks—which in those days meant clerics—into masonry. There was no known tradition among stonemasons that clerics were the original masons. Within the Knights Templar, however, we saw the green-robed clerics originally arose from among masons in the Holy Land.

On the face of it, this poem seemed to recommend that younger sons become stonemasons. Based upon that, one would have expected that if this well-preserved poem had some effect in the world, then history would have recorded a highly unusual trend of gentlemen forsaking their lofty station to work with their hands as stonemasons. Yet no such trend was reported. So the poem either had no effect at all, or its meaning was somewhat deeper.

The answer to this particular puzzle seemed to be reflected in the fact that Regius was not recognized as being connected to Freemasonry for many years. It was referred to simply as a poem of moral duties. Oddly enough, that description was one of the things that tied it to Freemasonry. As every Mason can attest, the tools and practices of the stonemason are used as allegories for life—which is to say that there is another meaning behind the superficial one. That second meaning reflects the Mason's moral duties in life.

Almost everyone knows that a "square" was an L-shaped tool used for making a block of stone or wood truly square or rectangular. Yet in a person's life it meant something was truly fair or correct. This led to expressions such as "a square deal," in which the words really do not make any sense outside of Freemasonry. Similarly, the stonemason's "level" insured the stone was being laid properly so that one side was not lower than the other. In life it meant that something was not being tipped or biased unfairly in one direction or another, as a person being "on the level," or people meeting "on the level" as equals who respected each other. For many generations, Freemasons actively discussed the use of the square, the level, and similar items as guides for life. Other members of society simply heard interesting expressions and repeated them. Influence in society is not always blunt and direct— sometimes it is quiet and indirect.

The same seemed to be true of Regius. If it was not an actual call for young gentlemen to give up their privileged life and dirty their hands by hewing stones, what was it? Perhaps it was originally intended to call younger sons to make their own way in the world as honest tradesmen and merchants rather than be a drain on the family. Or perhaps it was a straightforward call for young gentlemen to become Freemasons. Given that the poem went on to present the traditional history, articles and points that made up the Old Charges of Freemasonry, this third choice seems to be strongly indicated.

Since all the Old Charges and Constitutions[269] of Freemasonry copied and paraphrased this one document from the 1300s, it may be useful to consider the segment of society toward which this original appeal was directed. These younger sons of noble families—the same people who once formed the Templars' core membership—now seemed to be prime candidates for Freemasonry. Since it was normal for people to seek members similar to themselves, it speaks to the composition of the group making this proposal—a well-educated group of gentlemen.

Note that in those days the term "gentlemen" referred to well-to-do men who were not bound by contract to work for a lord or other owner. They were free to be merchants or simply live off their family's assets. Although the lords who owned large estates could sometimes be included in this group, they generally received a separate and higher recognition as "nobility."

Fig. 40   Freemasons meeting "on the level" in the 1700s

Having younger sons of noble families as members of such a group was attractive for other reasons as well. We saw one of the hallmarks of Freemasonry was that its members joined together to protect themselves from the arbitrary acts of powerful men, as they did when the Royal Society was formed. Arbitrary and powerful men had also crushed the Templars. On the other hand, younger sons of noble families were not men to be feared by anyone, since they were not going to inherit the family's estates and power. In fact they were valuable allies. Being brothers in those noble families, they were not as easily intimidated by the prospect of having to face an older brother or similar men if that need arose. There was also a further advantage. As younger sons, some of them had received a university education in preparation for going into the clergy. That would have made them similar to the green-robed clerics of the Templars, and similar to the well-educated author of the Regius Manuscript.

Unlike later versions of the Old Charges, the "traditional" history in Regius was quite short. In the equivalent of about eight paragraphs it covered what Anderson's *Constitutions* would cover in forty-eight.[270] The telling of this tale in Regius seemed to be enjoyed by all, and so it kept getting longer by being padded with imagined details as time went on.[271]

The seven arts and sciences were described in Regius, and were similar in form to what was found in Cooke as well as the other Old Charges. The prayer in Regius was considerably longer than that which appeared in later manuscripts, which would be appropriate for a group that retained influences from a religious order.

The Regius manuscript also referred to "the four crowned ones." These were four martyrs in Rome around 305 AD who refused to forsake their faith, even to the moment of death. The martyrs' situation seemed to resonate with the author. By some coincidence it also echoed the experience of the captured Templars.

> The art of the four crowned ones.
> Pray we now to God almighty,
> And to his mother Mary bright,
> That we may keep these articles here,

And these points well all together,
As did these holy martyrs four,
That in this craft were of great honour;
They were as good masons as on earth shall go,
Gravers and image-makers they were also.
For they were workmen of the best,
The emperor had to them great liking;
He willed of them an image to make
That might be worshipped for his sake;
Such monuments he had in his day,
To turn the people from Christ's law.

But they were steadfast in Christ's law,
And to their craft without doubt;
They loved well God and all his lore,
And were in his service ever more.
True men they were in that day,
And lived well in God's law;
They thought no monuments for to make,
For no good that they might take,
To believe on that monument for their God,
They would not do so, though he was furious;
For they would not forsake their true faith,
And believe on his false law,
The emperor let take them soon anon,
And put them in a deep prison;
The more sorely he punished them in that place,
The more joy was to them of Christ's grace,
Then when he saw no other one,
To death he let them then go;
By the book he might it show
In legend of holy ones,
The names of the four-crowned ones.[272]

The "emperor" sought to have them create a false image for all to worship and these men refused, paying the ultimate price. If it was meant to honor fallen Templars, it overlooked the fact that their faith wavered and they confessed to the false image of them.

But in the end they were resolute and told the truth, causing many of them to die in flames rather than yield.

The Knights Templar counted among their brothers not only noble-born knights and well-educated clerics, but also serving-men drawn from the rest of society. This point likewise seemed to have found its way into Regius, for it concluded with simple rules of etiquette when in public. Reflecting the different levels of society at that time, it suggested proper deference be shown to a person of higher station. This guidance to working men was brief or missing altogether in the later Old Charges.

> When thou meetest a worthy man,
> Cap and hood thou hold not on;
> In church, in market, or in the gate,
> Do him reverence after his state.
> If thou goest with a worthier man
> Then thyself thou art one,
> Let thy foremost shoulder follow his back,
> For that is nurture without lack;
>
> When he doth speak, hold thee still,
> When he hath done, say for thy will,
> In thy speech that thou be discreet,
> And what thou sayest consider thee well;
> But deprive thou not him his tale,
> Neither at the wine nor at the ale.
> Christ then of his high grace,
> Save you both wit and space,
> Well this book to know and read,
> Heaven to have for your reward.
> Amen! Amen! so mote it be!
> So say we all for charity.

Just as in the Cooke Manuscript, Regius ends with the traditional Masonic closing of "Amen," followed by "So mote it be." This was Freemasonry in its secretive, early days.

Chapter 25

So Mote It Be

Che combination of Regius, the other Old Charges, Medieval French words in Masonic ritual, the square-and-compass symbol and other pieces of evidence have shown more clearly than we could have expected that Freemasonry was alive and well in the 1300s. Drawn from all levels of society, Masonry was seen to include members of noble families, clerics and craftsmen.

In those early days the stonemason lodges were still in primitive and rustic condition. For the most part they were temporary affairs where a castle or cathedral was being raised, or were informal working places in town. Stonemasons' activities were little noted in most British cities. Only in the latter part of that century did stonemason lodges begin to get organized and recognized in the leading cities. London's stonemasons were granted the right in 1376 to send four representatives to serve on the city's Common Council.

The city of Edinburgh did not grant incorporation to its stonemasons until 1475, at which time its members were so few in number they had to join with the wrights to gain that charter. Official records from this time give no indication that any gentlemen were associated with this Scottish incorporation. Later known as the Lodge of Edinburgh (Mary's Chapel), this group's records from the 1500s still showed no members other than stonemasons and related crafts. Other lodges across Scotland and England had similar experiences.

Since Freemasonry already existed in the 1300s—and continued in the 1400s when the Cooke Manuscript was written—its members were clearly meeting separately from any stonemason activities. *The two existed in parallel during those days.* Stonemasons met in dusty lodge rooms filled with blocks of stone in various states of completion, or they met in corners of churches such as St. Giles or Mary's Chapel. Freemasons met in private lodgings or in the wooded countryside, bringing the instruments of their ceremonies with them.

Prior to the 1600s it is likely that a few stonemasons entered Freemasonry, since its early documents indicate it was open to all levels of society. But the opposite was not true. No gentlemen were recorded as being members of a stonemason lodge until the manipulations by the Scottish Master of Works in 1634, followed by a few other gentlemen who were admitted years later.

An example of parallel meetings held by Freemasons was the initiation of Elias Ashmole in 1646, which took place in a private home. It was attended by several gentlemen but no stonemasons.[273] As we have seen, other gatherings of gentlemen initiating gentlemen into Freemasonry were documented during these times at York and Scarborough. In 1686 Robert Plot described still more Freemason meetings—consisting of gentlemen and men from all levels of society—at locations across the length of England. These were white-glove affairs rather than rough-hands meetings.

This period of the late 1600s was also the time stonemasons' lodges began to lose membership and fall into disuse. London, Edinburgh and other cities began to trim protections from the workmen's lodges, allowing anyone to go onto a worksite and practice the craft without having to be a member of the lodge. With those damaging acts, these bodies lost their main purpose in life. Some lodges closed their doors and disappeared. In other lodges, particularly the flagship lodges in Edinburgh and London, a surprising number of gentlemen showed up and requested admission. It would be reasonable to ask why men of noble birth and wealthy merchants would want to do such a thing.

Given that stonemasons and Freemasons had been co-existing side by side for several hundred years, with Freemasons gathering allegories from their working brethren, it would have been natural for the gentlemen to feel an interest in going to a workshop and seeing the tools of the trade actually put into use. When the working lodges fell on hard times, those gentlemen were able to become patrons and contribute to the upkeep of the lodge. As the number of working members fell so low that the lodge had to consider closing its doors, the patrons may have felt a valued way of life was disappearing. In any event, rather than let the old lodges be turned into places of business or be torn down altogether, the gentlemen came forward in large numbers and took over the lodges. This preserved them—at least in name—in their original use. As we saw at the Lodge of Edinburgh (Mary's Chapel), there was no gradual transition from stonemasons to Freemasons. Over the course of one month, the gentlemen took over the fading lodge and that was that. The change came faster or slower at other lodges, but it came.

A similar process is happening today with the gentrification of historic buildings in cities all over the world. The old structures manage to avoid demolition by being kept in use, and their historic elements—sometimes accompanied by pictures and memorabilia—are preserved. It is not a new concept, especially in Europe.

An unexpected experience brought this to life for me during a trip to England. As a Mason, I felt drawn to see an actual stonemason lodge, and happened to find one that still functions at York Minster. The craftsmen took time from their work to let me examine and feel the heavy stones making their journey from rough blocks to expertly carved images. The back part of these stones were precisely squared and sized to fit exactly into the stone walls of the cathedral, replacing old and possibly broken pieces. It was fascinating to see the Masonic allegories and images of square and compass come alive in the real world. This experience became an indelible memory.

Yet I am not a stonemason by training. In fact, no Freemason I know is a stonemason. We live side by side, in two separate worlds. Yet if I was asked to send a donation to that working lodge in York to keep it open, I would feel obliged to do so. There is no way to explain it. This is just a bit of living history I do not want to disappear.

Did other Freemasons have similar thoughts when the old stonemason lodges began to close their doors? I do not know. But having stood among the stonemasons at York, I know what those Masons would have felt.

What kept these two groups going for several hundred years until the gentlemen took over those working lodges in the 1600s and early 1700s? For stonemasons, the answer was readily apparent. This was their job, their way of making a living. They were paid to be in the lodge, doing their work.

Freemasons came to their separate lodge meetings for a different reason. Some speculate they came for fellowship, and that certainly existed in great measure. Or that they came for the rituals which made them part of an ancient practice, prompting them to be a better person. Or for the outstanding dinners and social events that make life more enjoyable. All of these would be excellent reasons to attend—and yet they basically describe a social club. Social clubs come and go by the hundreds every year.

Freemasonry is, as Masons readily admit, a society with secrets that has managed to stay in existence for many centuries. Over the years it has been difficult to discern what driving force brought it into existence and propelled its growth over all those years. That was largely due to so much being lost from the early days of Masonry. But having drawn back the veil of secrecy surrounding so many things that happened during those early years, the inciting events now become easier to see.

The factors that brought Freemasonry and the Knights Templar closer together have also shed some light on that driving force. Seeing their captured brethren tortured and executed by king and church, the surviving Templars found the close bond between them to be a sturdy shield that allowed them to survive. They literally depended on that bond for their life. These men relied upon their brothers to come to their aid if they should be attacked, and swore a strong oath to aid any brother in distress.

During the years that followed the Templars' transformation into fugitives, excessive use of force by kings and church leaders against different groups of people continued relentlessly. These ongoing injustices reasonably drove an endless supply of refugees to seek protection in local lodges. Those who were found worthy would be accepted, and pledged themselves to come to the aid of their brothers. The new brothers clasped hands with those original Templars, gave thanks to God, and learned the secretive ways that had kept them free. As the years passed, those who were accepted would clasp the hand of a younger man, then teach him the secretive ways that would allow him to protect his freedom. And so it continued.

In the 1300s, religious protesters against the wealth of the Catholic Church became known as Lollards. These people had a surprising ability to avoid pursuit by the church's inquisitors. This was reportedly due to covert aid they received from supporters in the countryside. Along those same lines we saw the Peasants' Revolt in England during 1381, which claimed to have the support of a hidden "Great Society." Attested by multiple sources, these statements indicate a secretive society may have been giving them aid.

The Protestant Reformation found its roots in the followers of John Wycliffe and John Hus in the 1400s, then grew rapidly to encompass large multitudes of people in the 1500s. Those rebels desperately needed protection from the powerful Catholic Church that fought to preserve its way of life. Once that breakaway was successful, the bloody conflict moved from inquisition cells to the battlefield as Protestant armies and Catholic armies engaged in mutual carnage across Europe. Refugees fled the forces of both sides and needed sanctuary. Civil wars tore many countries, with England going through its worst in 1642-1651 as Royalists fought Parliamentarians on battlefields and died on executioners' scaffolds. Many on both sides found need of succor and shelter. Freemasonry thrived during these times.

And when the fighting finally ended, those who had been given shelter not only survived but tasted victory. The Vatican had lost its position of supremacy in the Christian world and could no longer order people burned to death, as had been done to the

Templars. The Catholic Church was still able to practice its ministry, of course, but now in balance with Protestant denominations.

The practices of Freemasonry had become visible when English Royalists and Parliamentarians finally came together to limit the powers of their king with a Bill of Rights in 1689. But Masonry was still a secret society in those days before 1717, so its practitioners continued to conceal their membership and passed unseen across that stage.

All of this changed prior to the American Revolution—because by then Masonry had already emerged into public view. Benjamin Franklin displayed his membership when he was chosen as Provincial Grand Master of Pennsylvania in 1734. And he promptly re-published *The Constitutions of the Free-Masons* for readers in the American colonies.

So Masons were much more matter-of-fact about their membership by the time the American Revolution broke out. One such Boston Mason named Paul Revere took a famous midnight ride across Massachusetts in 1775 to warn people in Lexington and Concord that British soldiers were coming to attack them. An important part of Revere's mission that night was to help a distressed fellow Mason in his lodge—John Hancock—escape capture by the British at Lexington.

Because of those deeds, Hancock was still free one month later when it was time to choose a president for the Continental Congress. This was the assembly that united and led Americans during the Revolutionary War. Hancock was elected to lead that revolutionary congress.

One of this body's first acts was to choose a Commander in Chief for its army, which in reality was a cobbled-together group of state militias. George Washington was quickly approved for that critical role. As he struggled to prepare his rag-tag troops to go up against the far more disciplined and well-prepared British forces, Washington was clearly a Mason in distress. His call for help was answered by brothers from across the colonies, and even by the Marquis de Lafayette from France and Baron von Steuben from Germany.

During the course of the war, almost fifty percent of all the generals who served under Washington were Masons. That was an extraordinary number because the highest figure I have ever seen reported for Masons in the USA was about nine percent of the male population.[274]

In a similar manner, this society was well represented among the founding fathers of the United States. Thirty-three percent of the signers of the Constitution were Masons.[275]

Even this Constitution was a strange occurrence. Before that time, there was no such thing as a nation being ruled by a constitution. Countries were ruled by kings who granted some rights to the people. Yet governance by constitution had existed in Masonic lodges for hundreds of years. We have even seen several of these lodge documents here. When it came time for the founding fathers to govern their new country, they went with something familiar to themselves that they had recently introduced to their states. They created a Constitution.

As for the number of presidents of the United States at that time, there was only one—George Washington—and he was a Mason. So this quiet society's representation at that level was 100 percent. In keeping with the hopes of the original Masons, he presided over a land where the use of excessive force by king or church was not possible. It was a new day.

Freemasonry had thrived for hundreds of years because it was based on bonds between men. Those bonds had enabled brothers to survive the many acts of excessive violence by leaders of nations and religions against the common people. This was the driving force that brought Freemasonry into existence, and caused it to grow stronger over the decades.

Perhaps the best way to say it is that Freemasonry was about freedom. It provided that freedom for a fairly compact band of brothers at first, but then grew from there.

The fugitive band of Templars set aside their white robe, red cross and honored name in order to survive. In place of those things they adopted the symbols of masons. And they took the name Free-Masons. Though bearing this name, these men were not builders of stone cathedrals. They were builders of free men.

Those free men then played essential roles in building free countries, whether founding the Royal Society, taking seats in Parliament, signing the American Constitution, or marching in the French Revolution.

Through oaths sworn in secret they kept those commitments alive. And their quiet society still creates the kind of man who comes to the aid of a brother in distress.

Appendix

*Fig. 41 Seated beside the Apprentice Pillar in Rosslyn Chapel
a man looks down the stairs to the Lower Chapel*

A Rosslyn Secret

$\mathcal{T}$here is no way to know exactly what happened in those first days after the Knights Templar began to be arrested, when most of them disappeared into "underground" places of safety. It was quite literally a matter of life or death that their whereabouts and activities not be revealed or recorded in any way. The secrecy that surrounded those days was almost airtight.

But we do know some things that appeared in the public record, and these open the door to events that may have occurred at Rosslyn Chapel and contributed to the mystique that has surrounded this church ever since those early days. Henry St. Clair, the 3rd Baron of Roslin, began to build a castle for his family home around 1205 AD, and chose to put it on the spot where Rosslyn Chapel would one day stand.[276] The land upon which this stone-block manor was built sloped downward to the east, and it was in this part of the residence that the family chapel was built. For the next one hundred years, this chapel rested only four miles from a similar chapel at the Knights Templar preceptory at Balantrodoch. In 1307, when John de Hueflete and the other Templars hastily departed from their nearby preceptory, the closest and safest place for them to take shelter would have been this chapel in the St.

Clair manor. While the Baron of Roslin could not shelter them openly due to the sentence of excommunication proclaimed by the pope upon all who aided the Templars, he was entirely capable of doing it privately. In fact the St. Clair family had a long history of sheltering those stung by the power of church or state. They even permitted outlawed gypsies to live on the grounds until representatives of the king protested loudly enough that the Baron of Roslin was forced to desist.[277] The St. Clairs were not only capable of harboring the fugitive Templars, but had a history of enjoying the performance of that act.

This chapel at the lower part of the St. Clair estate had two outside doors that allowed access directly from the surrounding hillside, thereby avoiding use of the main entrances to the manor employed by the family. Individuals could therefore come and go quietly at night without being observed. Of course any fugitives who took refuge there would have moved on to permanent housing when it was arranged. Yet the problem of having meetings in those housing units without being observed by neighbors would have still been an issue. So it would have been entirely reasonable for this private chapel on the St. Clair estate to continue in use as a meeting place for a considerable amount of time.

The only indication that this in fact happened was what occurred next. In 1441, when the St. Clairs had already built a larger and more secure castle nearby, they began to tear down the old manor house on the site of what would become Rosslyn Chapel. They removed all of the manor except for the small chapel. For some reason that single room was preserved exactly as it stood, even though its location interfered with the majestic design of Rosslyn Chapel, as we have seen. Were the early St. Clair lords and ladies buried here? No, there was a separate outdoor graveyard for them, and the future lords and ladies were buried in the main crypt of Rosslyn Chapel, not this ancient Lower Chapel, as it is called. Yet some strangely emotional reason existed for preserving this modest stone chapel—because we can still walk into the magnificently ornate Rosslyn Chapel today and descend those rustic stairs to the Lower Chapel below.

It is entirely possible that this was one of the first asylums for the fugitive Templars, and that it continued to be the hall in which

Fig. 42   The Lower Chapel

those men met when they began to be called Freemasons in the 1300s. The lord of the hall in which they met would almost certainly have been initiated into this group that gathered in his chapel. After more than a hundred and thirty years of lodge meetings in this hall—from 1307 to 1441—it would clearly be understandable if the lord of Roslin ordered the chapel to be retained. Known facts do not prove that this is what happened, but there is also no known reason why it cannot have happened this way. We can only hope that some day this mystery will be resolved. But if in fact this is one of the first Masonic lodge rooms that came into existence after 1307, then it may be the oldest such room that has not been torn down and can still be seen today.

*Fig. 43 Temple Church was built by the Templars in 1185
and still stands in London*

Templar Preceptory
In London Today

When Hugh de Payens, first Grand Master of the Knights Templar, toured England and Scotland in 1128 to recruit knights and donations to support the Templars' mission in the Holy Land, his efforts began in London. There he was soon rewarded with a particularly attractive bequest: an expanse of property between the walled city of London and the Abbey at Westminster. It was among the fields which would become known as Holborn, a half-mile north of the River Thames.

On it he established the Templars' headquarters in England, and immediately began to raise a round church—a practice that would become one of the identifying marks of the men he led. As their fortunes improved, the Templars in London purchased an even larger property directly to the south. This gave them all the land from what is now Fleet Street to the River Thames, extending from Temple Avenue in the east to about Essex Street in the west. This area is still called Temple to the present day. A larger, round Temple Church was raised there by these men in 1185, and it continues to be regularly open for services.

Charles G. Addison, who worked on what remained of the Temple properties in 1874, described those events this way.

The Knights Templars had first established the chief
house of their Order in England, without Holborn
Bars,[278] on the south side of the street, where Southampton House formerly stood, adjoining to which
Southampton Buildings were afterwards erected; and
it is stated, that about a century and a half ago,[279] part
of the ancient chapel annexed to this establishment, of
a circular form, and built of Caen stone, was discovered on pulling down some old houses near Southampton Buildings in Chancery Lane. This first house
of the Temple, established by Hugh de Payns himself,
before his departure from England, A.D. 1130, on his
return to Palestine, was adapted to the wants and ne-
cessities of the Order in its infant state, when the
Knights, instead of lingering in the Preceptories of Europe, proceeded at once to Palestine, and when all the
resources of the society were strictly and faithfully
forwarded to Jerusalem, to be expended in defense of
the faith. But when the Order had greatly increased in
numbers, power, and wealth, and had somewhat departed from its original purity and simplicity, we find
that the Superior and the Knights resident in London
began to look abroad for a more extensive and commodious place of habitation. They purchased a large
space of ground, extending from the White Friars
westward to Essex House without Temple Bar, and
commenced the erection of a convent on a scale of
grandeur commensurate with the dignity and importance of the chief house of the great religio-military
society of the Temple in Britain. It was called the *New*
Temple, to distinguish it from the original establishment at Holborn, which came thenceforth to be known
by the name of the *Old* Temple. This New Temple was
adapted for the residence of numerous military monks
and novices, serving brothers, retainers, and domes-
tics. It contained the residence of the Superior and of
the Knights, the cells and apartments of the chaplains
and serving brethren, the council chamber where the

Chapters were held,[280] and the refectory or dining-hall, which was connected by a range of handsome cloisters with the magnificent Church, consecrated by the Patriarch. Alongside the river extended a spacious pleasure-ground for the recreation of the brethren, who were not permitted to go into the town without the leave of the Master. It was used also for military exercises and the training of horses.[281]

The fall of the Templars in 1307 caused those magnificent halls, cloisters and dormitories to be handed over to others, then be leased to members of the legal profession, who occupy it still. Two Inns of Court—which call legal professionals to the Bar and enable them to practice as barristers—occupy what is almost the entirety of the former New Temple property. These Inns are known as Inner Temple and Middle Temple.[282] The remainder of the property extending westward is called Outer Temple, and has been mainly given over to commercial buildings. On Fleet Street one enters a gated archway and walks south toward Temple Church, passing beside the buildings of the Inner Temple, which have been largely rebuilt since the days of the Templars. Looming on the left is Temple Church, the knights' main legacy. It still stands as they built it, though repairs have been made during the seven centuries since men clothed in white mantles and red crosses last walked there.

One other ancient fragment remains, however, and it is found straight ahead, just south of the Church. A long building stands where the Templars' magnificent main hall once arrayed itself, and in fact the west end of that ancient building was retained and is part of the current structure. The several walls of weathered stone seen there constituted the "buttery" part of the Templar dining hall. This venerable collection of rooms remains an actively-used part of Inner Temple Hall. Farther west from the hall are the many buildings of the Middle Temple. Upon reaching Middle Temple Lane, if one turns south and follows the road downhill toward the Thames, an archway pierces through the connected buildings at or near the location of the original gate from the Templar properties. The walled-off privacy and grandeur of the

Inner Temple and Middle Temple buildings still evoke the presence of the confident and lordly Knights Templar who once lived and feasted in these halls.

Fig. 44   The remaining part of the original Templar dining hall

Phoenician Secrets

Here you have experienced an introduction to the mysterious Phoenicians involved in building Solomon's Temple, whose heirs had great value for the Knights Templar and then for Freemasons. Yet their impact on the ancient Mediterranean and the societies of the world today was much greater than what you have seen so far. In *Phoenician Secrets: Exploring the Ancient Mediterranean* all those things are explored in a remarkable level of detail. In the process of so doing, we see much deeper into the myriad other societies of those days including the Classical Greeks, Romans, Minoans, Hebrews and Egyptians.

All these things are possible because the Phoenicians were the international traders who constantly traveled back and forth among those other peoples. The sea traders carried with them the inventions, customs, skills and languages of all those lands, in addition to the vast array of goods that filled their famous cedar ships. As we saw here, the Phoenician traders arose around 3200 BC and were present at the building of the Great Pyramid in Egypt six hundred years later. They also made contributions to the Minoans when that brilliant culture flowered on the island of Crete.

Like honeybees gathering pollen, the Phoenicians visited these cultures and then the Classical Greeks and Romans when those golden societies began to emerge. It is fascinating to follow all these interactions and the remarkable cultures that grew from them. Even in warfare, which was not a Phoenician strength, enough was carried forward that the Romans chose to honor Hannibal as the *Father of Strategy*.

The great river of Greek literature drew from many streams, and the Greek historian Herodotus, who lived at the beginning of the Classical Age, gave credit to the Phoenicians as one of those streams.

> Now the Phoenicians who came with Cadmus, and to whom the Gephyraei belonged, introduced into Greece upon their arrival a great variety of arts, among the rest that of writing, whereof the Greeks till then had, as I think, been ignorant. And originally they shaped their letters exactly like all the other Phoenicians, but afterwards, in the course of time, they changed by degrees their language, and together with it the form likewise of their characters. Now the Greeks who dwelt about those parts at that time were chiefly the Ionians. The Phoenician letters were accordingly adopted by them, but with some variation in the shape of a few, and so they arrived at the present use, still calling the letters Phoenician, as justice required, after the name of those who were the first to introduce them into Greece.
>
> Herodotus 5:58

Illuminated with 100 photographs, maps and works of art, this is an intriguing voyage through the idyllic ancient Mediterranean you will long remember.

Phoenician Secrets:
Exploring the Ancient Mediterranean
by Sanford Holst

Fig. 45 Woman gathering saffron flowers, a fresco painted before 1600 BC on the island of Santorini in the Aegean Sea.

Illustrations, Acknowledgements

Figure

Figure

18 Clontarf Castle in Dublin, Ireland (Holst)

19 Richard the Lionheart (From Guizot, *History of France*, 1869)

20 Jacques DeMolay (By J. Williams in Burnes, *Sketch of the History of the Knights Templars*, 1840)

21 Templar preceptory in Paris (From Burnes, *Sketch...*, 1840)

22 Tomar Castle in Portugal (by Alvesgaspar)

23 Seal of the Knights Templar (From Burnes, *Sketch...*, 1840)

24 Tabard Inn (by Herbert Railton, c. 1897)

25 Roslin Castle (Holst)

26 Rosslyn Chapel (From Billings, *The Baronial and Ecclesiastical Antiquities of Scotland*, 1845)

27 William St. Clair, Grand Master (By Robert Patterson in Lyons, *History of the Lodge of Edinburgh no.1*, 1873)

28 Masons window in St. Giles Cathedral (Holst)

29 John Mylne the Younger (c.1650, National Galleries of Scotland)

30 Thomas Gresham (From the Mercers' Company of London)

31 Elias Ashmole (Painting by Cornelius de Neve, 1664)

32 Christopher Wren (Painting by Sir Godfrey Kneller)

33 Goose and Gridiron Ale House (Public)

34 Benjamin Franklin (Public)

35 Chinon Parchment (Public)

36 Square and compass (Holst)

37 Cooke Manuscript (Public)

38 Symbols of Freemasonry (From Mackey, *The History of Freemasonry*, 1898, and from the one dollar bill)

39 Regius Manuscript (Public)

40 Freemasons (From Anderson, *The New Book of Constitutions*, 1738)

41 Rosslyn Chapel (From *Heath's Picturesque Annual*, 1835)

42 The Lower Chapel (Courtesy of C Eileen Nauman)

43 Temple Church in London (Holst)

44 Original Templar dining hall in London (Holst)

45 Fresco of woman gathering saffron flowers (see note, Fig. 6)

Annotations

[1] Mackey, Albert G. *The History of Freemasonry.* (New York: Masonic History Co, 1898), Vol. 4, p. 877.

[2] Mackey, Albert G. *Washington as a Freemason: An Address Delivered before the Grand and Subordinate Lodges of Ancient Freemasons of South Carolina, at Charleston, S.C., on Thursday, November 4th, 1852, being the Centennial Celebration of the Initiation of George Washington.* (Charleston: Miller, 1852).

[3] Robinson, John J. *Born In Blood: The Lost Secrets of Freemasonry.* (New York: M. Evans, 1989), p.178.

[4] Hewitt, A.R. "Biographical Lists of Grand Masters" in *Grand Lodge 1717-1967.* (Oxford: United Grand Lodge of England, 1967), p. 265.

[5] The Rummer and Grapes lodge eventually merged with another and changed its name to the Royal Somerset House and Inverness Lodge, No. 4. Since Desaguliers belonged to several lodges it is not certain that the Rummer and Grapes was where he was active this particular year, but it is most often cited, and therefore used here. The Goose and Gridiron Lodge is today known as Lodge of Antiquity, No. 2. The Crown Lodge lapsed in 1736. The Apple-Tree

Lodge merged with another and became the current Lodge of Fortitude and Old Cumberland, No. 12.

[6] Anderson, James. *New Book of Constitutions*. (London: Grand Lodge of England, 1738), pp. 109-110.

[7] An Occasional Lodge was not a regular meeting of a lodge, but rather one that took place at another location, was held for a specific purpose, and theoretically was attended by at least six Masons, though records exist of fewer members being in attendance.

[8] Mackey, Albert G. "Desaguliers" in *The Masonic Trowel*, retrieved 14 Oct 2008,
www.themasonictrowel.com/masonic_talk/stb/stbs/36-05.htm

[9] Markoe, Glenn E. *Phoenicians: Peoples of the Past*. (Berkeley: University of California Press, 2000), pp. 10-13.

[10] Holst, Sanford. *Phoenicians: Lebanon's Epic Heritage* (Los Angeles: Cambridge & Boston Press, 2005) and *Phoenician Secrets: Exploring the Ancient Mediterranean* (Los Angeles: Santorini Publishing, 2011).

[11] *In eminenti* from the Vatican website *Papal Encyclicals Online*, bold font added, www.papalencyclicals.net/Clem12/c12inemengl.htm, retrieved 14 Nov 2008.

[12] It is not entirely clear if Robert the Bruce ordered the arrest of these men or whether it was done by Edward II of England, who claimed the Scottish throne, or by the papal representatives in Scotland.

[13] Addison, Charles G. *The History of the Knights Templars*. (London: Longman, Brown, Green & Longmans, 1842), pp. 226-228.

[14] This city was called *gbl* by the Phoenicians and is still called Jbeil by the local people today. However the Greeks celebrated it as Byblos, and that name has continued in wider popular use ever since.

[15] Herodotus. *The Histories*, 2:96.

[16] Known to the ancient Egyptians as Nekhen, the name of Hierakonpolis was bestowed by the Greeks and has continued in popular usage.

[17] Dunand, Maurice. *Byblos: Its History, Ruins and Legends*. (Beirut: Librairie Adrien-Maisonneuve, 1973), pp. 15-16. The archaeological remains of Byblos were discovered by French writer Ernest Renan in 1860. The detailed excavations that have revealed much of what we know about the early history of this city were performed by French archaeologists Pierre Montet and Maurice Dunand from 1921 to 1975.

[18] Khufu is sometimes also referred to as Cheops.

[19] Light is shed on this mystery by the events of 1075 BC at Byblos, as shown in the next chapter.

[20] For further discussion and source materials on formation of Minoan society see www.phoenician.org/minoans_phoenicians_paper.htm

[21] Bernal, Martin. *Black Athena, Volume I.* (New Jersey: Rutgers University Press, 1987), pp. 417-418.

[22] Herodotus. *The Histories*, 4:147.

[23] This building is identified as Xeste 3 in the excavation records.

[24] Various calculations on the date of this large and historic eruption have been made using different methods such as carbon dating, tree rings, and ice analysis, producing a variety of dates. The date of 1628 BC is one of the better-supported calculations within this band of dates. For example, Grudd, H, Briffa, KR, Gunnarson, BE, & Linderholm, HW. "Swedish tree rings provide new evidence in support of a major, widespread environmental disruption in 1628 BC". *Geophysical Research Letters* **27** (18): 2957–2960.

[25] Bikai, Patricia. *The Pottery of Tyre.* (Warminster, UK: Aris & Phillips, 1978), p. 65 and p. 72.

[26] The East Coast of the Mediterranean, comprising essentially what is now Syria, Lebanon, Jordan and Israel.

[27] This was recorded on the victory stele of King Merneptah which is now in the Cairo Museum.

[28] The original papyrus manuscript is in the Pushkin Museum of Fine Arts in Moscow, filed as Papyrus Pushkin 120. A transcript of the whole text can be found in: Holst, Sanford. *Phoenician Secrets.* (Los Angeles: Santorini Publishing, 2011), pp. 204-211.

[29] The year of David's death and Solomon's coronation is given by different sources as being between 1015 BC and 961 BC, however the year most frequently cited is 970 BC, so that is the date used here.

[30] The length of the temple was given simply as threescore (60) cubits, but a later verse clarified this was the total of the main room (40) plus the Holy of Holies (20).

[31] The statements shown here about the Master Mason's ritual have been published many times before, allowing it to be repeated once again.

[32] 1 Kings 14:25-26.

[33] 1 Kings 15:9-24.

[34] 2 Kings 12:17-18.

[35] 2 Kings 14:14.

[36] 2 Kings 16:8, 17-18.

[37] 2 Kings 18:15-16.

[38] 2 Kings 24:13; 2 Chr. 36:7; 2 Kings 25:9-17; 2 Chr. 36:19; Isaiah 64:11.

[39] Josephus. *Contra Apionem*, 1:17

[40] Markoe, *Phoenicians*, p.196.

[41] Today known as Larnaka.

[42] Cadiz was called Gadir by the Phoenicians, and then Gades by the Romans. Larache was called Lixis by the Phoenicians, then Lixus by the Romans. For the third city, Utica is the name that has come down to us but apparently was not the original name, since it meant "old city," and was so named when Carthage (which meant "new city") was established nearby in 814 BC.

[43] Baynes, Thomas Spencer (editor) *Encyclopaedia Britannica* (New York: Henry G. Allen, 1888), p. 806. "Strabo (i. 48) dates the settlements beyond the Pillars of Hercules soon after the Trojan War.... Lixus in Mauretania was older than Gades (Pliny, xix. 63) and Gades a few years older than Utica (Vell., i. 2), which again was founded in 1101 B.C. (Pseudo. Arist. *Mir. Ausc.*, 134; Bocchus, in Pliny, xvi. 216).

[44] Quintus Curtius Rufus wrote his works about 50 AD, basing his accounts of Alexander on earlier Greek writings.

[45] The Phoenicians made serious efforts to conceal these bonds, just as they did with most of their other internal affairs. That led a number of historians to erroneously conclude that their cities were separate and without bonds. However a long and detailed discussion is needed to clearly demonstrate what actually happened, and an academic paper is a more suitable forum.

[46] Livy. *The History of Rome*. (London: J.M. Dent & Sons, 1921), Vol. III, Book 21, pp. 3-4.

[47] The Sadducees strictly followed the written Torah, the five books of Moses which were also called the Pentateuch.

[48] The Pharisees believed the oral Torah and Rabbinic interpretations were also valid.

[49] Josephus. *Antiquitates Judaicae*, 14:4.

50 Byers, Gary. www.christiananswers.net/q-abr/abr-a022.html, retrieved on 16 Aug 2008.

51 As told in Matthew 21:2 and Mark 11:15.

52 Buckley, Jonathan. *The Rough Guide to Venice & the Veneto.* (New York: Rough Guides, 2004), p. 195.

53 Acts of the Apostles 1:1-11.

54 Some portions of the Roman wall are still visible today, most notably beside the Tower of London, then another section westward along the street called London Wall, and in several large sections near the Museum of London. There the wall turned southward and reached the Thames just west of St Paul's Cathedral.

55 The number of occupants fell drastically after the Romans left, not to be equaled again in London until the latter part of the Middle Ages.

56 York was called Eboracum in those days.

57 The city walls were enlarged and strengthened in the 11th and 12 centuries, but still followed the line of the original Roman walls, and remain largely intact around the old city of York today.

58 A good source on Constantine is Eusebius of Caesarea (c 263 – 339) (often called *Eusebius Pamphili*) who became the bishop of Caesarea Palaestina c 314, and wrote *Life of Constantine.*

59 Barber, Malcolm. *The New Knighthood: A History of the Order of the Temple.* (Cambridge: Cambridge University Press, 1994), pp. 9-10, who cited Albert of Aix, "Historia Hierosolymitana" in *RHCr. Occid*, Vol. IV, 12.33, pp. 712-713.

60 In English he is most commonly known as Hugh de Payens, yet the French prefer Hugues de Payns, with other variations also occurring. Since he came from the town of Payns in the Champagne region of France, there is some logic behind the French usage.

61 In formal usage he would be addressed as Hugh, Count of Champagne, but that is modified here to the more familiar Hugh de Champagne.

62 Addison, Charles G. *The History of the Knights Templars*, p. 11. "Hugh de Payens...fought with great credit and renown at the siege of Jerusalem." This indicated he was present at that time, contrary to the wonderings of some as to whether he arrived afterward.

63 Barber, *The New Knighthood*, note 21 on p.336. Also lamop.univ-paris1.fr/baudin/anglais/comtes/hugues/ hugues.htm retrieved 23 Aug 2008. Albéric gives the dates of Hugh de Champagne's visits to the Holy Land as 1113, 1121 and 1125, but the impacts on his life and the Knights Templar were the same.

64 Sainthood is only granted after a person's death, but St. Bernard was so well known by that name that it is occasionally used to refer to him during his life as well.

65 William of Tyre gave the founding year for the Templars as 1118, but he wrote many years after the event, and provided no supporting evidence. Malcolm Barber cited several documents written within nine years of the founding of the Templars, which point to 1119—or at the latest January 1120—as the proper founding date. Barber, Malcolm. *The New Knighthood*, pp. 8-9.

66 Daniel, Abbot "The Life and Journey of Daniel, Abbot of the Russian Land" in Wilkinson, J. (editor) *Jerusalem Pilgrimage*. (London: Hakluyt Society, 1988), p. 126. Also Barber, Malcolm. *The New Knighthood*, p. 3.

67 Also known as Geoffrey de St. Aldemar.

68 Andre de Montbard was the uncle of St. Bernard.

69 Kalman, Matthew. "Temple Mount discovery leads to dispute in Jerusalem" *San Francisco Chronicle*, November 18, 2007, p. A17.

70 During the reign of Emperor Julian, who died in 363 AD.

71 Genesis 22:4-14.

72 Tsafrir, Yoram. *Where Heaven and Earth Meet: Jerusalem's Sacred Esplanade*, editors Oleg Grabar and Benjamin Z. Kedar. (Austin: University of Texas Press, 2009), p. 80. Quotes the journal of the Pilgrim of Burdigala (Bordeaux) written in 333 AD.

73 Barber, *The New Knighthood*, p. 1 sets the total number of Templars at about 7000. This included 600 knights in the East with 2000 direct attendants. To that must be added the men staffing the Templars' Eastern residences and estates, plus administrators and priests, adding about 1600. In the West there were roughly 300 knights at the many preceptories, with about 2500 men staffing those preceptories and the rest of the 870 Templar estates.

74 Section LXI in *The Rule of the Poor Fellow-Soldiers of Jesus Christ and of the Temple of Solomon*. In the original Latin, this document was: *Regula Pauperum Commilitonum Christi et Templi Salomonis*.

[75] Addison, *The History of the Knights Templars*, pp. 69-70.

[76] *The Rule of the Poor Fellow-Soldiers of Jesus Christ and of the Temple of Solomon*, Section XXI, as shown in Addison, Charles G. *The History of the Knights Templars*, p. 19; also Barber, *The New Knighthood*, p.191.

[77] Granted to the Templars by the papal bull *Omne datum optimum* (1139); in Barber, *The New Knighthood*, pp.195-198

[78] *Italics added.* The relevance of wearing gloves will be seen later.

[79] Robinson, *Born In Blood*, p.72.

[80] Burgoyne, Michael Hamilton. "1187 – 1260" in *Where Heaven and Earth Meet: Jerusalem's Sacred Esplanade,* editors Oleg Grabar and Benjamin Z. Kedar. (Austin: University of Texas Press, 2009), pp. 157-58.

[81] The arrival of the alphabet at Greece was described by Herodotus in *The Histories* 5:58.

[82] Such as Columella xii. 39, 1, 2, who cited the agricultural records kept by Mago of Carthage.

[83] Templar castles identified in Barber, *The New Knighthood*, pp. 75-89.

[84] Harb, Antoine Khoury. *Lebanon: A Name through 4000 Years.* (Beirut: American University of Beirut, 2003).

[85] Bernard of Clairvaux. *Epistolae, in Sancti Bernardi Opera*, editors J. Leclercq and H. Rochais, Vol. VII, (Rome: 1974), ep. 31, pp. 85-86; in Barber, *The New Knighthood*, p. 11.

[86] Addison, *The History of the Knights Templars*, p. 13.

[87] In each region one estate was designated to house the leading Templar officials in that area, provide financial services, and watch over the smaller estates. Known as a preceptory, it could oversee anything from a small area to an entire country.

[88] Addison, *The History of the Knights Templars*, p. 26.

[89] Addison, *The History of the Knights Templars*, pp. 13-14.

[90] *The Rule of the Poor Fellow-soldiers of Jesus Christ and of the Temple of Solomon*, Section X, as shown in Addison, *The History of the Knights Templars*, p. 17.

[91] Per papal bull *Omne datum optimum* (1139); Barber, *The New Knighthood*, p.195-198.

[92] Barber, *The New Knighthood*, pp. 197-198, shows the Templars went to great lengths to confess only to their own chaplains, and that this was one of the charges against them at their trial—that they

did it to hide heresy. In their own defense, the Templars could only cite a few cases in which they confessed to outside priests, and some of those priests were tightly aligned with the Templars in other ways.

[93] This account was based on a journal attributed to Geoffrey de Vinsauf, who was said to have accompanied King Richard on his Crusade, as well as the writings of Jacques de Vitry and others. It was documented in Addison, *The History of the Knights Templars*, pp. 141-49.

[94] Addison, *The History of the Knights Templars*, pp. 45-46, who in turn cited *Anselmi Gemblacensis Chron.* ad ann. 1153; and *William of Tyre* lib. xvii. cap. 27.

[95] Addison, *The History of the Knights Templars*, p. 62, who in turn cited *William of Tyre* lib. xx, xxi, xxii.

[96] Addison, *The History of the Knights Templars*, pp. 28-29, who in turn cited *Histoire de Languedoc*, lib. xvii, p. 407; *Hist. de l'eglise de Gandersheim*; *Mariana de rebus Hispaniae*, lib. x. cap. 15, 17, 18.; *Zurita anales de la corona de Aragon*, tom. i, lib. i. cap. 52; and *Quarita*, tom. i, lib. ii. cap.4.

[97] Clontarf Castle Hotel, www.clontarfcastle.ie.

[98] By King Henry III in 1240 AD, when he was considering Temple Church as his burial place. He later opted for Westminster Abbey. There has been damage to the Church over the years, including during World War II when the dome was partially destroyed, but in each case it was repaired to be as close as possible to the prior construction.

[99] Addison, *The History of the Knights Templars*, p. 213.

[100] Barber, *The New Knighthood*, pp. 252-253.

[101] Addison, *The History of the Knights Templars*, p. 148.

[102] Addison, *The History of the Knights Templars*, pp. 186-192, who in turn cited De excidio urbis Acconis apud *Martene*, tom. v. col. 757. *De Guignes*, Hist. des Huns, tom. iv. p. 162. *Michaud*, Extraits Arabes, p. 762, 808. Abulfarag. Chron. Syr. p. 595. Wilkens, Comment. Abulfed. Hist. p. 231-234. *Marin. Sanut Torsell*, lib. iii. pars 12, cap. 21.

[103] Acre fell on 28 May 1291; the last of the other cities to fall was Atlit on 14 August 1291.

[104] Addison, *The History of the Knights Templars*, pp. 193-194.

[105] Barber, *The New Knighthood*, p. 120.

[106] Barber, *The New Knighthood*, pp. 199-200.

[107] Matthew of Paris *Chronica Majora*, vol. iv, p. 641; vol. vi, pi42. See Bulst-Thiele *Magistri*, p. 254, n.87; also Barber, *The New Knighthood*, pp. 199-200.

[108] Barber, *The New Knighthood*, pp. 296-297.

[109] Barber, Malcolm. *The Trial of the Templars*. (Cambridge: Cambridge University Press, 2006), p. 52.

[110] Barber, *The New Knighthood*, p. 289.

[111] Barber, *The New Knighthood*, p. 1; for additional information on their preceptories, baillies, estates, etc. see Barber, *The New Knighthood*, pp. 251-256.

[112] Barber, *The New Knighthood*, pp. 278-279.

[113] Addison, *The History of the Knights Templars*, p. 198.

[114] Addison, *The History of the Knights Templars*, p. 198.

[115] Addison, *The History of the Knights Templars*, p. 198.

[116] Barber, *The New Knighthood*, pp. 283-284.

[117] Addison, *The History of the Knights Templars*, pp. 200-201, and *Histoire de la Condemnation des Templiers*, by Pierre De Puy (Bruxelles, 1713), Vol. II, p. 309.

[118] Addison, *The History of the Knights Templars*, pp. 204-205.

[119] A papal bull is a formal letter sent to leaders of the Catholic Church setting forth actions, grants, policies, excommunications, etc, which are to be carried out among all members of the Church. It is so named from the bulla or seal at the end of the document. Variations of these letters are also called encyclicals or constitutions. These are still being issued today.

[120] This was down from their peak of 7000 in the 1200s noted in Barber, *The New Knighthood*, p. 1. Since the number of estates stayed roughly the same, the number of Templars in the West would have remained the same or fallen slightly to 2500. In the East, after the bloody loss of the Holy Land, about 1500 survivors remained on Cyprus.

[121] Baigent, Michael and Richard Leigh. *The Temple and the Lodge* (New York: Arcade, 1989), pp. 52-53.

[122] Dat. Apud Redyng, 4 die Decembris. Consimiles litterae diriguntur Ferando regi Castillae et Ligionis, consanguineo regis, domino Karolo, regi Siciliae, et Jacobo regi Aragoniae, amico Regis. Acta

Rymeri, tom. Iii. Ad ann. 1307, pp. 35-36; Addison, *The History of the Knights Templars*, pp. 206-207.

[123] Addison, *The History of the Knights Templars*, p.210

[124] Papal bull *Ad providam* issued on 2 May 1312.

[125] Mackey, *The History of Freemasonry*, p.223.

[126] Barber, *The Trial of the Templars*, p. 252.

[127] Barber, *The Trial of the Templars*, pp. 254-255.

[128] Barber, *The Trial of the Templars*, p. 254.

[129] Schottmüller, vol. 2, pp. 323-324; *Trial of the Templars in Cyprus*, ed. Gilmour-Bryson, p.289; Barber, *The Trial of the Templars*, p. 255.

[130] Schottmüller, vol. 2, pp. 376-400; *Trial of the Templars in Cyprus*, ed. Gilmour-Bryson, pp. 405-442; Barber, *The Trial of the Templars*, p. 256.

[131] Barber, *The Trial of the Templars*, pp. 279-80.

[132] Addison, *The History of the Knights Templars*, p. 213.

[133] Addison, *The History of the Knights Templars*, p. 17, who in turn cites *Chron. Cisterc. Albertus Miraeus*. Brussels, 1641. *Manricus ad ann*. 1128, cap. ii. *Act. Syn. Trec.* tom. x. edit. Labb.

[134] *In Praise of the New Chivalry* was written by Saint Bernard just after 1128. See Addison, *The History of the Knights Templars*, pp. 29-32.

[135] Barber, *The Trial of the Templars*, pp. 218-219.

[136] Thornbury, Walter and Edward Walford. *Old and New London: A Narrative of Its History, Its People and Its Places: The Southern Suburbs*. (London: Cassell & Company, 1893), Vol. VI, pp. 76-77.

[137] Thornbury, *Old and New London*, p. 76.

[138] Addison, *The History of the Knights Templars*, p.229.

[139] Grant, James. *Cassell's Old and New Edinburgh*. (London: Cassell & Co., 1882), Vol. III, p. 52.

[140] Addison, *The History of the Knights Templars*, p. 240.

[141] Addison, *The History of the Knights Templars*, pp. 279-280.

[142] Bulloch, John. *Scottish Notes and Queries*. (Aberdeen: A. Brown & Co, 1903), Vol. IV, issue 5 (November 1902).

[143] The date of 1070 is given by the Rosslyn Chapel Trust.

[144] Many good sources give conflicting details about the St. Clairs, so it has been necessary to examine and compare them to choose that which was best supported. In other cases, missing data is compiled from the facts available. For example the Rosslyn Chapel Trust gave the succession date of 1153 for the 3rd Baron of Roslin,

so this was then taken as marking the death of Henry, the 2nd Baron. Similar assessments were made regarding the later St. Clairs. Fortunately the central course of their history is well-agreed, and is shown here.

145 Hay, Richard Augustine. *Genealogie of the Saintclaires of Rosslyn.* (Edinburgh: Thomas G. Stevenson, 1835), p. 5. This collection of notes was written by Hay around 1700 using many actual documents owned by the St. Clair family, then was edited and published by James Maidment in 1835. Unfortunately, as Maidment noted, "It is to be regretted that the reverend gentleman was so careless in making his transcripts, as, in many instances, various evident mistakes have crept in...." In addition to troubling transcripts, Hay had the unfortunate habit of calling each Baron of Roslin "William" whenever he was unsure. Other sources have been used to determine the proper names and facts in those cases.

146 Bulloch, *Scottish Notes and Queries*, Vol. IV, issue 5, p. 66, tells us a year after David I became king of Scotland he issued a Charter of Confirmation that affirmed his predecessor's act of conferring on Sir Henry the title Baron of Roslin, and noted that the lifetime rights given to his father had been extended to make those rights hereditary to all his heirs.

147 Information on the first St. Clair castle was provided by Rosslyn Chapel Trust.

148 There is a possibility his son had not survived him, and that his successor named here might have been his grandson.

149 Dowden, John. (Editor J. Maitland Thomson) *The Bishops of Scotland.* (Glasgow: James Maclehose, 1912).

150 Hay, *Genealogie of the Saintclaires of Rosslyn*, p. 12.

151 Addison, *The History of the Knights Templars*, pp. 226-228.

152 That is to say, if a force from England did not arrive to give him relief from Scottish attack.

153 Bulloch, *Scottish Notes and Queries*, Vol. IV, issue 6 (December 1902), p. 83.

154 *Manuel des Chevaliers de l'Ordre du Temple* (Paris, 1825), p. 10. Also, James Burnes. *Sketch of the History of the Knights Templars.* (Edinburgh: Wm. Blackwood & Sons, 1840), p. 60—in which Burnes, a distant relative of Scotland's famous bard Robert Burns, noted "...we are told by a learned French writer, that having deserted

the Temple, they had ranged themselves under the banners of Robert Bruce, by whom they were formed into a new Order, the observances of which were based on those of the Templars, and became, according to him, the source of Scottish Free Masonry." And also, *Statutes of the Religious and Military Order of the Temple, as Established in Scotland; with an Historical Notice of the Order* (Edinburgh: Grand Conclave, 1843), p. viii.

[155] Baigent, *The Temple and the Lodge*, pp.35-36.

[156] Cooper, Robert L. D. *The Rosslyn Hoax?* (Hersham, Surrey: Lewis Masonic, 2007), pp. 264-72.

[157] Barbour, John. *The Bruce: Being the Metrical History of Robert the Bruce, King of Scots, Compiled A.D. 1375*, translated by George Eyre-Todd (London: Gowans & Gray Ltd, 1907), p. 194.

[158] Barbour, *The Bruce*, pp. 222-224.

[159] Bulloch, *Scottish Notes and Queries*, Vol. IV, issue 7 (January 1902), pp. 97-98.

[160] Lomas, Robert. *Turning the Templar Key.* (Beverly, MA: Fair Winds Press, 2007), pp. 142-168.

[161] The spelling of Rosslyn Chapel is different than that of the Barony of Roslin in which it stands. No conclusive reason has been given for this, it is just tradition.

[162] Hay, *Genealogie of the Sainteclaires of Rosslyn*, p. 27.

[163] Information concerning the preservation of the Lower Chapel from the original St. Clair family home was provided by staff of the Rosslyn Chapel Trust.

[164] Scott, Sir Walter. *Lay of the Last Minstrel.* (New York: C.S. Francis & Co., 1845), Canto Sixth, XXIII, pp. 178-179.

[165] Cooper, *The Rosslyn Hoax*, pp. 118-120.

[166] "...a model of this pillar had been sent from Rome, or some foreign place...." Cooper, *The Rosslyn Hoax*, p.108.

[167] The small enclosure that stands just outside this door today is clearly a modern addition and of no interest here.

[168] Lee, Sidney (editor) *Dictionary of National Biography* (New York: MacMillan Co, 1897), Vol. LII, p. 309-310.

[169] Burke, John. *Burke's Peerage: A General and Heraldic Dictionary of the Peerage and Baronetage of the British Empire – Fourth Edition.* (London: Colburn & Bentley, 1832), Vol. II, p. 440.

[170] Christian I was a Dane who held the triple crown, simultaneously ruling Norway, Denmark, and Sweden.

[171] Hay, *Genealogie of the Sainteclaires of Rosslyn*, pp. 82-87.

[172] In recent years it has been suggested that this William who became 15th Baron was the brother of Chief Justice St. Clair. That seems to be a confusion with the event in the 1400s where a St. Clair had two sons named William. This 15th Baron was then said to have died in 1610, passing the title to the same heir shown here, so everything got back on track at that point. The sole purpose of that deviation to a brother William seemed to be to avoid recognizing a disreputable younger William as the 15th Baron. Their name was St. Clair, but that does not mean they were all saints.

[173] Lomas, *Templar Key*, p. 183, Stevenson, *The Origins of Freemasonry*, p. 55.

[174] Lomas *Templar Key*, pp. 185-186, Stevenson, *The Origins of Freemasonry*, p. 56.

[175] Stevenson, *The Origins of Freemasonry*, p. 64.

[176] Richard Hay said clearly in *Genealogie*—which he wrote about the year 1700—that the present Baron of Rosin was Alexander. He also reported that James had passed away when Alexander was still a child and described the lad's early life. That means it was Alexander, at eighteen years of age, who became Baron in 1690.

[177] The author of *Genealogie* came into the St. Clair family when his widowed mother, Jean Spotswood, married James St. Clair--the younger brother of the 17th Baron--about 1667. That explains how he knew intimate details about the family, and how the private records of the St. Clairs became available to him. He knew family members able to testify that the grandfather of the then-current generation was a lewd man, which he reported in *Genealogie* on page 154.

[178] Mylne, Robert Scott. *The Master Masons to the Crown of Scotland and Their Works*. (Edinburgh: Scott & Ferguson, 1893), p. 5.

[179] Carr, Harry. "Freemasonry Before Grand Lodge" *Grand Lodge 1717-1967*. (Oxford: United Grand Lodge of England, 1967), p. 7.

[180] 13 shillings and 4 pence in sterling (silver).

[181] Carr, *Grand Lodge 1717-1967*, p. 9.

[182] St John the Baptist and St John the Evangelist, the patron saints of Freemasonry.

[183] Lee, Sidney (editor). *Dictionary of National Biography.* (New York: Macmillan, 1909), Vol. XIV, pp. 2-3.

[184] Mylne, *The Master Masons to the Crown of Scotland and Their Works,* pp. 47-48.

[185] Lee, *Dictionary of National Biography,* Vol. XIV, p. 3.

[186] He then passed away in 1605.

[187] In reporting the beginning of work on the Drum House in 1584, Lord Somerville identified John Mylne as already being "the King's Master Meassone" as excerpted in Mylne's *The Master Masons to the Crown of Scotland and Their Works,* p. 65.

[188] Stevenson, *The Origins of Freemasonry,* pp. 27-28.

[189] Schuchard, Marsha Keith. *Restoring the Temple of Vision.* (Leiden/Boston: Brill, 2002), pp. 198-199.

[190] From the Schaw Statute of 1598, translation by Holst.

[191] Stevenson, *The Origins of Freemasonry,* p. 51.

[192] Cooper, Robert L.D. *Cracking the Freemasons Code.* (New York: Atria Books, 2006), p. 18.

[193] Lomas, *Turning the Templar Key,* p. 172.

[194] As recorded in the records of the Lodge of Scoon in Scotland. Lomas, *Turning the Templar Key,* pp. 179-180.

[195] Cooper, *The Rosslyn Hoax,* p. 109.

[196] Schuchard, *Restoring the Temple of Vision,* p. 401.

[197] Schuchard, *Restoring the Temple of Vision,* p. 391.

[198] Carr, Harry. *The Minutes of the Lodge of Edinburgh, Mary's Chapel, No. 1 (1598-1738).* (London: Quatuor Coronati Lodge, 1962), p. 97.

[199] Carr, *The Minutes of the Lodge of Edinburgh,* p. 42. This entry translated by Holst. The actual text was: "Ultimo Julii 1599   The qlk day George Patoun maissoun granttit & confessit that he had offendit agane the dekin & m^{rs} for placeing of ane cowane to wirk at ane chymnay heid for tua dayis and ane helf day...."

[200] Schuchard, *Restoring the Temple of Vision,* p. 428.

[201] Carr, *The Minutes of the Lodge of Edinburgh,* pp. 99-101.

[202] Schuchard, *Restoring the Temple of Vision,* p. 429.

[203] Schuchard, *Restoring the Temple of Vision,* p. 430.

[204] Similarities between Freemasonry and Rosicrucianism have led to discussion over which came first, and therefore may have influenced the other. Rosicrucianism existed at least since 1601 when its works first became published, and its traditions say it goes

back to Christian Rosenkreuz around 1407. Those dates are earlier than 1717 when Freemasonry came into public view. However as seen in this book, evidence indicates Freemasonry already existed prior to 1407.

[205] John Mylne did not have children of his own so he mentored his brother's son, Robert. After John passed away in December of 1667, his nephew succeeded him as Master Mason to the Crown. For many years Robert performed projects all across Scotland. But in 1706 and 1707 the Acts of Union merged the kingdoms of England and Scotland to form the new United Kingdom. Thus there was no longer a need for separate Master Masons to the Crown in both lands. However, in recognition of Robert Mylne's long and distinguished service he was allowed to retain the title until his death in 1710. Altogether, the Mylne family served masonry and its lodges well during these centuries, acting as a bridge between the working men of the craft and the silk-stocking men of the king's court.

[206] Carr, *The Minutes of the Lodge of Edinburgh*, p. 119.

[207] Carr, *Grand Lodge 1717-1967*, p. 25.

[208] Masons' Livery Company, www.masonslivery.co.uk/html/about-the-company-the-masons-company, retrieved 1 Aug 2008.

[209] Carr, *Grand Lodge 1717-1967*, p. 36.

[210] Fellow Craft.

[211] Carr, *Grand Lodge 1717-1967*, p. 38.

[212] Medicine.

[213] Sometimes spelled as Scoon.

[214] Robert Moray was born between 10 March 1508 and 10 March 1509, based upon the official document presented in Robertson, Alexander. *The life of Sir Robert Moray: soldier, statesman and man of science (1608-1673)* (London: Longmans, Green & Co., 1922), p. 1.

[215] Carr, *Grand Lodge 1717-1967*, p. 28.

[216] Over the course of time, the botanical and biological specimens were moved to the Oxford University Museum of Natural History, being replaced by a wealth of archaeological finds. Sir Arthur Evans, who performed the Minoan archaeological excavations at Knossos on Crete, was the keeper of the Ashmolean Museum at that time.

[217] Josten, C. H. (editor). *Elias Ashmole (1617–1692): His Autobiographical and Historical Notes, his Correspondence, and Other Contemporary Sources Relating to his Life and Work.* (Oxford: Clarendon Press, 1966), vol. IV, pp. 1699–1701, provides additional quotes. In his latter years, Elias remained active in Freemasonry, noting in his diary on 10 March 1682, "About 5 H: P.M. I received a Sumons to appear at a Lodge to held the next day, at Masons Hall London." The next entry, on March 11, was, "Accordingly, I went.... I was the Senior Fellow among them (it being 35 yeares since I was admitted).... We all dyned at the halfe Moone Taverne in Cheapeside, at a Noble Dinner prepaired at the charge of the New-accepted Masons."

[218] In addition to Wren and Moray, the conspirators were Robert Boyle, John Wilkins, Alexander Bruce the 2nd Earl of Kincardine, Sir Paul Neile, William Balle, William Viscount Brouncker, Jonathan Goddard, William Petty, Lawrence Rook, and Abraham Hill.

[219] Weld, Charles Richard *A History of the Royal Society, with Memoirs of the Presidents* (London: John W. Parker, 1848), Vol. I, p. 39.

[220] Hearne, Thomas *Peter Langtoft's Chronicle* (Oxford, 1725), Vol. I, pp. 161-164. (Reprinted in London by Samuel Bagster in a collection titled *The Works of Thomas Hearne, Volume III*)

[221] The only known exception to this rule is the Grand Orient de France, which no longer required the prospective member state a belief in God after 1877, and a few other breakaway groups. All other grand lodges in Great Britain, the United States and the rest of the world still require belief in God as a requirement for membership.

[222] Teaching had begun at Oxford by 1096; the university at Cambridge was subsequently formed in 1209.

[223] Shown by Malcolm Barber on his map and list of significant Templar houses; Barber, *The New Knighthood*, pp. 252-253.

[224] The Hospitallers took possession of this estate in 1324.

[225] Only twenty-one received the honor of being named on the first Charter as original members, even though there were actually more by that time.

[226] Lomas, Robert *The Invisible College* (London: Headline Publishing, 2002).

[227] Anderson, *New Book of Constitutions* (1738), p. 109.

228 Adams, Colonel C.C. *The Oldest Lodge: the Prestonian Lecture 1949.* (Oldham: The Wellington Press, 1950). p. 2.

229 Jeffs, R. W. Bro. Julian. *A Short History of the Lodge of Antiquity, No. 2.* (London: Lodge of Antiquity, 2007), pp. 4-6.

230 Anderson, *New Book of Constitutions* (1738), p. 109.

231 Wren actually lived 90 years four months and 5 days, but is traditionally credited with having lived 91 years.

232 "Subtus conditur Hujus Ecclesias et Urbis Conditor, CHRISTOPHERUS WREN; Qui vixit annos ultra nonaginta, Non sibi, sed bono publico. Lector, si monumentum requiris, Circumspice. Obiit 25 Feb. MDCCXXIII., aetat. XCI."

233 Plot, Robert *Natural History of Staffordshire* (Oxford: Theatre, 1686), p. 316.

234 Quietism believed that each person should seek serenity, which brought them closer to God. Pope Innocent XI formally condemned it in his bull *Coelestis pastor* in 1687.

235 Cooper, *The Rosslyn Hoax*, p. 351.

236 That union was ordered by Pope Clement V in 1312 upon the dissolution of the Templar Order, but little came of it.

237 See www.papalencyclicals.net/Clem12/c12inemengl.htm

238 Clement V (c. 1264 – 20 April 1314) served as Pope from 1305 until his death.

239 Bianchi, Alessandro "Vatican to publish new papers on trial of Knights Templar," *USA Today*, 13 October 2007.

240 Barber, *The Trial of the Templars*, p. 129.

241 Addison, *The History of the Knights Templars*, p. 214, in which he cited *Processus contra Templarios* by W. Dugdale in *Monasticon Anglicanum* (1830) Vol. VI, part 2, pp. 844-46.

242 Addison, *The History of the Knights Templars*, pp. 242-43, in which he cited Arch. secret. Vatican. Registr. literar. curiae anno 5 domini Clementis Papae 5.—Raynouard, p. 152. And Acta Rymeri, tom. iii. ad ann. 1310, p. 224.

243 Addison, *The History of the Knights Templars*, p. 240, in which he cited Joan. can. Sanct. Vict. Contin. de Nangis ad ann. 1310. Ex secundâ vitâ *Clem.* V. p. 37.

244 Addison, *The History of the Knights Templars*, pp. 279-280.

245 Lomas, *Turning the Templar Key*, p. 32.

[246] Gould, R.F. with D. Wright (editor) *Gould's History of Freemasonry.* (London: Caxton Publishing, 1931), Vol. V, p. 279.

[247] Mackey, Albert G. *Encyclopedia of Freemasonry.* (London: Griffin, 1870), p. 132.

[248] Ward, J.S.M. *Freemasonry and the Ancient Gods.* (London: Simpkin, Marshall, Hamilton, Kent & Co., 1921), p. 303.

[249] The period of time was actually only two hundred years, from 1185 to 1381.

[250] Robinson, *Born in Blood*, pp. 57-58.

[251] Robinson, *Born in Blood*, pp. 30-31.

[252] Robinson, *Born in Blood*, pp. 239-240.

[253] The Bible is traditionally used, but the brother taking the oath may substitute another book that reflects his religion, reminding him that his oath is taken in front of God.

[254] Addison, *The History of the Knights Templars*, p. xi.

[255] Rijks Archieven in Limburg, Maastricht.

[256] Robertson, *The life of Sir Robert Moray: soldier, statesman and man of science*, p. 1.

[257] Anderson's *The Constitutions of the Free-Masons* in 1723 was followed by his *The New Book of Constitutions* in 1738.

[258] Printed copies of the Old Charges did not begin to appear until the 1700s.

[259] Cooke's translation was published by R. Spencer of London in 1861.

[260] The original manuscript now resides in the British Museum and is identified as Additional M.S. 23,198. The dating of this document was by William James Hughan, and confirmed by Begemann and others.

[261] For example, the *Constitutions of the Free-Masons*—which was based upon Cooke and the other Old Charges manuscripts—begins, "To His Grace the Duke of Montagu...."

[262] As discussed earlier, Pope Innocent II brought into existence this sub-order of clerics within the Templars in 1139, in his papal bull *Omne datum optimum*.

[263] Seven generations at thirty years per generation.

[264] The manuscript also cited the Polychronicon, the Master of History and others as sources, but they in turn only seemed to have the original Bible quotes from which to work.

265 The primary definition of "ordain" is to invest with ministerial or sacerdotal functions; to confer holy orders upon. Stuart Berg Flexner, (editor). *The Random House Dictionary of the English Language – Unabridged* (New York: Random House, 1987), Second Edition, p. 1362.

266 The Regius received this name because it was donated to the Library of the British Museum in 1757 by King George II from the regnal (royal) library. It was also called the Halliwell Manuscript due to the relationship of this document to Freemasonry having been first pointed out by James Halliwell-Phillips in a paper he read before the Society of Antiquaries in its 1838-9 session, and in an article he published the next year. The original manuscript can currently be viewed by appointment in the British Museum, where it is catalogued as Bibl. Reg. 17, A.1.

267 Line 143 of the Regius Manuscript reads, "By old time written I find," indicating that the writer of Regius consulted an older document for at least part of his information.

268 Had the author of Regius been willing to support the Hospitallers, that could have been an option here. But apparently the author was unwilling to do so. Given the rivalry between Templars and Hospitallers, it is likely that most Templars and descendants of Templars would have done what the Regius author did here.

269 After the emergence of Freemasonry in 1717 it became common practice to call the new editions of this document Constitutions instead of Old Charges.

270 This comparison is for the beginning of the tradition until the time of King Athelstan. Anderson's tradition continues after the 48th paragraph, to bring events up to the founding of the Grand Lodge in London.

271 The opposite seemed to happen with the articles and points that made up the "charges." In Regius there were fifteen articles and fifteen points. By the time of the Cooke Manuscript in the following century, the list was down to nine of each. The number would remain at approximately nine throughout the rest of the Old Charges. Two hundred and fifty years after Cooke, Anderson's *Constitutions* would list only six articles, with six subordinate items. Since they were not meant to be taken literally, the general agreement seemed to be that some of them could be deleted.

[272] Since the names of the four martyrs who died at Rome in 305 AD were not known, the names of five stonemasons who died for their faith in Hungary two years earlier were used in their place. The fact that there were four martyrs and five names did not seem to bother anyone. Four different names were later cited for the "four crowned ones." That phrase in the original Latin was *Quatuor Coronati*.

[273] Stevenson, *The Origins of Freemasonry*, p. 219.

[274] In 1958.

[275] That is to say *known* Masons for whom there are lodge records, etc. For many signers of the Constitution it has not been possible to determine whether they were Masons.

[276] While we examined Rosslyn Chapel in 2008, the Rosslyn Trust staff gave me the dates of construction for the original St. Clair manor as 1205-1210.

[277] Cooper, *The Rosslyn Hoax*, pp. 118-120.

[278] In those days the walled city of London referred to its gates as "bars." The usage here refers to being just outside Holborn gate from the walled city of that time, on the street now called High Holborn.

[279] About 1724, counting from the date of his writing.

[280] Religious orders often referred to the Abbot and monks in a location as a Chapter, and frequently had a special place to hold their Chapter meetings. For example, Westminster Abbey and York Minster both have Chapter Houses attached to their cathedrals.

[281] Addison, Charles G. and Robert Macoy. *The Knights Templar History*. (New York: Masonic Publishing, 1874/1912), pp. 475-476.

[282] The "Inner" Temple buildings were closer to Old London. The "Middle" Temple buildings were slightly farther west.

Bibliography

Addison, Charles G. *The History of the Knights Templars*. London: Longman, Brown, Green & Longmans, 1842.

_____ and Robert Macoy *The Knights Templar History*. New York: Masonic Publishing, 1874/1912.

Anderson, James. *The Constitutions of the Free-Masons*. Philadelphia: Benjamin Franklin, 1734.

_____ *New Book of Constitutions*. London: Grand Lodge of England, 1738.

Anderson, William. *The Scottish Nation*. Edinburgh: A. Fullarton & Co., 1877.

Appian. *Wars of the Romans in Iberia*. (Greek, translated into English by J.S. Richardson.) Warminster, UK: Aris & Phillips, 2000.

Arrian. *The Campaigns of Alexander*. (Greek, translated into English by Aubrey de Sélincourt.) London: Penguin Books, 1958.

Aubet, Maria Eugenia. *The Phoenicians and the West*. (Spanish, translated into English by Mary Turton.) Cambridge: Cambridge University Press, 2001.

Baigent, Michael, Richard Leigh and Henry Lincoln. *Holy Blood, Holy Grail*. New York: Delacorte Press, 1982.

Baigent, Michael and Richard Leigh. *The Temple and the Lodge.* New York: Arcade, 1989.

Barber, Malcolm. *The Trial of the Templars.* Cambridge: Cambridge University Press, First edition 1978, Second edition 2006.

_____ *The New Knighthood: A History of the Order of the Temple.* Cambridge: Cambridge University Press, 1994.

Barbour, John. *The Bruce: Being the Metrical History of Robert the Bruce, King of Scots, Compiled A.D. 1375.* (translated by George Eyre-Todd) London: Gowans & Gray Ltd, 1907.

Bard, Kathryn A. *Encyclopedia of the Archaeology of Ancient Egypt.* London: Routledge, 1999.

Baynes, Thomas Spencer, editor. *Encyclopaedia Britannica.* New York: Henry G. Allen, 1888.

Bernal, Martin. *Black Athena, Volume I.* New Jersey: Rutgers University Press, 1987.

_____ *Black Athena, Volume II.* New Jersey: Rutgers University Press, 1991.

Bernard of Clairvaux. *Epistolae,* in *Sancti Bernardi Opera.* (ed. J. Leclercq and H. Rochais) Rome: Editiones Cistercienses, 1974.

Bikai, Patricia. *The Pottery of Tyre.* Warminster, UK: Aris & Phillips, 1978.

Boardman, John et al, eds. *The Oxford History of the Roman World.* Oxford: Oxford University Press, 1986.

Bryce, Trevor. *The Kingdom of the Hittites.* Oxford: Clerendon Press, 1998.

Bulloch, John. *Scottish Notes and Queries.* Aberdeen: A. Brown & Co, 1903.

Burgoyne, Michael Hamilton. "1187 – 1260" in *Where Heaven and Earth Meet: Jerusalem's Sacred Esplanade.* (ed. Oleg Grabar and Benjamin Z. Kedar) Austin: University of Texas Press, 2009.

Burnes, James. *Sketch of the History of the Knights Templars.* Edinburgh: William Blackwood & Sons, 1840.

Cancik, Hubert and Helmuth Schneider, eds. *Brill's New Pauly Encyclopedia of the Ancient World.* Leiden, The Netherlands: Brill, 2002.

Carr, Harry. *The Minutes of the Lodge of Edinburgh, Mary's Chapel, No. 1 (1598-1738).* London: Quatuor Coronati Lodge, 1962.

_____ "Freemasonry Before Grand Lodge" *Grand Lodge 1717-1967.* Oxford: United Grand Lodge of England, 1967.

Casson, Lionel. *The Ancient Mariners.* Princeton, New Jersey: Princeton University Press, 1991.

_____ *Ships and Seamanship in the Ancient World.* Baltimore, Maryland: John Hopkins University Press, 1995.

Cooper, Robert L.D. *Cracking the Freemasons Code.* New York: Atria Books, 2006.

_____ *The Rosslyn Hoax?* Hersham, Surrey: Lewis Masonic, 2007.

Davies, Vivian and Renee Friedman. *Egypt Uncovered.* New York: Stewart, Tabori & Chang, 1998.

Diodorus. *Diodorus of Sicily.* (Greek, translated into English by Charles L. Sherman). Cambridge, Massachusetts: Harvard University Press, 1952.

Doumas, Christos. *The Wall-paintings of Thera.* (Greek, translated into English by Alex Doumas.) Athens: The Thera Foundation - Petros M. Nomikos, 1999.

Dueck, Daniela. *Strabo of Amasia.* London: Routledge, 2000.

Dunand, Maurice. *Byblos.* (French, translated into English by H. Tabet.) Paris: Librairie Adrien-Maisonneuve, 1973.

Fitton, J. Lesley. *Minoans.* London: British Museum Press, 2002.

Friedman, Renee. "The Ceremonial Centre at Hierakonpolis, Locality HK29A" *Aspects of Early Egypt.* (ed. A.J. Spencer) London: British Museum Press, 1996.

Gould, R.F. with D. Wright editor. *Gould's History of Freemasonry.* London: Caxton Publishing, 1931.

Grant, Michael. *The Ancient Mediterranean.* New York: Charles Scribner's Sons, 1969.

Haag, Michael. *The Templars: The History & the Myth.* New York: Harper, 2009.

Haunch, T.O. "The Formation-Part 1, 1717-1751" in *Grand Lodge 1717-1967.* Oxford: United Grand Lodge of England, 1967.

Hay, Richard Augustine. *Genealogie of the Saintclaires of Rosslyn.* Edinburgh: Thomas G. Stevenson, 1835.

Herodotus. *The History.* (Greek, translated into English by George Rawlinson.) New York: Tandy Thomas Co., 1909.

Hesiod. *Theogony.* (Greek, translated into English by Dorothea Wender). Harmondsworth, England: Penguin Books, 1976.

Holst, Sanford. *Phoenicians: Lebanon's Epic Heritage.* Los Angeles: Cambridge & Boston Press, 2005.

_____ *Phoenician Secrets: Exploring the Ancient Mediterrranean.* Los Angeles: Santorini Publishing, 2011.

Josephus, Flavius. *The Jewish War.* (translated into English by G.A. Williamson) New York: Dorset Press, 1985.

Josten, C. H. ed. *Elias Ashmole (1617–1692). His Autobiographical and Historical Notes, his Correspondence, and Other Contemporary Sources Relating to his Life and Work.* Oxford: Clarendon Press, 1966.

Knight, Christopher and Robert Lomas. *The Hiram Key.* Gloucester, MA: Fair Winds Press, 1996.

Lagassé, Paul et al, eds. *The Columbia Encyclopedia, Sixth Edition.* New York: Columbia University Press, 2001-04.

Lichtheim, Miriam. *Ancient Egyptian Literature: Volume II: The New Kingdom.* Berkeley: University of California Press, 1976.

Livy. *The Early History of Rome.* (First books of *The History of Rome from Its Foundation.* Latin, translated by Aubrey de Sélincourt) London: Penguin Books, 1960.

_____ *The War with Hannibal.* (Books XXI-XXX of *The History of Rome from Its Foundation.* Latin, translated by Aubrey de Sélincourt.) London: Penguin Books, 1965.

Lomas, Robert. *The Invisible College.* London: Headline Publishing, 2002.

_____ *Turning the Templar Key.* Beverly, MA: Fair Winds Press, 2007.

Mackey, Albert G. *Washington as a Freemason: An Address Delivered before the Grand and Subordinate Lodges of Ancient Freemasons of South Crolina, at Charleston, S.C., on Thursday, November 4th,*

1852, being the Centennial Celebration of the Initiation of George Washington. Charleston: Miller, 1852.

_____ Encyclopedia of Freemasonry. London: Griffin, 1870.

_____ The History of Freemasonry. New York: Masonic History Co, 1898.

Manuel des Chevaliers de l'Ordre du Temple. Paris: Chevaliers de l'Ordre du Temple, 1825.

Markoe, Glenn E. Phoenicians: Peoples of the Past. Berkeley: University of California Press, 2000.

Meyers, Eric, ed. Oxford Encyclopedia of Archaeology in the Near East. New York: Oxford University Press, 1997.

Moscati, Sabatino, ed. The Phoenicians. New York: Rizzoli International, 1999.

Mylne, Robert Scott. The Master Masons to the Crown of Scotland and Their Works. Edinburgh: Scott & Ferguson, 1893.

Not Applicable. The Holy Bible, King James Version. 1987.

Pliny. Natural History. (Latin, translated into English by John Bostock and H. T. Riley) London: Henry G. Bohn, 1855.

Plot, Robert. Natural History of Staffordshire. Oxford: Theatre, 1686.

Polybius. Histories. (Greek, translated by Evelyn S. Shuckburgh) London: Macmillan, 1889.

Redford, Donald, ed. The Oxford Encyclopedia of Ancient Egypt. New York: Oxford University Press, 2001.

Ritmeyer, Leen. The Quest: Revealing the Temple Mount in Jerusalem. Jerusalem: Carta, 2006.

Robertson, Alexander. The life of Sir Robert Moray: soldier, statesman and man of science (1608-1673). London: Longmans, Green & Co., 1922.

Robinson, John J. Born In Blood: The Lost Secrets of Freemasonry. New York: M. Evans, 1989.

_____ A Pilgrim's Path. New York: M. Evans, 1993.

Rufus, Quintus Curtius. The History of Alexander. (Latin, translated into English by John Yardley) London: Penguin Books, 2001.

Sasson, Jack M., ed. Civilizations of the Ancient Near East. New York: Charles Scribner's Sons, 1995.

Scott, Sir Walter. *Lay of the Last Minstrel.* New York: C.S. Francis & Co., 1845.

Stevenson, David. *The Origins of Freemasonry.* Cambridge: Cambridge University Press, 1988/2005.

Statutes of the Religious and Military Order of the Temple, as Established in Scotland; with an Historical Notice of the Order. Edinburgh: Grand Conclave, 1843.

Thucydides. *History of the Peloponnesian War.* (Greek, translated into English by Richard Crawley) London: Longmans, Green and Co., 1874.

Walbank, F.W. ed. *Cambridge Ancient History.* Cambridge: Cambridge University Press, 1989.

Ward, J.S.M. *Freemasonry and the Ancient Gods.* London: Simpkin, Marshall, Hamilton, Kent & Co., 1921.

Weld, Charles Richard. *A History of the Royal Society, with Memoirs of the Presidents.* London: John W. Parker, 1848.

Williams, Louis. "Sir Christopher Wren" in *Fiat Lux.* Sebring, Ohio: Philalethes Society, 2009.

Index

27863650R00218

Made in the USA
Middletown, DE
22 December 2015